STARTING WITH DERRIDA

Also available from Continuum:

Derrida and Disinterest, Sean Gaston

Impossible Mourning of Jacques Derrida, Sean Gaston

Jacques Derrida: Live Theory, James K. A. Smith

Derrida: A Guide for the Perplexed, Julian Wolfreys

STARTING WITH DERRIDA:
PLATO, ARISTOTLE AND HEGEL

SEAN GASTON

Continuum International Publishing Group
The Tower Building
11 York Road
London SE1 7NX

80 Maiden Lane
Suite 704
New York, NY 10038

www.continuumbooks.com

British Library Cataloguing-in-Publication Data
A catalogue record for this book is available from the British Library.

ISBN: HB: 0-8264-9785-3
9780826497857
PB: 0-8264-9786-1
9780826497864

Library of Congress Cataloging-in-Publication Data
A catalog record for this book is available from the Library of Congress.

Typeset by Servis Filmsetting Ltd, Manchester
Printed and bound in Great Britain by
MPG Books Ltd, Bodmin, Cornwall

CONTENTS

PROLOGUE:

PALINTROPES

On 2 October 1994 Jacques Derrida participated in a discussion to mark the opening of a new doctoral programme in the philosophy department at the University of Villanova. On two occasions Derrida tells his audience that the next day his latest work, *Politics of Friendship*, will be published in Paris: it is the day before the politics of friendship. Derrida goes on to say that his new work is 'mainly a book on Plato and Aristotle' and adds, 'I think we need to read them again and again and I feel that, however old I am, I am on the threshold of reading Plato and Aristotle. I love them and I feel I have to start again and again and again. It is a task which is in front of me, before me'.[1] Derrida reiterates not once but five times that when it comes to Plato and Aristotle one must *start again* – and again and again. At the same time, in *Of Spirit: Heidegger and the Question* (1987), written the year before he began his seminars in Paris on the politics of friendship, Derrida also insisted that 'it is already too late, always too late'.[2] One cannot, and must not, be beguiled by the possibility of a pure 'recommencement', by a 'return' that would 'signify a new departure . . . or some degree zero'. It is always *too late* to start again. The gesture of starting again is itself already part of the tradition of metaphysics: metaphysics always starts again – *and always with itself*, with Plato and Aristotle.

One of the ways that Derrida responded to the dilemma that to challenge or resist Western metaphysics one must somehow start again *and* recognize that it is always too late to start again was through the movement of what he calls a *palintrope*.[3] In Greek, *pálin* means to move back, to go backwards, *and* also to do something again, to do something once more. The word is perhaps best known today as a palindrome, a word or phrase or number that reads the same backwards and forwards. A palindrome starts and ends the same way. But a palintrope has a slightly different rhetorical flourish: it starts differently, with a start, it *startles* itself as it starts again.[4] It startles itself and, as Derrida says, loses the *logos*. Rather than moving backwards and forwards through the same word, or over the same ground, it suggests a turning backwards that happens *more than once*, a turning backwards that – already – repeats, splits, doubles and exceeds itself.

This book is divided into two parts. The first part, 'Histories – of Literature', explores Derrida's *palintropic* rereading of Plato and Aristotle through the question of the *possibility* of a history *of* literature. At the beginning of *Of Grammatology* (1965–67), Derrida had written of the importance of a reading that 'gets away, at least in its axis, from the classical categories of history: from the history of ideas, of course, and from the history of literature, but perhaps above all from the history of philosophy'.[5] But for this very reason, he was preoccupied with philosophy's difficult relationship *with* literature and history, and with the relationship *between* history and literature. One can see this in his summary of a seminar from the early 1980s on Kant and Kafka:

> I was concerned with the 'as if' (*als ob*) in the second formulation of the categorical imperative: 'Act as if the maxim of your action were by your will to turn into a universal law of nature.' This 'as if' enables us to reconcile practical reason with an historical teleology and with the possibility of unlimited progress. I tried to show how it almost introduces narrativity and fiction into the very core of legal thought, at the moment when the latter begins to speak and to question the moral subject. Though the authority of the law seems to exclude all historicity and empirical narrativity, and this at the moment when its rationality seems alien to all fiction and imagination – even the transcendental imagination – it still seems *a priori* to shelter these parasites.[6]

It is from his early readings on exceeding or resisting the ontological inheritance in Plato, and his redefinition of the concept of history (which I explore through that remarkable quasi pre-Socratic, Herodotus), that Derrida begins to sketch out the problem of a relation between history and literature that is not simply mediated or predetermined by philosophy. In his reading of Plato in 'The Double

Session' (1969), Derrida uses the phrase the 'history – of literature'. It is by taking the graphics of this line (or hyphen or dash) between 'history' and 'literature' seriously that one can follow his later retranslations of Heidegger in the 1970s to get a sense of the *trait* (the line, the trace) that is always *en retrait*, with-drawing or retreating from itself *as* itself, which Derrida places and dis-places in the ceaseless negotiation between history and literature.

The first part of the book ends with a possible 'history – of literature', by reading the entrance of TIME in Act Four of *The Winter's Tale* in relation to Britain's tortuous 170-year time lag (1582–1752) in changing from the Julian to the Gregorian calendar, which began in Shakespeare's lifetime. It is through Derrida's important differences with Heidegger over how to read Aristotle on the relation between time and space that one can get a sense of Shakespeare's own strange turning back, once more, to Aristotle.

The second part of the book, 'Histories – of the Senses', is concerned with Derrida's palintropic rereading of Aristotle and Hegel. In his long engagement with Aristotle's treatise *On the Soul* Derrida gestures to a 'new' history – of the senses. It is through that great reader of Aristotle, Hegel, that Derrida reads the irreducible gaps (*écarts*) *of* and *as* contact, and the reverberating *blows* from the outside (*les coups du dehors*) that challenge the history – of the senses as no-more-than-five, as always five-in-one. As he suggests in *On Touching – Jean-Luc Nancy* (1992–2000), there are blows *and* caresses, always somewhere in between, that exceed the Aristotelian inheritance of the diaphanous as the unseen origin of seeing, as a hearing that only hears itself, and the not x but the possibility of x at the heart of the legacy of Husserlian phenomenology.

It is from tracing the reliance of Husserlian phenomenology on Aristotle that Derrida turns back, once more, to Hegel. He begins *Glas* (1974), his remarkable reworking of the problem of a history of philosophy (on Hegel) in relation to the possibility of a history of literature (on Genet), with an unpublished seminar in 1967 devoted to the first chapter of Hegel's *Phenomenology of Spirit* on sensible certainty (*sinnliche Gewißheit*). Hegel opens the *Phenomenology* by defining sensible certainty as a simple, pure and undeveloped *being*. In his *Lectures on the History of Philosophy* Hegel keeps turning away, again and again, from this simple being of sensible certainty in his attempt to start again and to reach Plato and the beginning of philosophy.

In *Glas*, Derrida traces Hegel's impossible history of the *conception* of the immaculate concept. In gesturing to a new history of the senses, of blows and cuts, and leaps and gaps, Derrida also turns to the problem of *thinking* as thought thinking itself, of thinking as a memory that re-collects itself. Starting with *and* departing from Heidegger, Derrida argues for a resistance of thinking that remains to be thought, for a thinking that is unthinkable, startling even, because it no longer has the weight (the matter) or the weightlessness (the spirit) of a thinking *of* the senses: a thinking that turns backwards, once more, more than once, a thinking of *palintropes*.

10 November 2006

PART ONE

HISTORIES – OF LITERATURE

CHAPTER 1

STARTING WITH PLATO

> A beginning is that which is not itself necessarily after anything else.
>
> Aristotle, *Poetics*[1]

HUSSERL AND *THEORIA*

In a footnote to *The Problem of Genesis*, his 1953–54 dissertation on Husserl, Derrida wrote: 'One cannot fail to . . . regret that Husserl and numerous of his interlocutors and his disciples were not questioned, at least once in their lives, by a Socrates'.[2] In the early 1960s, it was this question about *not* being 'questioned . . . by a Socrates' that took Derrida back to Plato as a way of rereading Husserl and Hegel and examining the Platonic inheritance in the work of Foucault and Lévinas. Challenging the prevailing tradition that had dominated French philosophy since Hegel, Derrida *turns back* again, *once* more and always *more* than once, to Plato. It is in his early readings of Plato, before his celebrated 1968 essay 'Plato's Pharmacy', that Derrida both makes the case for a resistance of ontology within Plato's work and begins to sketch out the need for a *palintropic* reading of Plato and Aristotle.

Carrying on from his first criticisms in the mid-1950s of Husserl's inadequate response to Plato, in his 1961–62 introduction to Husserl's *The Origin of Geometry* (1936), Derrida uses Plato to question the origins of the phenomenological project. At first, he emphasizes the differences between Husserl and Plato. Unlike Plato, who believes that an ideal objectivity 'preexist[s] every subjective act', Husserl makes the case for a historicity *of* ideal objects. For Husserl, there is 'an original history' that 'primordially' grounds 'protoidealizations'.[3] But Derrida also starts to underline the similarities between Husserl and Plato. Like Plato, Husserl's ideal objectivity relies on a certain kind of fiction (hallucinations, dreams) to retain its 'intangibility'.[4] Husserl may make the case for a *history* and tradition of ideal objectivity, but he never stops arguing for an *absolute* ideal objectivity.

Derrida suggests that Husserl at once breaks away from *and* returns to Plato. On the one hand, he writes, 'as soon as phenomenology breaks from both conventional Platonism and historicist empiricism, the movement of truth that it wishes to describe is really that of a concrete and specific history – the foundations of which are a temporal and creative subjectivity's acts based on the sensible world and the life-world as cultural world'. On the other hand, for Husserl there can only be a tradition or 'transmission' of truth when it does *not* move away from its origin, and Derrida asks, 'Did not Plato describe this situation? Was not the eternity of essences for him perhaps only another name for a nonempirical historicity?'[5]

In his discussion of Husserl's notion of a 'prescientific cultural world' at the origin of geometry Derrida comes closest to linking Husserl directly to Plato. For Husserl, before there was geometry, there were bodies and shapes. From these shapes the protogeometer evoked *ideal* imaginary variations. However, these ideal imaginary shapes belonged to the 'sensible order' and were different from the later 'pure geometrical ideality' of geometry.[6] It would appear that for Husserl the *origin* of geometry is the *sensible* world. Sensibility precedes ideality, matter is the origin of form, and the body comes before the soul. Husserl somewhat qualifies this by describing a history of *two* idealities, the 'sensible morphological ideality' or 'pure sensible ideality' that precedes geometry, and the pure objective ideality of geometry itself, but it remains the case that the ideal starts *from* the sensible, or as Derrida puts it, geometry begins with geography.[7]

While recognizing that bodies, sensibility, imagination and culture precede the ideal objectivity of geometry, Husserl insists that this 'is not to be confused with the origin of geometry itself'. Ideal objectivity, the truth that does not change, cannot be sensible or imaginary. It is at this point, Derrida implies, that Husserl turns to a *second* origin of geometry. Starting from the sensible and the imaginary, geometry is born in the 'instituting act' of *philosophy* giving birth to itself. Philosophy can only be born in a 'philosophical act' – *and this is what Plato does*. For Husserl, 'Plato' becomes the name for the *possibility* of the historicity (*Geschichtlichkeit*) of ideal objects. As Derrida observes, in phenomenology 'the philosopher is the man who inaugurates the theoretical attitude'.[8] He is referring here to Husserl's late essay 'Philosophy and the Crisis of European Man' (1935) in which he describes the birth of philosophy in Greece as the appearance of a 'new attitude', 'a purely "theoretical" attitude'.[9] The origin of philosophy, the origin of philosophy as 'Plato', is *theoria*.[10]

The *OED* defines *theoria* as *contemplation*, *speculation* and *sight*, noting that the word comes from *theasthai* (to look on, to contemplate) and *theoros* (a spectator).[11] *Theoria* is a kind of contemplation, the action of a contemplative spectator. Contemplation comes from the Latin *contemplatio* or *con-templum*, to be together or jointly in an open and sacred space. In this Latin definition, the Greek *theoria* takes on the distinctly religious connotation of a shared meditation as one looks on and stands in the presence of the divine. If we leave aside the second definition offered by the *OED*, speculation, *speculatio*, which touches on both *specula* (a lookout or watch-tower) and *specere* (to see), and has strong associations with the speculative dialectics of Hegel, the Greek words *theasthai* and *theoros* link *theoria* with the act of looking. *Theoria* could be defined merely as *looking*. Socrates *looks* at, is a spectator of knowledge, wisdom, the good, etc. If one takes *theoria* as a looking at, as an *examining* or *viewing*, this does not necessarily imply that *theoria* describes the liberation from the sensible and the imaginary and the birth of ideal objectivity. As Aristotle himself remarks in the *Nicomachean Ethics*, when it comes to 'contemplation' (*theoria*), 'nothing results from it apart from the fact that one has contemplated'.[12]

But this is very much how Husserl interprets *theoria*. Breaking away from the 'mythico-practical' world, with the advent of *theoria* 'man becomes the disinterested spectator, overseer of the world, he becomes a philosopher'.[13] As I have argued elsewhere, from Hobbes to Kant, *disinterest* was understood primarily as a concept for attempting to mediate *between* the conflicting demands of the public and the private.[14] The association of the so-called 'disinterested spectator' with an *absolute* lack of interest in practical, social and ethical questions has very little to do with the concept of disinterest that flourished in the seventeenth and eighteenth centuries. This is a nineteenth-century conceit that arises in part from a narrow reading of Kant's analysis of disinterestedness in the *Critique of Judgement* and is perpetuated in the twentieth century in histories of aesthetics.[15] For Kant, interest was *indispensable* for the critiques of reason and ethics, and the disinterestedness of the third *Critique* should be seen as part of Kant's ongoing difficulties with the need for reason to be both interested *and* disinterested.

For Husserl, Plato is the philosopher as disinterested spectator (*theoria*) and is the start of a progressive history of (dis)interest. From an archaic preoccupation with 'vital interests', philosophy introduces an innovative 'theoretical interest' that will lead 'to the *theoria* proper to science'.[16] As with all claims to an apparent absolute disinterest, Husserl begins with the *theoria* of 'the disinterested spectator' and can then only *account* for this idealized disinterest through a *history* of interests. There can be no disinterest without a prior interest and there can be no move away from this primary interest without *another* interest, hence Husserl goes from vital interests to the theoretical interest of the disinterested spectator.

As Derrida asks in his reading of the apparent sensible origin of ideality in *The Origin of Geometry*, how can 'Plato' (*theoria* as philosophy) be concerned with 'truth in itself' if *before* the origin of philosophy *as* disinterest there is the origin of philosophy *as* interest? Husserl attempts to address this problem by *equating* the 'theoretical interest' and the act of disinterest, by placing them at the *same* moment in the progression from vital interests to the theoretical interest, to *theoria* as science. Husserl writes: 'It is important to explain the change from original *theoria*, from the completely "disinterested" (consequent upon the *epochē* from all practical interests) worldview (knowledge of the world based on universal contemplation) to the *theoria* proper to science – both states exemplify the contrast between *doxa* and *epistēmē*.' Husserl describes this move from *epistēmē* (Plato) to *epistēmē* (modern science) as a shift of focus from myths and traditions to the truth itself, to the truth freed from tradition thanks to the Platonic 'distinction' between the represented world and the real world.[17] Plato not only begins philosophy but accounts for its progression *beyond* Platonism: a very Hegelian proposition.

THE IMMACULATE BIRTH OF EXACTNESS

For Derrida, the fact that Husserl offers *two* origins of geometry (a sensible imaginary ideality in a prescientific culture *and* a pure geometrical ideality arising from the inauguration of philosophy) suggests that the *origin* of geometry is 'an idealizing operation'. *Idealization*, Derrida argues, describes the movement through which 'on the basis of a sensible ideality' Husserl 'makes a higher, absolutely objective, exact and nonsensible ideality occur'.[18] At the same time, what interests Derrida is that Husserl cannot avoid including the 'history' of this idealization in his argument for an absolute ideal objectivity. An absolute ideal objectivity (truth itself) cannot *begin*: it must have *always* been true. In his very inclusion of the origin – or, more accurately, the origins – of geometry, Husserl puts great strain on the concept of the *truth* as an unchanging, originless absolute.

Husserl's inclusion of the origin (as idealization) of geometry can be described as including the *possibility* of something within what is seemingly *already* possible. For example, I am halfway through a letter when I make the case for the *possibility* of writing letters. The origin – the possibility, the *question* of the possibility of the origin, the question of origin – appears in the *midst* of the work. In such cases, which already raise the question of writing and of literature, of the history *of* literature, there is a remarkable ripple of the text and one cannot avoid asking, how is it possible that this *began* and how is it possible that it can *go on*?

These are moments, fractures in writing, which should not be confused with some sort of ideal anticipation or clever self-reflectivity. A good century before the apparent assurance of the novel first appears, Cervantes touches on the precariousness of keeping a story going and the question of the very possibility of a narrative in *Don Quixote de la Mancha* (1605–15). In the midst of *Don Quixote*, 'one day in the exchange of Toledo' Cervantes finds 'some bundles of old papers'. By mere chance and a great stroke of good fortune these old papers touch on the adventures of Don Quixote and Sancho Panza. After having the papers translated from Arabic, Cervantes is able to finish his account of the battle between Don Quixote and Biscainer.[19] If Cervantes had not been wandering 'one day in the exchange of Toledo', the 'history' of Don Quixote would have 'stopped short'. To keep the story going, Cervantes suggests, the narrator must search without rest for the chance discoveries, the writings, parchments, archives, scraps and fragments that ensure the elusive – and impossible – *continuity* of the literary work. When the possibility of what appears to be already possible appears, it raises the disquiet of the *impossible*. This is what Derrida suggests in his reading of Husserl: the origin is impossible. In his 1964 essay 'Violence and Metaphysics: An Essay on the Thought of Emmanuel Levinas', Derrida describes this origin in the midst of the work as 'an *inscribed* origin'. 'The *inscription*', he writes, 'is the written origin: traced and henceforth *inscribed* in a system, in a figure which it no longer governs'.[20]

Boswell does much the same thing in his *Life of Johnson* (1791). He may have been inspired by Johnson's own strange moment of origin, of *beginning in the midst* of the work, in his *A Journey to the Western Islands of Scotland* (1775). Some thirty pages into his account, and very conscious of nature as a romantic and sublime scene of inspiration, Johnson describes the moment of the origin of his 'narration' as a *lacuna* of 'silence, and solitude', of blank nature:

> I sat down on a bank, such as a writer of Romance might have delighted to feign. I had indeed no trees to whisper over my head, but a clear rivulet streamed at my feet. The day was calm, the air soft, and all was rudeness, silence, and solitude. Before me, and on the other side, were high hills, which by hindering the eye from ranging, forced the mind to find entertainment for itself. Whether I spent the hour well I know not; for here I first conceived the thought of this narration.[21]

For his own part, because he is recounting the life of Johnson chronologically, Boswell can *only* describe the origin of the work, when he first meets Johnson on 16 May 1763, some 250 pages into the text. How is the distinctive claim of Boswell's biography, to have recorded the voice and conversation of Johnson, *possible*? Boswell must give the impression that he is able to write down everything as it happens. 'In my note', he remarks in a dispute about what took place on 16 May 1763, '*taken on the very day*, in which I am confident I marked everything material that passed, no mention is made of this gentleman'.[22]

At the same time, writing many years after this inaugural event, Boswell emphasizes that he is reliant on the half-forgotten partial views of the young man in his journal: 'On reviewing, at the distance of many years, my journal of this period, I wonder how, at my first visit, I ventured to talk to him so freely, and that he bore it with so much indulgence.' Boswell sounds almost surprised when he notes,

'I find in my journal the following minute of our conversation.' He later explains that after a day with Johnson, he would sit up all night 'recollecting and writing in my journal'.[23] It is some months after he first meets Johnson that Boswell relies on a *metaphor* to explain how his work is possible, which is not that far removed from Husserl's description of the origin as a process of idealization, of the move from *one* origin (sensible ideality) to *another* (pure ideality). Boswell writes:

> Let me here apologize for the imperfect manner in which I am obliged to exhibit Johnson's conversation at this period. In the early part of my acquaintance with him, I was so wrapt in admiration of his extraordinary colloquial talents, and so little accustomed to his peculiar mode of expression, that I found it extremely difficult to recollect and record his conversation with its genuine vigour and vivacity. In progress of time, when my mind was, as it were, *strongly impregnated with the Johnsonian æther*, I could, with more facility and exactness, carry in my memory and commit to paper the exuberant variety of his wisdom and wit.[24]

It is precisely this strange *history* of the origin as the move from the sensible to the *exact* that interests Derrida in his reading of Husserl. For Husserl, this is what starting with 'Plato' means: the *immaculate birth of exactness*. As Derrida writes, 'unlike morphological ideality, exact ideality has been produced without the essential aid of sensibility or imagination; it broke away by a leap from every descriptive mooring'. Though this 'leap drew its support or appeal from sensible ideality . . . it is "pure thinking" that is responsible for the leaping advance of idealization and for geometrical truth as such'. For Derrida, when it comes to the problem of 'pure thinking' it is all a question of a *leap* from the sensible to the ideal, and this is perhaps what he has in mind when he warns in *Glas* (1974) that 'it is always necessary to ask oneself why and on top of what one presses to leap'.[25] As Derrida had suggested in the introduction to *The Origin of Geometry*, what makes this leap so extraordinary is that it *erases* its *own* past: 'The inaugural character of the idealizing act, the radical and irruptive freedom which that act manifests, and the decisive discontinuity which uproots the act from its past conditions, all this hides the idealizing act from a genealogical description'.[26] The origin as pure ideality, as *theoria*, as 'Plato', is an act of erasure.

STARTING TO SPEAK

In his 1963 essay 'Force and Signification' Derrida argues that despite 'its anti-Platonism', phenomenology 'leads Husserl back [*reconduit*] to Plato'.[27] Having meditated for over a decade on the inadequacy of Husserl's engagement with Plato, Derrida offers the first glimpse of his own rereading of Plato in a footnote to 'Cogito and the History of Madness', his 1963 paper on Foucault and Descartes. One could be tempted to date the beginning of Derrida's engagement with Plato sometime between March 1963, when he gave his paper, and 1964 when the paper was published.

It all starts with a footnote, the first footnote. This footnote is itself about the beginning, the *style* of the beginning, of Derrida's paper:

> With the exception of several notes and a short passage (in brackets), this paper is the reproduction of a lecture given 4 March 1963 at the Collège Philosophique. In proposing that this text be published in the *Revue de métaphysique et de morale*, M. Jean Wahl agreed that it should retain its first form [*gardât sa forme première*], that of the spoken word [*la parole vive*], with all its requirements and, especially, its particular weaknesses: if in general, according to the remark in the *Phaedrus*, the written word is deprived of 'the assistance of its father', if it is a fragile 'idol' fallen from 'living and animated discourse' unable to 'help itself', then is it not more exposed and disarmed than ever when, miming the improvisation of the voice, it must give up even the resources and lies of style?[28]

This is more than an elegant and modest explanation for the reproduction of Derrida's lecture, which of course had already been written before it was delivered. Derrida's celebrated reading of Plato's account of writing in the *Phaedrus* begins with Foucault.[29]

Derrida emphasizes in his footnote that, according to Plato, writing (in contrast to speech) 'is deprived of "the assistance of its father" '. Derrida's lecture on Foucault starts with the very problem of starting without the assistance of the father. Derrida, the former student of Foucault, still has 'the consciousness of an admiring and grateful disciple'. But when the disciple 'starts, I would not say to dispute, but to engage in dialogue with the master' his consciousness becomes 'an unhappy consciousness'. 'Starting to enter [*en commençant*] into dialogue in the world, that is, starting to answer back [*à répondre*]', the disciple 'always feels "caught in the act", like the "infant" [*l'enfant*] who, by definition and as his name indicates, cannot speak and above all must not answer back'.[30] Both Foucault and Derrida were students of the Hegelian scholar and translator Jean Hyppolite, and Derrida is referring here to the so-called master–slave dialectic (which was also the cornerstone of Alexander Kojève's influential lectures on Hegel) and the unhappy consciousness in Hegel's *Phenomenology of Spirit* (1807).[31]

But Derrida is also raising the (Platonic) question of speaking (with the father, to the father and as the father), and writing (without the help of the father, without the father, without a father that may have never existed). He is, in effect, announcing a new kind of starting with Plato that moves on from the debates on Hegelianism that have dominated French philosophy since the war. Derrida begins with the problem of speaking, of being unable to speak (*infans*). He then turns to the Hegelian (and Foucauldian) master–disciple relationship. The disciple who tries to speak 'finds himself already challenged by the master's voice within him that precedes his own'. The disciple discovers *la voix du maître* 'within him and before him'.[32] The voice of the master has not only transported itself into the disciple, it also appears to be before the disciple, before him *and* in front of him. The disciple has 'interiorized the master', and is outmanoeuvred from the start, before he or she has even begun.

Derrida then turns away from this idealized power of speech, this *pure* transference of authority founded on the interiorization of the master's *voice*. 'The disciple', he argues, 'must break the glass, or better the mirror, the reflection, his infinite speculation on the master'. For Derrida, being able to 'start to speak' requires the recognition that in fact 'the master is perhaps always absent'.[33] As Derrida's first footnote already suggests, for Plato the absence of the master (Socrates), speaking without the assistance (or the hindrance) of the father, is the condition of writing. Derrida, who loved to speak, to deliver lecturers, papers and interviews, was always preoccupied with the assumptions behind speaking, the idealizations of speech, never with a denial of speaking or an idealization of writing as the only 'true' form of communication.[34] As he implies already in March 1963, it is only *from* writing, from a certain silence, that one can start to speak.

NOT X BUT THE POSSIBILITY OF X: *EPEKEINA TĒS OUSIAS*

In his first footnote to 'Cogito and the History of Madness' Derrida refers to a short passage in brackets that has been added to the text since the lecture was given in March 1963. It is perhaps not fortuitous that this addition is primarily concerned with Foucault having *not* started with Plato. Foucault, Derrida argues, has suggested both that the Socratic dialectic maintained the authority of reason by excluding madness and that 'the Greek Logos had no contrary'.[35] How, Derrida asks, can Plato use reason to keep its contrary (madness) in order and *at the same time* have no opposite (madness)? If the Greek *logos* had *no* contrary then it could not take care of the problem of madness. And if the Socratic dialogue has mastered madness, this can only suggest that there was a conflict and difference between reason and madness *before* the Greek *logos*. How are we to respond, Derrida asks, to what appears to have no symmetrical opposite (madness as the other *of* reason) *and* is also the source of the opposition between reason and madness?[36]

In his 1963 lecture Derrida addresses this question in Foucault's reading of Descartes by arguing that the *Cogito* gestures 'to an original point which no longer belongs to either a *determined* reason or a *determined* unreason'. The *Cogito* is mad in the sense that it points to a 'common origin of meaning and nonmeaning'. The opposition between reason and unreason can only be opened and founded by what *exceeds* this opposition.[37] To turn back and start differently with Plato we have to respond to what *exceeds* any possible totality. The dialectic of Socrates, Derrida notes, is hardly any more reassuring when it 'overflows the totality of beings, planting in us the light of a hidden sun which is *epekeina tēs ousias*'.[38] Derrida is referring here to the well-known passage in the *Republic* when Socrates insists that the good *exceeds* being (509b).[39]

Derrida had first cited this passage from the *Republic* in his introduction to *The Origin of Geometry*, and it plays a significant role in his 1964 article on Lévinas, 'Violence and Metaphysics'. Socrates introduces the discussion of 'the child of the good' (*ékgonós te tou agathou*) in the *Republic* by associating opinion (*doxa*) and 'the darkness of ignorance' with being blind (*tupheós*) (506e, a–c). Touching on 'the old story' of the one and the many, Socrates argues that the *many* belong to the visible and sensible, and are 'seen [*horasthai*] but not known [*noeisthai*]'. In contrast, the *one* belongs to absolute and essential ideas that are intelligible and 'known but not seen' (507b–c). Blindness is always a product of the visible world: it is a *seeing* without knowledge. Knowing, on the other hand, is an insight without the limitations of seeing. Blindness only *sees* the many. Knowing knows *what cannot be seen*: the one.

Socrates goes on to describe 'the most costly and complex piece of workmanship', sight. Unlike the other senses, the eye must be supplemented by light (507c). Light (*phos*) is 'the bond which links together sight and visibility', and it is the sun, the origin of light, 'which makes the eye to see perfectly and the visible to appear' (507e–508a). The sun (*hélios*) is the *possibility* of both sight and the appearance of the visible in general. The sun 'is not sight, but the author of sight' (508b). For Socrates, 'the child of the good', the good 'in the visible world' is like the sun: it is the possibility of the good *in* the sensible world without being *of* the sensible world. The good itself is concerned with the possibility of knowledge in the intelligible world. As the eye in relation to light (and the sun), 'when resting upon that on which truth [*alétheia*] and being [*ón*] shine, the soul perceives and understands and is radiant with intelligence' (508d). The idea of the good 'imparts truth': it is the *possibility* of knowing without seeing. The good is not the truth, but the *possibility* of the truth (509a). Like the sun, the good is also the possibility 'of generation and nourishment and growth, though he himself is not generation'. Socrates then remarks, 'in like manner the good may be said to be not only the author of knowledge to all things known, but of their being [*einai*] and essence [*ousían*], and yet the good is not essence, but far exceeds essence [*epékeina tēs ousías*] in dignity and power' (509b).

As Derrida notes in 'Cogito and the History of Madness', Socrates' claim that the good even exceeds being is greeted as an *excessive* and extravagant statement. 'It implies', he writes, 'the fundamental derangement and excessiveness of the hyperbole which opens and founds the world as such by exceeding it.'[40] The profound and influential Platonic logic of *not x but the possibility of x* cannot avoid its own hyperbole, its own excess. For Derrida, this excess can never be a *pure* possibility, it can never be an untouchable guarantee, an inexhaustible resource for the presence of the thing itself. This excess is always exceeding itself, exceeding the claims of any claim to *itself*.[41] If it starts, it does not start *with* itself, it starts by *startling* itself.

Derrida identifies this excess in the 'proper and inaugural moment' of the *Cogito* because 'it first awakens to itself in its war with the demon, the evil genius of nonmeaning, by pitting itself against the strength of the evil genius, and by resisting him through the reduction of the natural man within itself'.[42] He had already traced the similar threat of an unavoidable *reduction* of the natural in his introduction to *The Origin of Geometry*. Husserl's notion of ideal objectivity relies on a 'nonimaginary irreality' that can *only* be 'the sense and possibility *of* factual reality to which it is always related'. If 'just for one instant' this relation becomes excessive, 'then the whole phenomenological enterprise risks becoming 'a *novel*'. The 'Idea in the Kantian sense', which is not itself part of phenomenology but is the *possibility* of phenomenology, *the not x but the possibility of x*, is 'always "beyond being" (*epekeina tēs ousias*) . . . [and] as the Telos of the infinite determination of being, it is but being's openness to the light of its own phenomenality, it is the light of light, the sun of the visible sun, a hidden sun which shows without being shown'.[43] As Derrida suggests in his readings of Husserl and Foucault, for Socrates it is always a question of *two* suns, the visible sun *and* the hidden sun. The hidden sun, the sun that cannot be seen, is both the non-sensible origin of the visible ('the light of light . . . which shows without being seen'), and an internal insight that exceeds being (the light 'in us . . . which is *epekeina tēs ousias*').[44]

PALINTROPES: PARMENIDES AND THE *PARMENIDES*

It was after a conversation with Paul Ricoeur in 1962 that Derrida read Emmanuel Lévinas' *Totality and Infinity* (1961) in the summer of 1963.[45] It is in 'Violence and Metaphysics' that Derrida explicitly starts with Plato. When it comes to Plato, it is always the question of how one starts with the *father*. For Derrida, Lévinas repeats the Platonic gesture in the *Phaedrus* of evoking a speech that, in contrast to writing, is *never* without 'the assistance of its father'.[46] Always helped by its father, it is *always* 'able to assist itself'.[47] Speech, which assumes the ideality of an intelligible hearing that *transcends* the sensibility of sound and sight, is invisible. In this first transcendence, *thought* is speech.[48] Derrida will return to this question of thinking in his later readings of Aristotle and Hegel.

For Lévinas, Derrida argues, 'the sun of the *epekeina tēs ousias* will always illuminate the pure awakening and inexhaustible source of thought'. This Greek sun is the 'ancestor of the Infinite which transcends totality'. The *epekeina tēs ousias should* exceed the 'light *of* Being', the light of the one and the same, and announce a different paternity, a creation *of* the other. But in trying to avoid the visible sun (of phenomenology and ontology), Lévinas has returned to the invisible, hidden and intelligible sun *of* Platonism. The good beyond being has always been 'the father of the visible sun', the unseen origin of the light of being.[49] In evoking *the not x but the possibility of x as* the good beyond being, Lévinas has reconstituted the father, has started again *with* Plato. Derrida will later emphasize that the intelligible sun is *also* a source of a fatal blindness, of 'the death that one cannot look at face to face'.[50]

In 'Violence and Metaphysics' Derrida is concerned not only with Lévinas' reading of the *Republic*, but also with his understanding of the relationship between Plato and Parmenides. It is with Parmenides that Derrida will suggest a different way of turning back, a turning back that cannot simply start again with itself. Parmenides of Elea was a student of Xenophanes, who if nothing else should be remembered for his profound observation that if cows had hands they would draw their gods like cows.[51] In the *Sophist*, the Stranger says that the belief of the Eleatics 'that all things are many in name, but in nature one . . . goes back to Xenophanes' (242d).[52] As far as one can tell from the few surviving fragments of his work, behind Xenophanes' criticism of an eminently Greek anthropomorphic relation to the gods is an argument for an *arkhē* (origin, first principle) that exceeds all human categories, that is always one.[53]

One can see the influence of Xenophanes in Parmenides' emphasis on the unity and totality of the *arkhē*. For Parmenides, *being* is 'ungenerated and indestructible, / whole, of one kind and unwavering, and complete. / Nor was it, nor will it be, since now it is, all together, / one, continuous'.[54] Parmenides' lasting influence rests on a fragment of his poem where he argues that there are *only* two 'roads of enquiry': being and non-being. For the sake of truth and of knowledge, we can *only* concern ourselves with what exists, with being. For non-being to *be*, it must *already be being*. We can neither recognize nor speak about non-being: non-being is impossible. The choice is clear, because there is no choice. This is the celebrated and much disputed birth of ontology. Derrida had already touched on this primal scene in 'Cogito and the History of Madness', observing that Parmenides' poem demands a decision, a moment of madness, that is akin to the apparent *separation* of reason and madness in the *Cogito*. From the start, we are presented with

> the choice and division between the two ways [*les deux voies*] separated by Parmenides in his poem, the way of the logos and the non-way, the labyrinth, the 'palintrope' [the turning back, again] in which the *logos* is lost; the way of meaning and that of non-meaning; of being and of non-being. A division [*partage*] on whose basis, after which, *logos*, in the necessary violence of its irruption, is separated from itself as madness, is exiled from itself, forgetting its origin and its own possibility.[55]

To start with *and without* Parmenides, with *and without* ontology, Derrida suggests, one must start with a *palintrope*, with a labyrinthine turning back, a backwards turn that turns again, that turns once more *and* always more than once – *and loses the logos*.

The question of Plato's relationship to Parmenides is infinitely complicated by both Plato's own work, the *Parmenides*, and the position taken by the Stranger from Elea in the *Sophist*. The *Parmenides* can be taken as a mad dialectical monologue that somehow at once makes the case for, and illustrates the impossibility of making the case for, the inescapable unity of being.[56] The opening of Plato's *Parmenides* is itself labyrinthian and marked by many strange *palintropes*. It all begins with the narrator forgetting a name.[57] Cephalus the Clazomenae arrives in Athens, meets Adeimantus and Glaucon in the agora and asks Adeimantus for the name of his half-brother (Antiphon), which he has forgotten. Antiphon, who has now given up the study of philosophy, knew Pythodorus who 'remembers a conversation which took place between Socrates, Zeno, and Parmenides many years ago' (126d). Cephalus (who forgets the name of the narrator) then narrates from memory Antiphon's recollection of the dialogue that Pythodorus remembers. *Turning back* (in the absence of Socrates) and turning back *again*, everything that follows rests on the palintropes of this unpredictable and frail link between remembering and forgetting.[58]

When encouraged by the others to undertake to train Socrates in the proper style of philosophical argument, the 65-year-old Parmenides experiences 'a trembling when I remember through what an ocean of words [*tosouton pélagos lógon*] I have to wade at my time of life' (137a). Parmenides remembers and he trembles.

He trembles, he starts, because to start again, he must wade through a palintropic 'ocean of words'.

LÉVINAS, PLATO AND PLOTINUS

As Derrida points out in 'Violence and Metaphysics', at the end of his 1946–47 lectures, *Time and the Other*, Lévinas makes it clear that when it comes to the unity of being, Plato and Parmenides are *one*:

> Sexuality, paternity, and death introduce a duality into existence, a duality that concerns the very existing of each subject. Existing itself becomes double. The Eleatic notion of being is overcome. Time constitutes not the fallen form of being, but its very event. The Eleatic notion of being dominates Plato's philosophy, where multiplicity was subordinated to one . . . Plato constructs a Republic that must imitate the world of Ideas; he makes a philosophy of a world of light, a world without time.[59]

But by the early 1960s, Lévinas had developed a more complex view of the relationship between Parmenides and Plato, primarily to support his interest in 'the Platonic idea of the Good beyond being' (*du Bien au-delà de l'Être*).[60]

As one would expect from the author of *Time and the Other*, in *Totality and Infinity* Lévinas argues that the idea of infinity *in us* (which he takes from Descartes) leaves as 'purely abstract and formal the contradiction the idea of metaphysics is said to harbour, which Plato brings up in the *Parmenides* – that the relation with the Absolute would render the absolute relative'.[61] But he goes on to cite a passage from the *Theaetetus* in which Socrates discusses Protagoras' idea that 'man is the measure of all things' and that, since we can only rely on individual perceptions, everything must be relative. Socrates then remarks that in such conditions we should describe everything not as 'being' but as 'becoming', because 'nothing ever is'. Parmenides alone, Socrates notes, does not agree with this view.[62] For Lévinas, this suggests that 'a multiplicity of sentients would be the very *mode* in which becoming is possible – a becoming in which thought would not simply find again, now in movement, a being subject to a universal law, producing unity'. Plato's text provides the seeds of a notion of becoming that can be 'radically opposed to the idea of being'.[63]

In *Totality and Infinity*, Lévinas begins the rehabilitation of the *Parmenides*, separating Plato's text from 'Eleatic unity'. He starts by marking a gap between knowledge and being and notes that the 'modification that knowledge brings to bear on the One, which in cognition loses its unity, is evoked by Plato in the *Parmenides*'.[64] The reason that the *Parmenides* can never simply make the case for the unity of being is because the unity of being is *beyond* knowledge. For Lévinas, 'the ancient privilege of unity' which is affirmed by Parmenides can only be resisted by the relation of 'a separated being' with 'an other absolutely other', and this relation is founded on the idea of the infinite in us, an absolute *interior* separation.[65] Greek metaphysics is always trying to close, redeem and unify this separation. But for Lévinas, it also 'conceived the Good as separate from the totality of essences, and in this way . . . caught sight of a structure such that totality could admit of a beyond [*un au-delà*]'.[66] Plato, Lévinas argues, never 'deduces being from the Good: he posits transcendence as surpassing the totality'. He recognizes the idea of infinity.[67]

In 'The Trace of the Other' (1963), which Derrida notes was published just as he finished writing 'Violence and Metaphysics', Lévinas returns to 'the enigmatic message of the beyond being'.[68] In *Totality and Infinity* Lévinas had appeared to contrast Plato's recognition of the good *beyond* being to Plotinus, whom he argues 'returns to Parmenides' and *starts* from the unity of being.[69] But by the time Lévinas writes 'The Trace of the Other', Plotinus has become part of the rehabilitation of the *Parmenides*. To *illustrate* 'the Good with respect to being *epekeina tēs ousia*', Lévinas writes:

> The One in Plotinus is posited beyond being [*posé au-delà de l'Être*], and also *epekeina nou*. The One of which Plato speaks in the first hypothesis of the *Parmenides* is foreign to definition and limit, place and time, self-identity and difference with respect to oneself, resemblance and dissemblance, foreign to being and to knowledge – for which all these attributes constitute the categories of knowledge. It is something else than all that, *other* absolutely and not with respect to some relative term. It is the Unrevealed [*l'Irrévélé*], but not the unrevealed because all knowledge would be too limited or too narrow to receive its light. It is unrevealed because it is *One*, and because making oneself known implies a duality which already clashes with the unity of the One.

> The One is not beyond being because it is buried and hidden; it is buried because it is beyond being, wholly other than being [*au-delà de l'être, tout autre que l'être*].[70]

In *Otherwise than Being, or Beyond Essence* (1974), which was published a decade after Derrida's essay, Lévinas reiterates and expands on the association of Plotinus with the Platonic idea of the good beyond being and reaffirms the opposition of the *Parmenides* to Parmenides.[71]

THE *SOPHIST* AND THE RELATIVE RELATION TO BEING

In 'Violence and Metaphysics', Derrida begins his analysis of Lévinas' reading of Plato by turning to the *Sophist*. In the *Sophist*, the Stranger from Elea is 'a disciple of Parmenides' (216a). Socrates recalls that he heard Parmenides speak when he was a young man and asks the Stranger 'whether you like and are accustomed to make a long oration on a subject which you want to explain to another, or to proceed by the method of question and answer'. Given that the so-called dialogue in the *Parmenides* is essentially a monologue, it is perhaps *impossible* to choose between a serious veneration and an ironic deflation when Socrates goes on to say, 'I remember a very noble discussion in which Parmenides employed the latter of the two methods' (217b). It is precisely the *indeterminacy* of the relationship between Plato and Parmenides as a question of style and language that Derrida alludes to in the opening pages of 'Violence and Metaphysics'. After having linked the *Parmenides* and Plotinus to going beyond being in 'The Trace of the Other', even Lévinas must ask if 'the Platonic hypothesis concerning the One, which is One above being and knowledge' is 'not the development of a sophism'.[72] As Derrida will suggest, it is a testament to the difficulty of determining the exact relationship between Plato and Parmenides that in the *Sophist* the hunt for the nature of the sophist turns into a going *beyond* Parmenides.

In his discussion with Theaetetus, the Stranger cites Parmenides' insistence that it is impossible to 'show that non-being is [*mē ón einai*]' (237a), and comes to the conclusion 'that not-being [*mē ón*] in itself can neither be spoken [*phthégksasthai*], uttered [*eipein*], or thought [*dianoethenai*], but that it is unthinkable [*adianóetón*], unutterable [*árreton*], unspeakable [*áphthegkton*], indescribable [*álogon*]'

(238c).[73] The Stranger then qualifies this, noting 'a little while ago I said that not-being is unutterable, unspeakable, indescribable', but that 'when I introduced the word "is" [or the verb "to be", *éinai*], did I not contradict [*enantía*] what I said before?' (238e–239a). Acknowledging how hard it is to find 'the right way of speaking about not-being' (*tèn orthologian peri tò mē ón*), the Stranger warns that he is in danger of being seen 'as a parricide', because 'I must test the philosophy of my father [*patrós*] Parmenides, and try to prove by main force that in a certain sense non-being is [*mē òn os ésti*], and that being [*òn*], on the other hand, is not [*ouk ésti*]' (241d). Having 'proved that things which are not are', the Stranger goes on to acknowledge that not-being 'is distributed over all things in their relations to one another, and whatever part of the other is contrasted to being' (258c). The Stranger then observes that the dialogue has taken them 'beyond the range of Parmenides' prohibition' to follow what Derrida calls 'the non-way, the labyrinth, the "palintrope" in which the *logos* is lost'.[74]

The complexity of this passage is critical to understanding Derrida's reading of Lévinas and his starting again with Plato. To go *beyond* Parmenides is to argue that not-being *is* and that it is not 'unutterable, unspeakable, indescribable', but 'distributed over all things in their relations to one another'. In other words, going beyond Parmenides is to say *at once* that the other *is* – *and* that the other is *not* an absolute other, but a relative other in relation to being. By saying that the other *is*, the Stranger is reaffirming the inescapability of being. But by saying at the same time that the other is not *absolute*, that it has a relative relation to being, the Stranger is also suggesting that being is not absolute, is not *one*, and challenges 'the way of the logos' as the *one and only way* of being. The *absolute* difference, the *absolute* 'break' with Parmenides that Lévinas calls for in his evocation of an *absolute* other, does not take us beyond Parmenides.[75]

As Derrida observes, 'the great and fearful white shadow [*la grande ombre blanche et redoutable*] which spoke to the young Socrates continues to smile' when we attempt to make the other *absolutely* other.[76] Everything begins with the Stranger recalling the 'is' when one *says* 'not-being *is* unutterable, unspeakable, indescribable' and the recognition of the difficulty of finding 'the right way of *speaking* about not-being', and for Derrida it is the question of language that announces this *alterity* in Plato.[77] Derrida writes:

'The Eleatic stranger and disciple of Parmenides had to give language its due for having vanquished him: shaping non-Being according to Being, he had to "say farewell to an unnameable opposite of Being" and had to confine non-Being to its relativity to Being [*confiner le non-être dans sa relativité à l'être*], that is to the movement of alterity'.[78] The Stranger knows that in 'differing from Being, the other is always relative'.[79]

When Derrida wrote in the mid-1950s in a footnote to *The Problem of Genesis* that 'one cannot fail to evoke here – as in many other places – the Platonic dialectic of the One and the Many, nor to regret that Husserl and numerous of his interlocutors and his disciples were not questioned, at least once in their lives, by a Socrates', it is likely that he was referring to a passage from the *Sophist* and that he *began* his reading of Plato with the *Sophist*.[80] He will later argue in 'Plato's Pharmacy' that the *Sophist* is indicative of what happens when Plato himself *starts* writing in the absence of Socrates, the text becoming at once a record of an original parricide and the beginning of a ceaseless effort to supplement and replace the absent father.[81] From the start.

STARTING YESTERDAY

It all starts with Plato. And Plato's beginnings are so strange.

First, there are the texts where Socrates narrates in the first person with their odd temporal and spatial displacements. In the *Charmides*, Socrates *begins* with 'yesterday'. 'Yesterday [*proteraia*] evening', he says, 'I returned from the army at Potidaea' and was greeted by Chaerephon 'who is a kind of madman' (153a–b). Writing or speaking in the past tense the day *after* his return, Socrates goes on to relate how he had managed to arrive back in Athens *before* the full report of the battle.[82] The *Lysis* begins with Socrates being diverted in mid-step from his intended destination: 'I was going from the Academy straight to the Lyceum, intending to take the outer road, which is close under the wall. When I came to the postern gate of the city, which is by the fountain of Panops, I fell in with Hippothales [who] . . . asked whence I came and whither I was going' (203a).[83] 'Where do you come from?', the unnamed companion asks Socrates at the beginning of the *Protagoras*. Socrates says that he has 'just come' from seeing Alcibiades, and goes on to say that he has 'just come' from a discussion with the celebrated

Protagoras (309a). Both men were in fact present at the same discussion, but for a moment it seems as if Socrates was in two different places at the same time. He goes on to explain how 'last night, or rather very early this morning' (once again, it is a narration after the fact), he was woken by Hippocrates who was eager to be taught by the famed sophist (310b).[84]

Like the *Charmides*, the *Euthydemus* begins with yesterday, with Crito asking, 'Who was the person, Socrates, with whom you were talking yesterday [*khthès*] at the Lyceum?' (271a). In the crowd of listeners Crito was able to see but not to hear whom Socrates was talking with yesterday. Socrates goes on to 'repeat the whole story' of his conversation with Euthydemus and Dionysodorus which started when Socrates was once again caught in mid-step and *just about* to leave the Lyceum (272d–273a).[85]

The *Republic* also opens with yesterday, as Socrates says, 'I went yesterday [*khthès*] to the Piraeus with Glaucon.' By chance, Socrates goes on to say, he was seen 'from a distance' by Polemarchus and then grabbed by his cloak and held back by Polemarchus' servant to ensure that he waited for his master (327a–b). It is the odd combination of this chance sighting of Socrates with his being physically detained to guarantee that this leads to an actual encounter that opens the great dialogue of the *Republic*. Like so many of the dialogues, everything depends on a chance meeting: on being *startled* by the other.

The *Cratylus*, the *Gorgias* and the *Phaedrus* all begin as dialogues in which Socrates participates but is no longer a *narrator* opening and overseeing the scene. It is *only* without Socrates as narrator that these dialogues take place not yesterday, but *today*. When Socrates narrates it is always *yesterday*. In the *Cratylus* Socrates is *pulled into* a pre-existing and seemingly irresolvable dispute about names (383a). The dialogue has started *before* Socrates and he must re-start it, he must mimic and take the dialogue away from Cratylus. The *Gorgias* also starts with Socrates being *late* and the dialogue having to *start again*. Socrates has been detained by Chaerephon in the agora and missed the 'exhibition' of Gorgias. Chaerephon says, 'Never mind, Socrates . . . for Gorgias is a friend of mine, and I will make him give the exhibition again' (447a–b). In his dispute with Gorgias, Socrates will insist in the middle that they 'resume [*analabóntos*] the argument from the beginning' (506c).[86]

The *Phaedrus* opens with Socrates asking the wandering Phaedrus 'whence come you, and whither are you going?' While Phaedrus tries to convince Socrates to walk with him 'outside the wall', Socrates tries to persuade Phaedrus to repeat 'the speech of Lysias' that he has just tried to memorize (227a–c). Finally, Phaedrus says, 'Let me begin at the beginning' (*arkhsámenos apò tou prótou*). Socrates then interrupts him, saying 'but first of all show me what you have in your left hand under your cloak', and Phaedrus is forced to reveal the written text of Lysias' work (228d). It is only *after* the beginning has been interrupted (and inscribed) by writing that Socrates and Phaedrus walk along the banks of the Ilissus and sit down under a plane tree to carry on their conversation (230b).[87]

Like the *Parmenides*, the *Symposium* is neither narrated by Socrates nor presented as a dialogue of today and this leads to all sorts of disparate and tenuous chains of memory and repetition. As Cervantes, Johnson and Boswell after him, Plato cannot avoid inscribing the possibility of the origin of the work in the work itself. It all starts with a chance meeting. Apollodorus describes to an unnamed companion how, 'the day before yesterday', he was walking from his 'home at Phaerum to the city' when he was met by Glaucon. Glaucon has heard from an unnamed person who heard from Phoenix, the son of Philip, about the supper at Agathon's house where speeches in praise of love were made. Glaucon has got the date and time wrong, thinking that this supper had taken place recently. Apollodorus tells him that it happened many years ago and that he also heard the story from the 'same person who told Phoenix', one Aristodemus, who 'was a little fellow, who never wore any shoes'. Apollodorus then reassures Glaucon that he did not only rely on this short shoeless narrator but also asked Socrates 'about the truth of some parts of his narrative' (172a–b, 173a–c).[88] Socrates is not dead, but he is absent.

Both the *Timaeus* and the *Sophist* begin as dialogues without a narrator that take place the *day after* another event: 'one, two, three; but where, my dear Timaeus, is the fourth of those who were yesterday [*khthès*] my guests and are to be my entertainers today?' (17a); 'Here we are, Socrates, true to our agreement of yesterday [*khthès*]; and we bring with us a stranger from Elea, who is a disciple of Parmenides and Zeno, and a true philosopher' (216a).[89] While the dialogue that took place the day before the *Timaeus* is unrecorded, the *Sophist* is set the day *after* the *Theaetetus*. However, like the *Parmenides*, the *Theaetetus* is a dialogue marked by the absence of Socrates. Euclid and Terpsion meet and discuss the news that

Theaetetus has been wounded fighting in Corinth and Euclid mentions that many years ago he 'took notes' during a conversation between Theaetetus and Socrates. Euclid observes that as the author, he has 'introduced Socrates, not as narrating to me, but as actually conversing with the persons' who were present. Euclid then orders a servant to read the written text (142–3). Once again, the origin of the work is included in the work and as with the openings of the *Parmenides* and the *Symposium*, the start of the *Theaetetus* and the *Sophist* reverberate with the finitude, the absence and the death of Socrates the father. As Derrida suggests, from the start for Plato it is already too late, it is always *yesterday*.

'Where shall I begin?' (*póthen oun dè arksómetha*) the ageing Parmenides asks in Plato's dialogue (137b).

'Let's begin again' (*recommençons*), Derrida writes at the start of 'Plato's Pharmacy'.[90]

CHAPTER 2

HERODOTUS: ALMOST PRE-SOCRATIC

> Is not the quest for an *archai* in general, no matter with what precautions one surrounds the concept, still the 'essential' operation of metaphysics?
>
> Jacques Derrida[1]

KOSMOS, PHUSIS, ARKHĒ, LOGOS

If Derrida's early reading of Plato begins with a palintrope that startles ontology, it also raises the question of history, and it is through turning back once again to the eminently Heideggerian question of the *pre*-Socratics, and that *quasi* pre-Socratic and 'father' of history, Herodotus of Halicarnassus, that one can discern Derrida's very different journey towards the *possibility* of a history – of literature.

There seems to be little that did not interest Herodotus in the early fifth century BCE from Asia Minor to Greece, from Egypt to the Persian Empire and beyond. As Jean-Pierre Vernant and Pierre Vidal-Naquet suggested, fifth-century Greece saw the decline of the great Homeric myths of heroes and gods and the emergence of tragedy as the representation of the irresolvable conflict between the individual and the city-state.[2] It also saw the *historia* (the research, the inquiry, the history) of Herodotus. Born sometime at the start of the fifth century (490–480), Herodotus was a near contemporary of the philosophers Anaxagoras and Empedocles. He was familiar with such sixth-century philosophers as Thales and Pythagoras, and probably aware of the most influential philosopher at the time of the outbreak of the Persian wars, Heraclitus.

Socrates (470–399) was in his early forties when Herodotus died (c. 430–425). Plato, who refers to many of the principal characters in *The Histories* – Croesus, Cambyses, Cryrus, Darius, Xerxes, Themistocles – never mentions Herodotus. While Herodotus is thought to have spent some time in Athens between the 450s and 440s and may have visited again in 431–30, it is most likely that he was completing his research and writing just as Socrates was beginning his teaching in earnest.[3] *The Histories* were written in the lifetime of Socrates *and* engaged with what has been called 'pre-Socratic' thought. Herodotus' work neither simply precedes the thought of Socrates, nor can it be considered as merely contemporary with it. Herodotus is *almost* pre-Socratic.

The thinkers before Socrates were described variously as men of understanding (*sunetous*), wise men (*sophous*), or lovers of wisdom (*philosophous*).[4] As Jonathan Barnes notes, Aristotle called them natural philosophers (*phusikos*), a term that ranged from questions of physics to psychology.[5] Herodotus was a writer who undertook an inquiry and research (*historia*) into the causes and outcome of the Persian wars and the customs and stories of the non-Greeks.[6] Many of the so-called *phusikos* presented their ideas in long poems and, as Homer before him, Herodotus often presents the views of his protagonists in extended speeches and dialogues. While Plato displays a preoccupation with classification that has become integral to Western philosophy, it is likely that Herodotus' expansive concept of *historia* would have included some *phusiologia*. It is also possible that Herodotus' concept of *historia* offers an unclassified and broader scope for the work of philosophy than survived the fourth century and, in this sense, it could be called 'pre-Socratic'.

What is pre-Socratic? With the Aristotelian precision that one would expect from a distinguished editor of Aristotle, Jonathan Barnes characterizes pre-Socratic thought through four concepts: *kosmos* (the ordered whole); *phusis* (things that have grown, the essence of something, and opposed to things that are made, *tekhnē*); *arkhē* (the origin and beginning); and *logos* (speech, reason, reasoning through speaking).[7] If we accept this 'Aristotelian' definition as only one of a number of possible views of pre-Socratic thought, we can say that Thales, Anaximander, Pythagoras and Heraclitus invented 'philosophy' as a discipline concerned with *reasoning about the origin and essence of ordered wholes*. The pre-Socratics *invented* 'nature', 'whole', 'origin', 'reason' – and we are still trying to recover.

In 'Anaximander's Saying' (1946), his remarkable forty-page reading of one fragmentary line of Heraclitus, Heidegger warns that 'the implicit standard for explicating and judging the early thinkers is the philosophy of Plato and Aristotle'.[8] For Heidegger, this anachronistic reading rests primarily on assumptions about *phusis* (nature). Reading from the perspective of Plato and Aristotle, we would separate *phusis* from *mythos* and *logos*, and insist on the fundamental opposition between *phusis* (that which 'brings itself forth by arising out of itself') and *tekhnē* (what is 'brought forth through human planning and production').[9]

It is only after Plato, Heidegger argues, that we also begin to separate and to oppose *mythos* and *logos*.[10] Heidegger prompts the question of how we (those who come after Plato and Aristotle) can encounter a *phusis* that is *not* separated from *mythos*, *logos* and *tekhnē*. How can there not be a clear distinction between what grows (naturally) and what is made (artificially)? Today, as strains of GM crops blow across the fields and gardens of the world, it is far more likely that we would ask, how can there ever be a clear and *absolute* distinction between what grows naturally and what is made artificially?

Hegel said that 'we can do no better in Greek philosophy than study the first book of Aristotle's *Metaphysics*', and it is not fortuitous that Jonathan Barnes' list of the four fundamental concepts of pre-Socratic thought – *kosmos*, *phusis*, *arkhē* and *logos* – all appear in Aristotle's brief overview of philosophy from Thales to Plato at the opening of the *Metaphysics* (980a–984a).[11] As Hegel observes, Aristotle represents 'the unity of what has come before' (*Vereinigung der Bisherigen*).[12] In his 1966–67 seminars on Heraclitus with Eugen Fink, Heidegger warns that it is only after Aristotle that one can begin to call *kosmos*, *phusis*, *arkhē* and *logos concepts*.[13] Prior to their classification and assured and commonly understood definition, these words did not have a fixed or single meaning. For example, Heidegger argues that Heraclitus understands *arkhē* (later defined as the origin, beginning or first principle) as both 'the origin of ruling and directing' *and* 'the origin of movement'.[14] *Arkhē*: the origin that moves.

NOT PRE OR POST, BUT QUASI

In following Heidegger, in acting as a 'post-Heideggerian', there is the danger of reading Herodotus as an absolute pre-Socratic and treating *The Histories* as an archaic work that has no antecedents and few contemporaries.[15] Nonetheless, it is certainly the case that Herodotus is treated today more as the 'father of history' and less as the 'father of lies'.[16] As Arnaldo Momigliano observed more than forty years ago, 'it is a strange truth that Herodotus has really become the father of history only in modern times'.[17] Recent scholarship on *The Histories* has focused on the ethnographic aspects of the work, the digressions from the Persian wars on the customs, habits, laws and beliefs of the non-Greeks. There is a general agreement that *The Histories* are distinguished by an emphasis on custom (*nomos*) – and clearly *historia* includes both military and political history and an analysis of customs, traditions and beliefs – but there is ongoing debate over the relationship between custom and nature in Herodotus' work.[18]

On the other hand, such is the influence of Plato and Aristotle on all aspects of Western thought that Gadamer *begins* his reading of the pre-Socratics *with* Plato and Aristotle as 'the sole philosophical access to an interpretation of the Presocratics'.[19] Heidegger himself opened his reading of Plato's *Sophist* with 150 pages on Aristotle's *Nicomachean Ethics* and *Metaphysics*, arguing that only Aristotle can give the 'proper standpoint' and 'orientation' from which 'to watch Plato at work'.[20] We can only see Plato *from* Aristotle. The challenge that Heidegger opens, which perhaps risks a certain ahistoricism, is to read Herodotus without concepts, without the assurance that there is a single definition or meaning for any given word in *The Histories*. At the same time, as Derrida first suggested in 'Cogito and the History of Madness' (1963–64), one should be wary of the 'fascination' with the pre-Socratics which began with Nietzsche and became indispensable to Heidegger's preoccupation with the original thinking of being that predated Plato and Aristotle.[21] Derrida never stopped warning about both the inherent ahistorical *and* historicist assumptions behind any assured 'pre-ism' or 'post-ism'.[22]

To treat the pre-Socratics as a *pure resource*, as an ideal world that was entirely separated from the *fallen* and compromised world of Plato and Aristotle, is not only to return to the very Platonism and Aristotelianism that one apparently wishes to escape but also to imbue this division with a Christian pathos. As Derrida asks of Heidegger's work in '*Ousia* and *Grammē*' (1968), 'suppose, despite powerful presumptions, that one may eliminate it from any other provenance, is there not at least some Platonism in the *Verfallen*?'[23] At the beginning of *Of Grammatology* (1965–67), Derrida argues that 'from the pre-Socratics to Heidegger' the 'origin of truth in general' has *always* been assigned 'to the *logos*', and that 'the history of truth [*l'histoire de la vérité*], of the truth of truth' has always been founded on 'the debasement of writing, and its separation outside "full" speech'.[24] As he later remarks in 'Heidegger's Ear' (1989), in evoking the pre-Socratics, Heidegger 'clearly intends to return to a pre-Aristotelian, indeed pre-Platonic, hearing of *lógos*'.[25] And somewhat like Herodotus, when Derrida begins his own reading of Plato, it is not with the pre-Socratics, but with the Egyptians, with the non-Greeks, the barbarians, who came before the Greeks.[26]

How do we then read Herodotus, who is almost, but not quite, pre-Socratic? Commenting on the dialogue between Solon and Croesus in his translation of *The Histories*, David Grene notes, 'Herodotus keeps altering the nouns and adjectives with which he describes the desired object of human life . . . He is not a philosopher, using his terms to fix a definition, but a conversationalist, employing subtle differences in common usage'.[27] According to Grene, Herodotus is not a philosopher (not Plato or Aristotle) because in the discussion about happiness (*eudaimonia*) Solon suggests that being blessed by the gods (*olbios*) – being given divine attention – can also mean *not* being blessed (*olbios*) and can be distinguished from mere human good luck (*eutykhia*). Herodotus is a 'conversationalist', because he suggests that the same word can have two different meanings – much as Hegel did with the word *Aufhebung* – and that some words cannot be given a single fixed definition.[28]

It is possible, to put it in anachronistic terms, that for Herodotus *historia* is not a concept (if there is such a thing as a concept, of the concept as a single fixed definition). But how do we address *historia*? How historical or ahistorical is *historia*? How much is *historia*, the inquiry into the military and political events of the past and the inquiry in the customs, beliefs and traditions of non-Greeks, 'historical' or 'ahistorical', or even neither 'historical' nor 'ahistorical'? Whatever *historia* is, as Heidegger and Derrida both argued, we should not take it for granted that *historia* simply 'is', that it can be incorporated without pause into an ontology that always starts – with itself.

NIGHT CAME FIRST – BY A DAY

Of the so-called pre-Socratic philosophers, Herodotus only explicitly refers to Thales (1. 74–5, 170) and Pythagoras (2. 81; 4. 95). Isocrates tells us that Pythagoras of Samos 'went to Egypt and studied with the Egyptians'.[29] It is possible that Pythagoras' travels may have inspired Herodotus to undertake his own journey to Egypt. Evidently aware of Pythagoras' most notable idea, the immortality and transmigration of the soul, Herodotus makes it clear that this idea originated in Egypt:

> The Egyptians are the first who have told this story also, that the soul of man is immortal and that, when the body dies, the soul creeps into some other living thing then coming to birth; and when it has gone through all things, of land and sea and the air, it creeps again into a human body at its birth. The cycle for the soul is, they say, three thousand years. There are some Greeks who have used this story, some earlier and some later, as though it were something of their own. I know their names but will not write them down. (2. 123, Grene trans.)

Though Herodotus does not name Pythagoras, it is likely that he has him in mind. On the one hand, this implicit criticism of one school of Greek philosophy can be taken as a very pre-Socratic preoccupation (if we follow Aristotle). Herodotus wants to correct the order of precedence: the Egyptians came first (*protoi*). On the other hand, unlike the so-called *phusikos*, he does not say that the Egyptians were the *first* to do this (*arkhein*), simply that they did so *before* (*próteron*) the Greeks. Herodotus makes no claims here about the *arkhē*, about the origin as first principle, about a principle that might be above and beyond the *problem* of what came before. The fact that this problem of precedence concerns the relationship between the Greeks and the non-Greeks (or the 'barbarians' as they were called by the Greeks) is Herodotus' great theme: from the start, *historia* takes account of the constant *oscillation* of precedence between the Greeks and the non-Greeks.

According to Diogenes Laertius, when someone asked Thales of Miletus 'which came first, day or night, he answered, "Night came first – by a day"' (*he núks éphe mia eméra próteron*).[30] In his *Lectures on the History of Philosophy* (1805–31), Hegel warned against putting too much weight on the 'clever sayings' (*sinnreichen Sprüchen*) of the early Greek thinkers, but allowed that 'some of these sayings could not merely be regarded as thoughtful or good reflections, but in so far, as philosophic and speculative, they have a comprehensive, universal significance ascribed to them, which, however, does not explain them'.[31] Thales' 'clever saying' can be taken as a response to the need for an ordered sequence, a single or assured definition: a first principle (*arkhē*). When asked, '*What comes first: x or y*?' he answers, '*Y comes first*'. But he then adds, '*After x*'. '*Y comes first – after x.*' In other words, what comes *first* has already been *preceded* by something else. It still comes first, but 'first' is something that cannot be distinguished from what it follows. It is possible that Herodotus was aware of this famous saying of Thales which, already, puts into question Plato's later confidence in the self-idealizing origin as *the not x but the possibility of x*.

As Derrida argued in *The Post Card* (1980), since Plato and Aristotle it has been understood that 'Socrates comes *before* [avant] Plato'. It is 'an order of generations, an irreversible sequence of inheritance'. But when Derrida sees a postcard of a drawing in the Bodleian Library depicting Plato standing *behind* Socrates, it suggests that 'Socrates is before, not in front of, but before Plato, therefore behind him [*Socrates est avant, pas devant mais avant Platon, donc derrière lui*]'.[32] Derrida echoes Thales: what comes before suggests *at once* what is *behind* (before) and what is *in front* (before). What 'precedes us', Derrida later writes in the *Spectres of Marx* (1993), is 'as much *in front of us* as *before us* [*aussi bien* devant nous *qu'* avant nous]'.[33] What comes first, day or night? Night, by a day: before *and* in front, *avant et devant*. As Heidegger suggested, the first principle, the principle that is first (*arkhē*) *moves*, and it moves *from the first.*

In the *Physics*, Aristotle himself also recognizes an unavoidable indeterminacy in the concept of 'before' in relation to both time and place. We will come back to Aristotle and the question of time, for now in his discussion of *place* Aristotle turns to the question of direction and the 'distinctions' of 'up and down and right and left'. 'To *us*,' he writes, 'they are not always the same but change with the direction in which we are turned: that is why the same thing is often both right *and* left, up *and* down, before *and* behind [*prósthen kai ópisthen*]. But in *nature* each is distinct, taken apart by itself' (208b).[34] While allowing that the same thing can *appear to us* as both before *and* behind, Aristotle insists that nature (*phusis*) is immune from this relative difference: nature abhors what is at once before *and* behind. Derrida challenges the natural immunity of *phusis* from the interminable oscillations of the before *and* in front.

HISTORIA AND *PRÓTERON*

'Night came first – by a day'. If we follow Diogenes Laertius, Thales says night came before, came in front (*próteron*) – by a day. From the start, *historia* is preoccupied with the *problem* of what came before. Herodotus begins with how the conflict between the Greeks and the Persians *started*. The Persians *say* (*légousi*), he writes, that it *all began* (*arkhen*) with the Phoenician abduction and rape of Io and the Greek abduction and rape of Europa and Medea. The Greek invasion of Troy to avenge the abduction and rape of Helen was seen by the Persians as the first act of Greek aggression in their sphere of influence (1. 1–4). Herodotus notes that the Phoenicians 'disagree with the Persians' about the start of the conflict and say that Io left Argos voluntarily (1. 5). Herodotus describes these *claims* to *the* 'beginning' (*arkhen*), to the *arkhē*, as 'stories' (*légousi*): 'These are the stories [*légousi*] of the Persians and the Phoenicians. For my part I am not going to say about these matters that they happened thus or thus, but I will set my mark upon that man that I know began [*proton*] unjust acts [*àdíkon érgon*] towards the Greeks' (1. 5, trans. Grene). Herodotus *includes* the stories of the Persians and Phoenicians about 'the beginnings of their enmity toward the Greeks', but he does not accept them as the origin. He then turns to Croesus, where he believes the conflict began. In David Grene's translation, Herodotus writes, 'I will set my mark upon that man that I myself know began unjust acts against the Greeks'. In Aubrey de Selincourt's translation, Herodotus writes, 'I prefer to rely on my own knowledge, and to point out who it was in actual fact that first injured the Greeks.'[35] The difference between these two translations opens the very problem of *historia*: how far does an inquiry into what has come *before* also claim to be an account of what came *first*? For what it is worth, Herodotus does not say here that Croesus was *the* first (*arkhein*) to do unjust acts towards the Greeks. If Herodotus knows that Croesus 'began unjust acts towards the Greeks', this does not necessarily mean that he knows that Croesus was *the* first to do this. *Historia* may begin without an assured *arkhē* or, at the very least, with an irreducible gap – the gap of and as *historia* – between *arkhē* and *próteron*.

Herodotus goes on to give us the first explicit attribute of *historia*:

> I will set my mark upon that man that I myself know began unjust acts against the Greeks, and, having so marked him, I will go forward in my account, covering alike the small and great cities of mankind. For of those that were great in earlier times [*próso*] most have now become small, and those that were great in my time were small in the time before [*próteron*]. Since, then, I know that man's good fortune never abides in the same place, I will make mention of both alike. (I. 5, trans. Grene)[36]

Historia registers or defines 'the time before' as that which is more often than not *greater* than or *smaller* than what is 'in my time'. The 'time before' is, in most cases, that which was disproportionate to 'my time'. Tracing the rhythm and order of these contractions and expansions, *historia* teaches us 'that man's good fortune never abides in the same place'. The *disproportion* of the before teaches us a law of *displacement*. The disproportionate before displaces the (first) place. This is what *historia* is concerned with. It takes account of, it has to work with, the displacement of the *first* place, the origin or first principle, the good order of the whole that is always in one place, the *arkhē* and *kosmos* of the place.

Starting with what comes before, comes in front (*próteron*), *historia* must contend with the original displacement of the *arkhē* and *kosmos*. As Derrida writes in 'Cogito and the History of Madness' (1963–64) about Foucault's attempts to write a history or archaeology of madness beyond and outside of reason:

> A history, that is, an archaeology against reason doubtless cannot be written, for, despite all appearances to the contrary, the concept of history has always been a rational one. It is the 'meaning' of history or *archia* that should have been questioned first, perhaps [*qu'il eût peut-être fallu questionner d'abord*]. A writing that exceeds [*une écriture excédant*], by questioning them, the values of origin, of reason and of history could not be contained within the metaphysical closure of an archaeology.[37]

Questioning Foucault's characterization of the *origin* of history as the decisive separation of reason and madness, in which an idealizing *historicity* becomes the 'condition of meaning and of language, the condition of the tradition of meaning', Derrida asks how one would write the *history* of such an *origin of* history. 'The *hysteron proteron*', he argues, 'would not here be a simple "logical fallacy," a fallacy within logic, within an established rationality'.[38] In the same 1963–64 work where he turns to the *palintrope*, Derrida evokes the *hysteron proteron*, a sixteenth-century rhetorical figure, to describe an argument or phrase that has erroneously put what should come last (*husteros*, come late, be behind) in front, before or first (*proteron*).[39] For Derrida, 'if there is a historicity of reason in general, the history of reason cannot be the history of its origin (which *already* demands the historicity of reason in general), but must be that of one of its determined figures'.[40]

PAN ÈSTI ÁNTHROPOS SUMPHORÉ

It is a testament to Herodotus the quasi pre-Socratic that he introduces Solon as Solon the *sophist* (1. 29). Solon is not a *phusik*, but a *sophist* – a wise and learned man, a seeker of wisdom, who also travels. And one is tempted to ask why Solon, the political, legal and ethical philosopher, is excluded by Barnes from the pre-Socratic pantheon. Diogenes Laertius has no hesitation in including Solon among the eminent philosophers that lived before Socrates.[41] Diogenes also notes that Plato was most likely a descendant of Solon.[42] Hegel compares Solon the law-giver to Moses.[43] For Herodotus, Solon is the pre-eminent *sophist* of the sixth century and can in no way be confused with the later Platonic invention of the sophist as the Socratic *other*, as the dubious thinkers (Protagoras, Gorgias) who believe that virtue can be taught for a price and make Platonic propriety *possible*.

In his discussion with Croesus, Solon argues that it is precisely because the inquiry into what has come before can *only* respond to its disproportion with what is now (the greater becoming smaller and the smaller becoming greater) that one can judge whether a life has been happy or fortunate *only* by how well it ends (I. 32). A life (*bios*) can only be judged at the end, by the end (*telos*). For Hegel, Solon begins philosophy because he starts with 'the whole of life' (*das ganze Leben*). Solon recognizes 'a totality of enjoyment which is a universal', and directs the work of philosophy to go beyond 'sensuous enjoyment' and 'immediate pleasure'.[44] Philosophy begins with the end (*telos*) as a universal totality. But part of what distinguishes *historia* from the Aristotelian summation of pre-Socratic philosophy (*kosmos*, *phusis*, *arkhē* and *logos*) is not only the problem of the *gap* between what has come before and the origin, but also the problem of what is to come, of the end (*telos*), of teleology and eschatology.

For Solon, the *telos* can be illustrated by dying well, by the good death (I. 31). By linking the good death to the ability to make a judgement about what has come before (the indeterminacy of the smaller becoming greater, the greater becoming smaller), Solon suggests that *I* can never make such a judgement. The end, the final position of the expansions or contractions of good fortune, will always elude *me*. I am always *after*, in excess of, the end, of the *telos*. As Solon says to Croesus, he will make no judgement 'until I hear that you have brought your life to an end well' (I. 32). It is only the *other* who can make an inquiry (*historia*) into my life. *Historia* must always begin with the other.

But perhaps what is most remarkable about Herodotus of Halicarnassus, and gives him the status of a pre-Socratic on the margins, is his record of the words of Solon the Sophist. Solon has done something extraordinary: long before the early church historians began to calculate the time remaining till the end of days, he has counted 'all the days' of a man's life. 'All the days of man's life', he tells Croesus, 'are twenty-six thousand two hundred and fifty.' From this exceptional act of teleology he concludes, 'of all those days not one brings to him anything exactly the same as another. So, Croesus, man is entirely what befalls him' (I. 32). The *telos* of the *próteron* teaches us that not one day of the past is *ever the same*. When it comes to *historia* nothing is the same (*homoios*). *Historia* can *only* work with what is always different (*heteros*). For Solon, this suggests that 'man is entirely what befalls him' (*pan èsti ánthropos sumphoré*), or as another translation says, 'the whole of man is but chance'.[45] This short phrase invites an infinite reading, a reading *without rest*. Not just man, but the *whole* of man 'is but chance'. Man (*ánthropos*) is chance, the chance happening, the assurance of an *event*, of something happening, that is always unforeseeable.[46] In the last years of Herodotus' life, Sophocles has Jocasta say in *Oedipus the King* (c. 430):

> It's all chance [*tukhē*],
> chance rules our lives. Not a man on earth
> can see a day ahead, groping through the dark.[47]

What *historia* perhaps teaches us about the past, about what has come before, is that the *future* of the past always remains *to come*. It was Heidegger, who was always trying to re-gather the *logos* in the pre of the pre-Socratics, who also recognized the importance of the future *of* the past, of a '*handing down* to oneself' (*Sichüberliefern*) that, in its finitude, is always *open* to the future possibilities of the past.[48]

THE HISTORY OF THE DEPARTURES FROM TOTALITY

As both Herodotus and Derrida suggest, history must always contend with the heading of the other, with the other heading. As Derrida observed in 1991, 'Like every history, the history of culture no doubt presupposes an identifiable heading, a *telos* toward which the movement, the memory, the promise, and the identity, even if it be as difference to itself, dreams of gathering itself: *taking the imitative, being out ahead, in anticipation* (*anticipatio, anticipare, antecapere*). But history also presupposes that the heading not be *given*, that it not be identifiable in advance and once and for all.'[49] With all its rigour of getting the order right, with its searching for chronology and its grasping at linearity, history must also begin with the digression of the unforeseeable.

It is perhaps not fortuitous that the 'father' of history devoted his work both to a war between the Greeks and the non-Greeks, and to long digressions on the non-Greeks.[50] Reflecting in 'Violence and Metaphysics' (1964) on Lévinas' attempts to counteract the Hegelian totality and colonization of alterity through an absolutely other that embodies the ethics of an absolute peace above and beyond the negation and violence of speculative history, Derrida offers his own description of a history that cannot escape a certain warfare and digression, of a history that is always *departing* from the whole of man since, as Herodotus had written sometime in the late fifth century, *pan èsti ánthropos sumphoré*:

> There is war only after the opening of discourse, and war dies out only at the end of discourse. Peace, like silence, is the strange vocation of a language called outside itself by itself. But since *finite* silence is also the medium of violence, language can only indefinitely tend toward justice by acknowledging and practicing the violence within it. Violence against violence. *Economy* of

violence. An economy irreducible to what Levinas envisions in the word. If light is the element of violence, one must combat light with a certain other light, in order to avoid the worst violence, the violence of the night which precedes or represses discourse. This *vigilance* is a violence chosen as the least violence by a philosophy which takes history, that is, finitude, seriously; a philosophy aware of itself as *historical* in each of its aspects (in a sense which tolerates neither finite totality, nor positive infinity), and aware of itself, as Levinas says in another sense, as *economy*. But again, an economy which in being history, can be *at home* neither in the finite totality which Levinas calls the Same nor in the positive presence of the Infinite . . . *Within history* which the philosopher cannot escape, because it is not history in the sense given it by Levinas (totality), but is the history of the departures from totality [*l'histoire des sorties hors de la totalité*], history as the very movement of transcendence, of the excess over the totality without which no totality would appear as such.[51]

CHAPTER 3

THE HISTORY – OF LITERATURE

> We cannot think of a line without *drawing* it in thought, we cannot think of a circle without *describing* it, we cannot represent the three dimensions of space at all without *placing* three lines perpendicular to each other at the same point, and we cannot even represent time without . . . *drawing* a straight line.
>
> Kant, *Critique of Pure Reason* [1]

L'HISTOIRE – DE LA LITTÉRATURE

In the essays collected in *Writing and Difference* (1963–67) and in *Dissemination* (1968–72), Derrida attempted to redefine the traditional role played by history and literature in philosophy. From Plato to Hegel, he suggests, philosophy (as unchanging truth, science, *epistēmē*) has reinforced its authority by dismissing, relegating and colonizing history (as external changes in time) and literature (as subjective opinion, *doxa*). As we have seen, in 'Violence and Metaphysics' (1964), Derrida argued that while Lévinas attempts to escape Hegel by placing the absolutely other beyond and outside of history, it is only through an alterity within history that one can resist Hegelianism. Derrida redefines history as 'the history of departures from totality', as an excess that is at once the possibility *and* the ruin of any totality.[2] Eight years later in 'Outwork, Prefacing' (1972), Derrida suggested that far from simply being a *doxa* that *epistēmē* can always refute and outmanoeuvre, literature confronts philosophy with a disruption of the part–whole relation, the basic architecture of inductive and deductive reasoning. Derrida writes: 'But if the formula for this absolute knowledge [*savoir absolu*] can be thought about and put in question, the whole is treated then by a "part" bigger than itself [*le tout s'agit alors d'une "partie" plus grande que lui*]; this is the strange subtraction of a *remark* whose theory is borne by dissemination and which constitutes the whole, necessarily, as a *totality-effect*.' 'Literature', he argues, can then be seen as 'a part that, within *and* without the whole [*dans* et *hors le tout*], marks the wholly other, the other incommensurate with the whole'.[3]

It has perhaps not always been recognized that from his earliest work on Husserl and Heidegger Derrida was concerned with the question of history, and in his readings of Plato and Aristotle in the late 1960s and his retranslations of Heidegger in the 1970s he gestures to the *possibility* of a history *of* literature.[4] The problems that Derrida raises about writing a history of literature can also be seen in attempts from the sixteenth to the twentieth century to establish 'The History of English Literature'.

In the midst of his 1969 seminar, which was published in 1970 as 'The Double Session', Derrida wrote the phrase 'the history – of literature –' (*l'histoire – de la littérature –*).[5] He did not write 'the history of literature', but 'the history – of literature –'. If you read this phrase out loud, you introduce a pause, a caesura or lacuna between 'the history' and 'of literature'. To begin to contemplate what a history of literature might entail, Derrida suggests, we have to take account of this pause, this graphic pause marked by a short line between 'the history' 'of literature'. For Derrida, the graphic can never simply be *separated* from the phonic nor can it be entirely *subsumed* to the phonic: this very desire is at the heart of much of the Graeco-Christian tradition that shapes Western philosophy. For Socrates, philosophy only truly *begins* when one is able finally to dispense with the body and listen to the soul. Socrates says this in the *Phaedo* just before he dies, and since Plato there has been this death-wish in philosophy, a death-wish that Derrida spent a lifetime fighting.

So, we must take the *graphics* of 'the history – of literature –' seriously. To start with, what exactly do we call this line, this printed straight line between 'the history' 'of literature'?[6] Is it a hyphen, a dash, an *en* or an *em* rule?

HYPHEN, DASH, EN RULE, EM RULE

The word hyphen comes from the Greek *huphen* meaning together and is defined by the *OED* as 'a punctuation mark used to connect two words together'. It is also used 'to indicate a missing or implied element'. A hyphen connects, brings together two words: it is a bridge. At the same time, like any bridge, it also indicates that there is a space between these two words. A few sentences after Derrida writes 'history – of literature' in 'The Double Session', he writes 'being-present' (*étant-présent*).[7] The hyphen in 'being-present' marks at once a bridge *and* a gap between 'being' and 'present'. When there is a hyphen, there is a bridge *and* there is a gap that *cannot be closed*. The hyphen brings together what can never *absolutely* be brought together: there is always a gap. As Derrida suggested in *Artaud le Moma* (1996), the hyphen appears to make *one* out of two, but this two-in-one also indicates what is always *more than one*.[8]

What are we to make of a 'small phrase between dashes', Derrida asks in *Glas* (1974)?[9] The dash has a multitude of dynamic meanings in the *OED* (a violent blow, part of the Morse code, a small quantity of something, showy behaviour, a race), which include a *straight line* that marks 'a parenthetical clause, break in sense, omission, substitution, etc.'. *Between* history and literature Derrida places a graphic mark, an instance of a 'break in sense', a moment of non-meaning. It is a graphic mark that Derrida *places* between history and literature to indicate something that is without place, something that can be dis-placed and re-placed. Unlike the hyphen, which brings together what cannot be brought together without a bridge (and an irreducible gap), the dash is associated with a speed and violence. It is not so much a bridge, as a *stroke* that strikes the paper in a single line, opening a sudden division or separation that can never be bridged, and that – for a moment – makes no sense.

It is difficult to think of the dash without Emily Dickinson, that violent queen of dashes.[10] Her early poems have an occasional dash at the end of a line. After the mid-1850s, these strange hovering pauses begin to appear in the middle of a line, not as the caesura of the single dash – that literary convention that apparently cuts a line perfectly in two – but as *two* dashes for a parenthetical observation, a conversational aside:

> And the Earth – they tell me –
> On its axis turned![11]

From the late 1850s, Dickinson's dashes begin to multiply, until every line and every phrase seems to be suspended by a dash, by a hovering *stroke* of non-sense, a mute onomatopoeia that makes sound and meaning possible:

South Winds jostle them –
Bumblebees come –
Hover – hesitate –
Drink, and are gone –[12]

While the dashes 'hover – hesitate' and become an index of incalculable speeds, they also become an explicit shorthand for an incalculable and insurmountable silence:

I have a King, who does not speak –
So – wondering – thro' hours meek
I trudge the day away –[13]

'We can find no scar, / But internal difference, / Where the Meanings, are –.'[14] 'The space – began to toll.'[15] The dashes in Dickinson's work mark an indispensable and relentless silent speed, a speeding silence, the dashing *strokes* of a soundless violence, of a spacing without which there can be no rhythm, no words, no voice, no meaning, no poetry:

How many times these low feet staggered –
Only the soldered mouth can tell –
Try – can you stir the awful rivet –
Try – can you lift the hasps of steel!

Stroke the cool forehead – hot so often –
Lift – if you care – the listless hair –
Handle the adamantine fingers
Never a thimble – more – shall wear –

Buzz the dull flies – on the chamber window –
Brave – shines the sun through the freckled pane –
Fearless – the cobweb swings from the ceiling –
Indolent Housewife – in Daisies – lain![16]

In Barbara Johnson's translation of 'La double séance', Derrida's strange phrase '*l'histoire – de la littérature –*' is translated as 'history—the history of literature—'. This repetition of history in the second part of the phrase effectively negates the strange gap of the hyphen and soundless stroke of the dash. The hyphens and dashes have become no more than a parenthetical emphasis. A bridge without a gap has been built between the words, erasing the resonating pause, the hovering silence, between 'the history – of literature –'. The English translation also belies Derrida's earlier caution around the phrase 'the history of literature'.[17]

The English translation has also changed the length of the hyphen or dash from an *en rule* to an *em rule*. In the wonderful language of printing, in the words coined for printing words, a straight line in the text is known as a *rule*. Taken from the Latin *regula* for a straight stick or bar, the gap of the hyphen and the stroke of the dash are recast as a rule, as a line or principle of regulation, governance, custom, discipline and power. This translation is an invitation to Michel Foucault! A rule is also a 'standard of discrimination or estimation; a criterion, a test, a measure'. Translated from a hyphen or a dash into a rule, the graphic marks that Derrida placed between history and literature become a self-measuring standard for the clear discrimination between history and literature. It is the law (the straight line) that divides and discriminates 'history' and 'literature'. By changing the rule from a short unit of measurement (en rule) to a long unit of measurement (em rule), the translation emphasizes that this straight line cannot be crossed.

LE TRAIT AND THE LINE OF TRUTH

In French, a line, a stroke or a mark is *un trait*, and the hyphen a *trait d'union*, a line that combines or juxtaposes.[18] A dash is *un tiret*, and comes from the verb *tirer*, to pull, to draw open, to draw out, to shoot, to fire. *Tirer un trait* is to draw a line. A *tiret* or a *trait de plume* is a stroke of the pen, a dash.[19] While the French echoes the English connotations of hyphen (the bridge as irreducible gap) and dash (the violence of a silent stroke), *un trait* also means a *trace*. In English, the hyphen and the dash are kinds of lines. In French, the *trait d'union* and *trait de plume* are lines that are also traces. A trace is a mark, but it is also a mark of the *past*, from the past, it has a temporality: a *history*.

It is perhaps not fortuitous that when Derrida first turns to the *question* of a history of literature at the start of 'The Double

Session', *le trait* is not far away. Having begun the seminar juxtaposing two long citations from Plato's *Philebus* and Mallarmé's *Mimique*, Derrida writes:

> Because of a certain fold [*pli*] that we shall outline [*dessinerons*], these texts, and their commerce, definitely escape any exhaustive treatment. We can nevertheless begin to mark out, in a few rough strokes [*à gros traits*], a certain number of motifs. These strokes [*traits*] might be seen to form a sort of frame, the enclosure or borders of a history [*une sorte de cadre, la clôture, les bordures d'une histoire*] that would be that of a certain play between literature and truth.[20]

These strokes (*traits*) indicate the *history* of 'a certain interpretation of *mimesis*' that has taken place from Plato to Mallarmé. 'This history', Derrida goes on to write, 'was also a history of literature [*une histoire de la littérature*] if one accepts the idea that literature was born of it and died of it, the certificate of its birth as such, the declaration of its name, having coincided with its disappearance, according to a logic that the hymen will help us define'. Based on the Platonic understanding of *mimesis*, this history of the birth and death of literature has been a history *of* truth.[21] At the same time, Derrida argues, it has also marked another history, the history of the spatio-temporal differing and deferring of the *between* (the hymen), of what remains '*between* literature and truth' (entre *littérature et vérité*).[22]

What is perhaps most striking here is that for Derrida *le trait* accounts for this *history* of the *difference* between a literature *of* truth and a literature *between* truth. It is only a few pages later that Derrida writes of '*l'histoire – de la littérature –*':

> Perhaps, then, there is always more than one kind of *mimesis*; and perhaps it is in the strange mirror that reflects but also displaces and distorts one *mimesis* into the other, as though it were itself destined to mime or mask itself, that history – the history of literature – is lodged, along with the whole of its interpretation [*que se loge l'histoire – de la littérature – comme la totalité de son interprétation*].[23]

Derrida goes on to suggest that it is the *trait* that accounts for 'the history – of literature' as a literature *between* truth, a literature in which 'there is always more than one kind of *mimesis*'. The 'presence of the present' is the 'invariable feature' (*le trait invariant*, the invariable stoke, line, trace) of the unity of *mimesis* that only works for truth:

> The invariable feature [*le trait invariant*] of this reference sketches out [*dessine*] the closure of metaphysics: not as a border enclosing some homogeneous space but according to a noncircular, entirely other, figure. Now, this reference is discreetly but absolutely displaced in the workings of a certain syntax, whenever any writing both marks and goes back over its mark with an undecidable stroke [*marque et redouble la marque d'un trait indécidable*].[24]

In marking itself, in referring *to* itself, in *re*-marking itself, *mimesis* (as truth, as the presence of the present) exceeds itself. It exceeds the truth, and the truth becomes a part *of* 'the history – of literature'. The *possibility* of 'the history – of literature' is 'an undecidable stroke' (*un trait indécidable*). Three years later in *Spurs: Nietzsche's Styles* (1972), Derrida once again links the question of history and of the history of truth to the graphics of *le trait*: 'The truth has therefore not always been woman. The woman is not always truth. The one and the other have a history, form a history – history itself perhaps [*une histoire – l'histoire elle-même peut-être*], if the precise value of history is always presented as such in the movement of truth – that philosophy alone cannot decode, itself being included in it.'[25]

Derrida had first touched on the *graphics* of the *trait* (the stroke, the line, the trace) in his 1961–62 introduction to Husserl's *The Origin of Geometry* (1936). In this late essay, Husserl attempts to resolve the problem of the incompatibility of history and truth through a phenomenological *tradition* of truth (the historicity *of* ideal objects). For Husserl, truth (ideal objectivity) uses language as its representative while maintaining its absolute independence. Language assists the truth, it never compromises it. Along with speech, which provides a present and immediate subjectivity to support the truth, writing offers a 'virtualizing' (an absent and non-immediate communication) that reflects 'absolutely permanent ideal objectivities'.[26] This is how writing works *for* truth.

Confronted with the 'sensible spatiotemporality' of language, Derrida argues that Husserl treats the graphic as the most spiritual of bodies. Writing incarnates, embodies the truth, but Husserl gives 'the impression that ideal objectivity is fully constituted as such *before* and *independently* of its embodiment'.[27] At the same time, Husserl suggests that a tradition of truth *relies* on the 'graphic possibility', and this *absolute* before, this absolute independence, is not so assured. As a tradition of truth, writing already accounts for 'the possibility of truth's disappearance': the graphic mark can always be erased, effaced, torn, burnt. The *trait* (stroke, line, trace) of a history of truth, of a history *as* truth, can never rule out the accidental or the catastrophic.[28]

For Husserl, the straight line has a significant role in the origin of geometry. As we have seen, according to Husserl before geometry there were bodies and shapes, *sensible* idealities that became, with the advent of geometry, *pure* geometrical idealities. The increasing accuracy and rigidity of the line is part of the *origin* of geometry. As Derrida writes,

> by a practical necessity of daily life, certain shapes and certain processes of transformation could be perceived, restored, and progressively perfected; for example, rigid lines, even surfaces, and so forth. Every morphological, i.e., pregeometrical, determination works according to qualitative graduations of sensible intuition: *more or less smooth* surfaces, sides, lines, or *more or less rough* angles, and so on.

With the institution of geometry, these approximate and partly sensible lines become pure and infinite straight lines.[29] The origin of geometry is the *idealization* of straight lines, the birth of non-sensible, non-imaginary lines: the line as the truth, the truth of the line. The line of truth is a line without sense, a line that always transcends a history – of the senses.

THE TIME OF THE LINE OR THE LINE OF TIME

Aristotle had argued in *De Anima* that the straight line begins with a *point* or 'a unit having position'. A unit is a basic indivisible whole: it has no parts or interior differences.[30] A point is an *indivisible whole*, a *one* that has a position, a one *in* space and *of* space: a concept of space that endures and supports an undivided primal one. A line is a *point extended in space*. Derrida notes in 'Force and Signification'

(1963) that this is precisely how structuralism defines the line: a line *of* space, a line without *time*.[31] Derrida traces this structuralist inheritance from Aristotle to Leibniz in its assumption that 'confronted with a literary work, one should always be able to find a line [*trouver une ligne*], no matter how complex, that accounts for the unity, the totality of its movement, and all the points it must traverse'.[32] In 'Force and Signification', Derrida also quotes from Delacroix that 'there are lines which are monsters' (*il y a des lignes qui sont des monstres*), and he ends his essay by contrasting the structuralist-Husserlian 'epiphany of lines' to the 'force and movement which displaces lines'.[33] He develops this argument in *Of Grammatology*, making the case for a *text* – the traces of and as *différance* – that 'disturbs the time of the line or the line of time' (*dérange ainsi le temps de la ligne ou la ligne du temps*).[34]

In *Of Grammatology*, Derrida links the profound and lasting influence of the 'concept of *linearization*' to Heidegger's description of 'a concept of time thought in terms of spatial movement or of the now'.[35] As we shall see, for Heidegger the lamentable spatialization of time begins with Aristotle.[36] What interests Derrida, on the contrary, is that in relying on the now to *account* for time in the *Physics*, Aristotle cannot avoid *comparing* time to space, to a line.[37] As he notes in '*Ousia* and *Grammē*' (1968), the influence of this comparison can still be seen in Kant, who argues in the *Critique of Pure Reason* that because 'time is nothing other than the form of inner sense' (*die Zeit ist nichts anders, als die Form des innern Sinnes*), and has nothing to do with the 'determination of outer appearances', with shapes or positions, we 'attempt to remedy this lack through analogies, and represent the temporal sequence through a line progressing to infinity'.[38] For Kant, the 'straight line' (*gerade Linie*) is 'the external figurative representation [*Vorstellung*] of time'.[39]

For Aristotle, like a point in relation to a line (*grammē*), the now gives *continuity* to the before and after, and it *limits* the before and after.[40] As Derrida observes, 'it is because movement is determined according to the before and after [*l'avant et l'après*] that the graphic linear representation of time is simultaneously required and excluded by Aristotle'. Aristotle does not want time to be seen simply as a line. Time is not a series of discrete points that are always the same, as a 'continuous, extended unfolding of punctuality'.[41] For Aristotle, when you use 'the same point' as *both* 'the beginning and the end', 'a pause is necessary' (220a). In other words, as Derrida notes, if one treats the boundary of the now as a point there is an unavoidable pause, *un arrêt*, a *gap*.[42] Comparing time to a line leaves a gap – in time.

Aristotle attempts to resolve this problem of space as an arresting limit in time by turning to his great resource: potentiality and actuality. If one treats the point as potentiality and the line as actuality, the now as a point is never actually there: it is always *waiting* for actuality, for presence. For Aristotle, this means that the line in relation to *time* is not matter, but form. And, Derrida argues, it also means that the line can only become a *circle*. Aristotle's account of time requires the comprehension of spatialization: the point becomes a line becoming a circle. The line as actuality, as presence, is a tracing that *erases* its own traces: it keeps going in circles.[43] For Derrida, this is the *limit* of the line as presence: it can *only* trace the erasure of its own traces (*grammē*: line, trace). The line, the linearization of the straight line, can only erase its *own* traces of *différance*, of space becoming time *and* time becoming space.[44]

Derrida argues in *Of Grammatology* that 'the work of spacing' already limits the *imperium* of the straight line: 'What cannot be thus represented by a line [*une ligne*] is the turn (trick/trope) of the re-turn [*le tour du re-tour*] when it has the bearing of re-presentation. What one cannot represent is the relationship of representation to so-called originary presence. The re-presentation is also a de-presentation. It is tied to the work of spacing.'[45] In almost the last line of *Writing and Difference*, in a short essay on Edmond Jabès, Derrida observes, 'the time of writing [*le temps de l'écriture*] no longer follows the line [*ne suit plus la ligne*] of modified present tenses'.[46] To start, we can only begin with *le tour du re-tour*, with a turning backwards, again, with the *palintrope* of a turning back that also turns once more *and* always more than once. Before we have even started, the *trace* brings us to 'the impossibility of beginning at the beginning of the straight line [*cette impossibilité de commencer par le commencement de droit*]'.[47]

A *RE-TRAIT EN RETRAIT*

Before we have even started, *une ligne* becomes *un trait*. By 1969, Derrida had translated this history of and as linearization into the graphics of *le trait* and 'the history – of literature', and by 1972 into 'a history – history itself perhaps'. By 1978, he would describe the four essays collected in *The Truth in Painting* (1974–78) as being preoccupied with 'le trait *lui-même*'.[48] The stroke, the line, the trace, the trait itself: always somewhere in between. The trait *itself*, Derrida will argue, is a *re-trait* always *en retrait*. In other words, the trait *itself* is always repeating, withdrawing or retreating *from* itself as itself and giving itself *to* the other: re-tracing, re-drawing and with-drawing.[49]

From his earliest work on Husserl in the 1950s, Derrida had been concerned with the inescapable *oscillation* between a history of philosophy *and* a philosophy of history, and the problem of the oscillation between philosophy and history is at the heart of Derrida's 1973–74 seminar on the question of 'art', which was published in fragments in *The Truth in Painting* under the title 'Parergon'.[50] The fragments of the seminar explore the presupposition of a truth of art that unveils itself '*through* history' (à travers *l'histoire*). This presupposition lends itself to both a *historicism* (as 'the determining character of the historicity of meaning') and an *ahistoricism* (as history 'transfixed in the direction of meaning'). For Derrida, 'history' then becomes the problem of an oscillation that can be determined *neither* as historicism *nor* as ahistoricism, in other words, as a history *of* meaning:

> As for history [*l'histoire*], we shall have to deal with the contradiction or the oscillation between [*à l'oscillation entre*] two apparently incompatible motifs. They both ultimately come under one and the same logical formality: namely, that if the philosophy of art always has the greatest difficulty in dominating the history of art, a certain concept of the historicity of art, this is, paradoxically, because it too easily thinks of art as historical. What I am putting forward here obviously assumes the transformation, from one statement to the other, of the concept of history. That will be the work of this seminar[51]

In *The Truth in Painting*, Derrida argues that the event – the event even perhaps of 'the history – of literature' – 'makes a contract with itself only at the instant when the singularity of the trait divides itself [*la singularité du trait se divise*]', doubles itself and exposes itself to the unforeseeable.[52] The trait opens a gap, a gap that cannot be closed or bridged or used as an enabling separation or division (a gap that is always waiting-to-be-closed). The trait is a gap that *moves*.[53] Throughout the 1970s, Derrida in part developed the trait *en retrait* or the gap that moves by retranslating Heidegger's use of *Entfernung*, *Riss*, *Aufriss* and *Entziehung*.

In *Being and Time* (1927), Heidegger had argued that 'Dasein does not have the kind of Being which belongs to something merely present-at-hand [*vorhanden*] within the world, nor does it ever have it.' Being-in-the-world (*In-der-Welt-sein*), *Dasein* cannot be described as merely inside or outside of the world, nor characterized as simply a subject or object.[54] When it comes to *space*, to the spatiality of Being-in-the-world, '"spatiality" [*Räumlichkeit*] cannot signify anything like occurrence at a position in "world-space", nor can it signify Being-ready-to-hand [*Zuhandensein*] at some place'. For *Dasein*, space is indicated through an *Ent-Fernung*, which Macquarrie and Robinson translate as *de-severance*. Heidegger marks a gap between *ent* (negation, reversal, removal) and *fern* (far, distant, remote), and *Ent-fernung* (withdrawal) becomes the *removal* of the far or the distant. *Ent-fernung* 'amounts to making the farness vanish – that is, making the remoteness of something disappear, bringing it close'. Withdrawal removes the far and brings the close. To bring something close, one has to *start* with the distant and remote. The relative relation of *Dasein* to closeness and farness cannot be determined as present-at-hand.[55]

In both *Spurs* (1972–78) and *Parages* (1976–79), Derrida retranslates *Ent-Fernung* as *é-loignement*, as 'the distancing of distancing'.[56] While Heidegger insists that *Dasein* can never simply be close (present-at-hand) or far (present-at-hand), he also argues that '*in Dasein there lies an essential tendency towards closeness*'. For Derrida, this relative differing of approximation is always *on its way to* proximity and propriety. In retranslating *Ent-fernung* as *é-loignement* Derrida redefines the movement of *withdrawal* as both the possibility *and* the ruin of proximity, of the presence of the present. There is neither the time nor the space to start or end with *the* near or *the* far.

Throughout *The Truth in Painting*, Derrida refers to and defers from another retranslation of Heidegger, which he eventually published in the paper 'The Retrait of Metaphor' (1978). He begins with *le trait* as a translation of *der Riss*, the stroke, tear, rip, gap, the sketch or outline. In 'The Origin of the Work of Art' (1936–37) Heidegger writes, 'The rift is the drawing together, into a unity, of sketch and basic design, breach and outline' (*Der Riss ist das einheitliche Gezüge von Aufriss und Grundriss, Durch – und Umriss)*.[57] Derrida suggests that there are at least two ways of reading this passage.

On the one hand, he argues, Heidegger 'names the "stroke" [le "*trait*"] (*Riss*) which not only opens above the gulf but also holds together the opposite edges of it [*tient ensemble les rives adverses*]'.[58] Heidegger evokes *der Riss* (the 'trait') as that which rips, tears and cuts open a gap (*Aufriss*) and *maintains* this gap: it holds its edges in place, it brings it together, and stops it from moving. It gathers itself together 'into a unity'. The trait opens *and* closes the gap.

On the other hand, Derrida points out, in describing the *line*, the trait, the trace (*Riss*) of drawing as a tearing open of an outline or sketch (*Aufriss*, *Umriss*) and as the attraction or contraction 'into a unity' (*Gezüge*, *Zug*), Heidegger *also* suggests in his later *On the Way to Language* (1959) that the line and the trait furrows, hauls, pulls and draws itself along, removing, retracting and withdrawing (from) itself (*Ziehen*).[59] The trait opens, it brings together – *and* it withdraws (*Entziehen*). It attracts, contracts – and retracts.

While he retranslates *Ent-fernung* as *é-loignement*, Derrida also retranslates *Riss* as *trait*, *Aufriss* as *entame* (incision, breaching, broaching, first cut), and *Entziehen* as *re-trait*. For Derrida, the *line* that draws (tears, pulls and with-draws), 'the line which frames the picture, cutting it off from its outside', cannot avoid moving.[60] It cannot avoid an interlacing (*Geflecht*), a weaving at once inside *and* outside of its edges, its borders.[61] The line always crosses the outline. The line diverges and withdraws (*écarter*). Interlacing (from) itself, the 'line [*ligne*] is already a tracing [*tracé*] of coming and going between the outside and the inside [*d'aller-retour entre le dehors et le dedans*]'.[62] From the start, it is a question of the 'divergences [*écarts*, the gaps] . . . of the trait', of 'the essential parasitizing which opens every system to its outside and divides the unity of the line [*trait*] which purports to make its edges [*le border*]'.[63] The straight line is always *en retrait*, from the start: 'A trait never appears, never itself [*lui-même*], never for a first time. It begins by retrac(t)ing [*il commence par se retirer*].'[64]

It is worth noting that in making the case for his slightly abusive translation of *Entziehung* in 'The Retrait of Metaphor', Derrida also distinguishes the *re-trait* of the line from the hyphen (*trait d'union*).[65] Marking itself, the trait can only *re-trait* (from) itself, re-mark and exceed itself and indicate 'a discourse whose rhetorical border is no longer determinable according to a simple and indivisible line, according to a linear and indecomposable trait'.[66] The *re-trait* of the line is a 'tracing of fraying which cuts, tears [and] marks the divergence' (*tracement de frayage qui incise, déchire, marque l'écart*). The *re-trait* of the line marks the gap that *moves*, that diverges from itself. It frays the ideality of the straight line with '*un écart différentiel*'. Derrida concludes that in the passage from 'The Origin of the Work of Art', the trait (*Riss*) 'attracts adversity to the unity of the contour', it contracts an 'ensemble of reassembled traits' that 'open the delimitation, the de-marcation from which ontological discourse on substance, predicate, proportion, logic and rhetoric, can then be stripped away'. 'The *Grundriss* is *Aufriss*': from the start, the ground plan is the *first* cut of the trait re-tracing itself, beyond ontology.[67]

Retranslating Heidegger, Derrida suggests that the *re-trait* between history and literature does not simply bring them close, nor does it merely set them clearly apart: it leaves them both *in the vicinity* (*parages*) of themselves. Oscillating, not vacillating. The *re-trait between* history and literature can be seen as a 'common origin' that is 'neither fully originary and autonomous, nor, as fraying, purely derivative'.[68] The line, the trait *en retrait* is at once the *possibility* of 'the history – of literature' *and* 'it does not appear itself, it has no proper and independent phenomenality, and in not disclosing itself, it withdraws, it is structurally in withdrawal as a divergence [*en retrait, comme écart*]'.[69] The *re-trait* can never be a gap that fills itself, or a bridge that delivers history *to* literature or gives literature *to* history.[70] For Derrida, the strange suspensions of literature that make a part greater than the whole that would encompass it, cannot be reduced to *either* a historicism *or* an ahistoricism.

THE HISTORY – OF ENGLISH LITERATURE

'The history – *re-trait* – of literature': has English literature ever not been anxious about this elusive and unbridgeable gap between history and literature? Has English literature ever escaped the anxiety that somehow the literary will tip over the edge and become the historical or that the historical will fall into the literary? Has English literature been worrying about anything else since it began as the writings of the Angles, Jutes and Saxons, since Beowulf faced the monster Grendel?

In the introduction to his poem *Annus Mirabilis: The Year of Wonders, 1666*, John Dryden worried about his status as a poet chronicling contemporary historical events. One of the self-proclaimed fathers of literary criticism, Dryden treated the Restoration as a chance to restore, to elevate, to clarify and to define, the work of literature. 'I have called my poem *historical*, not *epic*', he writes, 'though both the actions and actors are as much heroic, as any poem can contain. But since the action is not properly one . . . I have judged it too bold a title for a few stanzas . . . For this reason (I mean not of length, but broken action, tied too severely to the laws of history), I am apt to agree with those who rank Lucan rather among historians in verse, than epic poets.'[71] One can glimpse the Aristotelian inheritance at work here. Since the 'action is not properly one . . . but broken action', Dryden judges that his work cannot claim the title of an epic. According to Dryden, a literary work that is called *historical* is a work of 'broken action' that is 'tied too severely to the laws of history'. The 'laws of history' are strange laws, laws that *break* the unities of action, time and place. Dryden forecloses these complexities by ending with the remarkable distinction between a *historian in verse* and an *epic poet*, a distinction worthy of the seventeenth century. The moving gap that cannot be bridged between 'the history – of literature' is as profound, as frail and as tenacious as this distinction between a historian in verse and an epic poet. Dryden overcomes or bypasses the frailty of this distinction by according a *common* origin to 'the composition of all poems', 'wit writing' or 'the faculty of the imagination in the writer, which, like a nimble spaniel, beats over and ranges through the field of memory, till it springs the quarry it hunted after'.[72]

In his later *An Essay of Dramatic Poesy* (1668) Dryden returns to the need to distinguish historians and poets. The work of the poet, Eugenius argues, is the 'imagining' of 'the movements of . . . minds'. The work of the historian is concerned with 'the changes of . . . fortunes'.[73] This is a distinction that Hegel would appreciate. Poets (and philosophers) are concerned with *internal* developments, historians with *external* changes. From this later distinction, it seems we should treat *Annus Mirabilis* as a work of history and could hardly imagine a historian in verse that writes epic poems and that somehow takes account of both internal movements and external changes. But these definitions and distinctions are never pure or absolute and for Dryden, as for many others, there remains a persistent and unsettling oscillation between history and literature.

A few pages later, Lisideius praises the French writers of the day for interweaving truth and fiction and tempering or incorporating history into dramatic poesy: 'He so interweaves truth with probable fiction that he puts a pleasing fallacy upon us, mends the intrigues of fate, and dispenses with the severity of history, to reward the virtue which has been rendered to us there unfortunate.'[74] But the uneasy oscillation continues. Having made the case for history in dramatic poesy, Lisideius then immediately criticizes Shakespeare's history plays for unduly diminishing and contracting the events of history:

> On the other side, if you consider the historical plays of Shakespeare, they are rather so many chronicles of kings, or the business many times of thirty or forty years cramped into a representation of two hours and a half, which is not to imitate or paint nature, but rather to draw her in miniature, to take her in little, to look upon her through the wrong end of a perspective, and receive her images not only much less, but infinitely more imperfect than the life.[75]

When it comes to the relation between history and literature, Dryden suggests there is an *economy* of perspective, a telescoping economy: as history diminishes literature grows larger, as history expands literature grows smaller. As Plato had argued in the *Symposium*, this is nothing less than an economy of *life*, the rhythm of a changing perspective (larger–smaller, smaller–larger) that always protects and maintains history from literature and literature from history.[76] It is an economy without gaps, an economy of life that cannot risk the economy *of* death *in* life, as Derrida called it.[77]

Nonetheless, this balanced and balancing economy of changing perspective is also a *departure* from Aristotle. In the *Poetics*, Aristotle had argued that the poet's task was 'to describe not the thing that happened, but a kind of thing that might happen'. History (*historia*) is concerned with 'the thing that has been', poetry (*poiesis*) with 'the thing that might be'. History traces singularities while poetry proclaims universals.[78] Poetry is the wide expanse of the future and of the possible. History is the narrow record of the past. If Dryden had followed Aristotle to the letter he could have never written his *historical* poem *Annus Mirabilis*. Some ninety years before Dryden's *An Essay on Dramatic Poesy*, Sir Philip Sidney had reiterated this tradition of the *Poetics* in his *The Defence of Poesy* (c. 1580), disparaging the historian as 'laden with old mouse-eaten records' and 'authorising himself (for the most part) upon other histories, whose greatest authorities are built upon the notable foundation of hearsay'. Historians, Sidney concludes, have always 'been glad to borrow both fashion and, perchance, weight of the poets' and, as Aristotle had said, remain 'tied, not to what should be but to what is'.[79] So much for the historian in verse, so much for Dryden's remarkable descriptions of the fire of London winding and racing its way through the narrow streets of the capital in 1666!

Over the first 25 years of the nineteenth century, Hegel grappled in his many prefaces and introductions to his *Lectures on the History of Philosophy* with the problem of how one can write a *history* (that changes) of philosophy (that doesn't change). A history of philosophy can only be written, he argued, if one *already begins* with a *philosophy* of history, that is, with an unshakeable conviction in the unchanging and unchangeable truth. One can write a history of the Church (external changes), but one can never write a history of Christianity (the truth).[80] As Derrida suggests in 'Parergon', a *history* of literature, of poetry, would only be possible, would only be faithful to Aristotle, if it assumes that poetry (whether epic, dramatic, lyric or even historical) is neither *doxa* (subjective opinion) nor *epistēmē* (objective knowledge), but the expression of *aletheia*, *etuma* (truth). A history of poetry would be a history – of the soul, the form, the meaning, the speech – of the poem as the expression of the *truth*.[81]

But as Dryden himself suggested in *An Essay of Dramatic Poesy*, in the very articulation of this goal, the Greeks themselves bequeathed a profound legacy of qualification – of an 'or', of a line *or* trait *or re-trait* – *between* literature and truth. Dryden quotes from those oldest of pre-Socratics, Homer and Hesiod: 'The spirit of man cannot be satisfied but with the truth, or at least verisimility, and a poem is to contain, if not *ta etuma* [the truth], yet *etumoisin omoia* [things resembling the truth], as one of the Greek poets has expressed it.'[82] A poem is *speaking* truth (*etumeoros*), the true name (*etymon*) – *or* something resembling it, something like it (*mimesis*), making truth come *back* to itself *as* something like itself (*homoios*).[83] In 'Parergon', in the context of the question of art and the history of art, Derrida addresses the implications of *starting* with the *etymon*:

> What it [the question 'What is art?'] begins by implying is that art – the word, the concept, the thing – has a unity and, what is more, an originary meaning, an *etymon*, a truth that is one and naked [*une vérité une et nue*], and that it would be sufficient to unveil it *through* history [*dévoiler* à travers *l'histoire*].[84]

As we have seen, for Derrida the presupposition of the *etymon* leads to the reduction and determination of 'history' as either a historicism or an ahistoricism. For Dryden, when it comes to dramatic poesy, it is all a question of *verisimilitude*, of verses (of furrows, of *lines*, of lines of writing) that tend *towards* the truth.[85] Literature: truth – *or* something like it. As Derrida had argued in 'The Double Session', since at least Plato, the work of *mimesis* (imitation *from* the truth, *as* the truth, or on its way *to* the truth) has always been trying to *close* this gap, this oscillation of the *re-trait* between literature and truth – *or* something like it.

How can one *start* to write 'the history – of literature (of truth – *or* something like it)'? David Daiches begins his *A Critical History of English Literature* (1960) with the acknowledgement that English literature began as German literature, and that *Beowulf*, the first articulation of Old English or Anglo-Saxon literature, is preoccupied with 'the shortness of life and the passing away of all things except the fame a man leaves behind'.[86]

> This gruesome creature was called Grendel
> notorious prowler of the borderland, ranger of the moors,
> the fen and fastness.[87]

The *histories* of English literature have been fighting Grendel (the 'prowler of the borderland') ever since, the half-English half-German man-eating monster that announces – at the very beginning – the finitude of man, and the possibility that a *historian in verse* can never simply be separated from an *epic poet*.[88]

GRENDEL AND DIA-SYNCHRONIC HISTORY

'But there was a monster named Grendel, who lived in the darkness of lonely morasses', Jusserand writes at the beginning of his *A Literary History of the English People* (1894).[89] Starting with and departing from Grendel, English literature is always marked by a 'history – of literature' that it has at once tried to avoid and to idealize. In 1907, in *The Cambridge History of English Literature*, Grendel is both acknowledged as the origin of English literature and immediately incorporated into a very Edwardian sensibility. 'English literature, as we know it', the authors note, 'arose from the spirit inherent in the Viking makers of England before they finally settled in this island.' Beowulf and the battle with Grendel has become indicative of 'a reflective spirit, attachment to nature, a certain carelessness of "art", love of home and country and an ever present consciousness that there are things worse than death [dishonour] – these have, in the main, continued unaltered'.[90]

In 1774 Thomas Warton began his *History of English Poetry* in the twelfth century, thus avoiding both the German barbarians and Grendel (two years before Gibbon would remind his readers that the 'barbarians of Germany' were 'the rude ancestors of the most polished nations of modern Europe').[91] Nonetheless, Warton describes his history as 'tracing the transitions from barbarism to civility'. By starting 'from a rude origin and obscure beginnings', Warton argues, the history of poetry 'teaches us to set a just estimation on our own acquisitions, and encourages us to cherish that cultivation, which is so closely connected with the existence and exercise of every social virtue'. The history of poetry overcomes its 'obscure beginnings', overcomes the problem of beginning obscurely, by *reflecting* not our finitude but our progress and 'perfection in a polished age'.[92]

Having started his history with polish and perfection, Warton goes on to describe the difficulties of writing a *history* of poetry. He has chosen to organize his work into 'a chronological series' and not to disturb this diachronic structure with 'detached articles' or 'periodical divisions'. But much like Kant, who a few years later in the first edition of the *Critique of Pure Reason* (1781) will have problems with form and content and have to *introduce* his argument for *deduction* with an inductive digression and put four parts before the whole,[93] Warton cannot maintain a chronology of easy and progressive transitions:

> Yet I have not always adhered so scrupulously to the regularity of annals, but that I have often deviated into incidental digressions, and have sometimes stopped in the course of my career, for the

> purpose of collecting scattered notices into single and uniform points of view, for the more exact inspections of a topic which required separate consideration, or for a comparative survey of the poetry of other nations.[94]

Writing a *history* of poetry Warton cannot write *history* ('the regularity of annals'). Even though he has left out the time 'before the Norman accession' when 'we were an unformed and unsettled race', Warton's history of poetry does know how to begin and he starts his 'chronological series' with five thematic, five synchronic, dissertations, 'to prepare the reader by considering apart, in a connected and comprehensive detail, some material points of a general and preliminary nature, and which could not either with equal propriety or convenience be introduced, at least not so formally discussed, in the body of the book'.[95]

Warton can only begin his history *of* poetry with what Derrida described in a 1980 article as the unavoidable and impossible demand of a 'dia-synchrony'.[96] As Derrida had first noted in his introduction to Husserl's *The Origin of Geometry*:

> If the history of geometry were only the development of a purpose wholly present from the beginning, we would have to deal only with an explication or a quasi-creation. We would have on one side a synchronic or timeless [*uchronique*] ground and, on the other side, a purely empirical diachrony with its indicative function but without any proper unity of its own. Neither pure diachrony nor pure synchrony makes a history.[97]

Having avoided the 'unformed and unsettled' beginnings of English literature and started *after* Grendel, in his prefatory dissertations Warton must still contend with monsters and the impossible 'dia-synchronic' histories of poetry. Warton argues that romantic fiction in Europe originates not with the Goths, but with the Arabs. It is at the time of the Crusades that the Arabs introduce the *first* 'monstrous and arbitrary fictions' into Europe. The romantic fictions with 'giants, enchanters, [and] dragons', Warton concludes, 'were written at a time when a new and unnatural mode of thinking took place in Europe'.[98] When it comes to the origin of *The History – of English Literature*, we are always dealing with monsters.[99]

WITHOUT REST

If we are still following Aristotle, if it is possible not to follow him, how can one write the history of literature, the dia-synchronic history – of literature (of truth – *or* something like it)? How, we still ask Aristotle, can one write a history (only what is or what has been) of literature (only what might be, what should be and should always remain possible)? 'The history – of literature', according to Aristotle, would be 'the has been – of the possible', 'the past – of the future'. But we cannot write a history of the future. Since Aristotle, this impossibility has at once maintained the formal identity of history (the has been) and literature (the might be) *and* retained the strange hoverings and oscillating separations of the gap, of the trait or *re-trait* between 'history' and 'literature'.

For Derrida, there is perhaps another response to this Aristotelian inheritance. One cannot minimize or close the gap between history and literature. But one can read it differently. 'The history – of literature' is not as much 'the past – of the future' as 'the future – of the past'. The future *of* the past. 'The history – of literature' is 'the future – *re-trait* – of the past': a turning back again that demands a ceaseless *negotiation* with what remains to come. As he suggests in an interview from 1987, for Derrida this negotiation without rest between history and literature was always a question of an institutional negotiation, a negotiation with the history – of the institution:

> One does not negotiate between exchangeable and negotiable things. Rather, one negotiates by engaging the nonnegotiable in negotiation. And I have the feeling that, both in my work and in my political-institutional engagements, but also in my manner of being that is the most, how shall we say it, personal, affective, the style is what imposed itself on me: I cannot do otherwise. Thus, when I think negotiation, I think of fatigue, of this without-rest, this enervating mobility preventing one from ever stopping. If you would like to translate this philosophically, the impossibility of stopping, this means: no thesis, no position, no theme, no station, no substance, no stability, a perpetual suspension, a suspension without rest.[100]

The line, the trait *en retrait* that Derrida marks between 'the history – of literature', between a history *of* literature and a literature *of* history, is always with-drawing, retreating and repeating and exceeding itself, re-marking a *gap* that is at once irreducible and ungraspable. The gap, the trait between 'the history – of literature' *moves* – it oscillates, exposing history *to* literature and literature *to* history, without one ever resolving itself entirely into the other or without one separating itself entirely from the other – without rest.

CHAPTER 4

ENTER TIME

This tragedy of dating has become apparent to me today, too late.
Jacques Derrida[1]

THE WIDE GAP

After some twenty years of meditating on time, time itself at last takes the stage in Shakespeare's work. Time, that thing that so tormented Hamlet ('The time is out of joint. O cursèd spite / That ever I was born to set it right!'), has *arrived*.[2] At the beginning of Act Four of *The Winter's Tale*, TIME enters and speaks:

> *Enter* TIME, the *Chorus*.
> I that please some, try all; both joy and terror
> Of good and bad; that makes and unfolds error
> Now take upon me in the name of Time
> To use my wings. Impute it not a crime
> To me or my swift passage that I slide
> O'er sixteen years and leave the growth untried
> Of that wide gap, since it is in my power
> To o'erthrow law, and in one self-born hour
> To plant and o'erwhelm custom.[3]

Beyond the familiar appearance of Father Time on the sixteenth- and early seventeenth-century stage to account for the 'swift passage' of time, it is hard to overestimate how strange this arrival is.[4] Imagine that it was not TIME that entered at the beginning of Act Four of *The Winter's Tale*, but space. *Enter* SPACE. How do we keep watching, how do we keep reading *after* the arrival of TIME? What was happening *before* the arrival of TIME?

Since at least Aristotle, the arrival of time *itself* has been the philosopher's dream, the disquieting, long hoped for and always dreaded moment of arrival. But can time ever *arrive*? Can time *itself* arrive? We are no longer waiting, look Godot has arrived, he is *here*! *Enter* TIME.

The arrival of TIME in *The Winter's Tale* can be taken as a wonderful conceit, an impossible gathering, an amazing act of theatrical bravado. It is also possible that Shakespeare was sensitive to the entrance of this most difficult, most elusive of characters. As he writes, TIME enters and announces a 'wide gap', a gap that can neither simply be filled, nor entirely closed. *The Winter's Tale* perhaps marks the extraordinary *entrance* of that which *cannot arrive* – as itself. This exceptional arrival of the 'wide gap' of time can be read as a possible 'history – of literature'.

The reaction against this 'wide gap' was so great in the eighteenth century that when David Garrick and Charles Marsh both adapted and reworked *The Winter's Tale* in 1756, they *closed* the gap and removed TIME from the stage.[5] For the most part, this removal of TIME in the eighteenth century from Shakespeare's play met with approval. As Tobias Smollet commented in a review of Marsh's adaptation, 'he cuts off fifteen years of the tale and opens the scene immediately before the arrival of the deputies from *Delphos*. This expedient of curtailing in some measure removes the improbability that shocks the imagination of a person that sees the performance acted.'[6] But there was some criticism of this heavy-handed intervention. In a review of Garrick's work, Theophilus Cibber complained that Shakespeare's play had been 'lop'd, hack'd, and dock'd'.[7] In trying to *close* 'the wide gap' of *The Winter's Tale*, Garrick had only *opened* more gaps.

This anxiety in 1756 about the wide gaps *of* time on the stage may have also been a remote and rippling eddy from the great 'wide gap' that had appeared four years earlier in 1752 when Britain and its colonies had finally adopted the Gregorian calendar: 'that calendar trick where chance will have marked an epoch'.[8] In an attempt to resolve the long-standing problems that had arisen from trying to ensure that Easter would never coincide with Passover, in 1582 a Papal Bull had introduced the Gregorian calendar in Catholic Europe.[9] For the next 170 years every correspondent to and from

Britain would have problems with dating, and every traveller to and from Britain would experience an exceptional time lag.

Until 1752, the New Year began in Britain not on 1 January but on 25 March: the dating of the previous year and the year to come were always nearly three months out of sequence with much of Europe. On 24 March 1751 in Paris it was still 1750 in London. There was also a discrepancy of 11 days between the Julian and Gregorian Calendars, and for 170 years if you sailed from France to England you could *arrive* ten days *before you had left*. This remarkable 'wide gap' of time – that led to the traveller arriving *before* departing and suggested that the *entrance* of time could disorder the accustomed sequence of 'before' and 'after' and 'behind' and 'in front' – began in 1582 when William Shakespeare was 18 years old.

Though it has recently been argued that there were probably no riots (as has often been thought) when the 11 days were removed and the calendar jumped from Wednesday 2 September to Thursday 14 September 1752, as with Garrick and Marsh's adaptations of *The Winter's Tale* four years later, it was apparent that one could only *close* a gap of time by *opening* another 'wide gap'.[10] One can only wonder what happened to those in Britain and its colonies who had a birthday or an anniversary of some kind between 3 September and 13 September 1752.

In fact, this extraordinary 'wide gap' in September 1752 is remarkably elusive. The Earl of Chesterfield, who first proposed changing the calendar in 1751, is rather coy in his letters to his son, leaving a gap in the correspondence from 21 July 1752 to 15 September 1752, the second day of the new calendar.[11] David Garrick wrote a letter on 1 September 1752, two days before the calendar changed, but no other letters have been preserved until 14 October 1752.[12] Samuel Johnson dates a letter to Charlotte Lennox from February of that year as 1751/2, hinting at the confusion of dating the New Year from 1 January.[13] It is only to be regretted that the antiquarian Joseph Ames, who noted with such care that on 'Friday evening 21st day August 1752 at Eleven a Clock' he was 'accompanied by Mr. John Rook to the Angell Inn [at] the back of St. Clemons church in the Strand', leaves a gap in his travel diary from Sunday 23 August to Saturday 18 October 1752.[14] It is a testament, however, to the impact of the changing of the calendar that in July 1789 and again in August 1795, Horace Walpole was still referring to the events of September 1752.[15] Most eighteenth-century writers seem to have left a silent and eloquent gap in their correspondence to mark the difficulties of accounting for this entrance of time and the wide gap of the loss of 11 days in September 1752.

THE DISUNITIES OF ARISTOTLE

This muted reaction may in part be due to the incremental move away from the Aristotelian inheritance in representing time and space in the arts. Three years before the changing of the calendar that playwright and novelist Henry Fielding had included in *The History of Tom Jones* (1749) a familiar swipe at the continuing influence of the so-called Aristotelian unities of time, place and action in theatrical productions:

> Who ever demanded the reasons of that nice unity of time or place which is now established to be so essential to dramatick poetry? What critick hath been ever asked, why a play may not contain two days as well as one? Or why the audience (provided they travel, like electors, without any expence) may not be wafted fifty miles as well as five?[16]

Earlier in his work, Fielding suggests that he has found in the novel a literary form that will allow him to break the laws of 'the antient critic'. 'Tho' we have properly enough entitled this our work, a history, and not a life', he says that he will not be following the method of the historian who, 'to preserve the regularity of the series, thinks himself obliged to fill up as much paper with the detail of months and years in which nothing remarkable happened'. He goes on to write:

> Now it is our purpose in the ensuing pages, to pursue a contrary method. When any extraordinary scene presents itself, (as we trust will often be the case) we shall spare no pains nor paper to open it large to the reader; but if whole years should pass without producing anything worthy of his notice, we shall not be afraid of a chasm in our history.

For Fielding, contrary to the edicts of Aristotle in the theatre, in the novel there can be 'wide gaps'. Some of his chapters will be very short and others much longer, and his 'history sometimes seems to stand still, and sometimes to fly'.[17] The novel, he argues, has its own speed, its own narrative time, which is neither that of biography nor that of history: it is the time of the novel.[18]

If the experiments of the emerging form of the novel provided an opportunity to escape from Aristotle, the theatre was something else and throughout the eighteenth century it was generally believed that the 16-year gap announced by TIME at the beginning of Act Four of *The Winter's Tale* contravened the so-called Aristotelian unities. Charles Gildon, writing in 1710, was one of the first critics to insist that the entrance of TIME in *The Winter's Tale* could only be read as an *apology*:

> Natural Reason indeed show'd to Shakespeare the Absurdity of Making the Representation longer than the *Time*, and the *Place* more extensive than the Place of acting, as is plain from his Choruses in his Historical Plays, in which he apologises for the Absurdity, as in the Beginning of the fourth Act of *The Winter's Tale* among other things.[19]

Despite what Gildon says of the history plays, there seems to be little apology when RUMOUR enters triumphantly at the beginning of *The Second Part of Henry the Fourth*.[20] When CHORUS twice asks for the audience's 'pardon' in the opening of *The Life of Henry the Fifth* it is perhaps more to *celebrate* the fact that the 'vast fields of France' can fit 'within this wooden O'.[21]

Fifty years after Gildon, George Colman in 1756 reiterated this tradition of apology in his review of Johnson's edition of Shakespeare:

> All Liberties may be carried to an Excess, and the Violation of these Unities may be so gross as to become unpardonable . . . and for the same Reason he [Shakespeare] brings in the Personage of Time in the Character of Chorus in *The Winter's Tale* to apologise for the lapse of sixteen years.[22]

While the critical response to Shakespeare has long since moved on from measuring his strict adherence to the so-called Aristotelian unities, it is worth recalling that in the eighteenth century it was widely believed that Shakespeare introduced TIME in *The Winter's Tale* to apologize *to* Aristotle. Constrained by his source material,

Robert Greene's *Pandosto*, Shakespeare brings TIME on stage to apologize to all those readers of Aristotle in his audience and, ultimately, to the great philosopher himself. Of course, one problem with this interpretation is that Shakespeare apologizes and *still* breaks all the rules. At least one critic in the eighteenth century described the appearance of TIME as an apology but added, 'in the Days of our great Poet the Unities of the Drama were very little understood'.[23] Shakespeare was apologizing, but he didn't even know what he was apologizing for.

If the entrance and 'wide gap' of time was almost uniformly condemned in the eighteenth century, from the 1950s it has been celebrated as 'a breathing space', as an 'orderly and spacious' division, a graceful changing of tone, a shift from death to life, a move from tragedy to comedy: *a perfect hinge* that separates the play in two symmetrical halves.[24] In the second half of the twentieth century the entrance of TIME became a scene of order, of decorous transition, of symmetry and structure. In short, it is only in the twentieth century that time becomes a genuinely eighteenth-century concept.

More recently, *time* also has been linked to 'a time that lacks any sense of causality, development, fullness, or even duration'.[25] Rather than linger in this dreamtime, this time without time, or set our watches to the *Zeitalter der Aufklärung*, it is perhaps worth holding on to the eighteenth-century preoccupation with Shakespeare as a negligent reader of Aristotle. And if we question the predominant eighteenth-century assumption that Shakespeare is *apologizing* to the Aristotelians, what is Shakespeare trying to say when he *addresses* Aristotle?

PLAYING GREEK PHILOSOPHY

Though perhaps more equivocal about the representation of time than some of his eighteenth-century readers, in the *Poetics* Aristotle was primarily concerned that a theatrical production be a 'whole' (*ólon*) and 'complete in itself', a seamless coherent unity of action: a play without gaps (1450b).[26] As John Dryden had already pointed out in his *An Essay of Dramatic Poesy* (1668), it was not Aristotle who came up with the *three unities* (of action, time and place), but Pierre Corneille in his *Trois Discours sur le poème dramatique* (1660).[27] Corneille himself had been inspired by Ludovico Castelvetro in his *Poetica d'Aristotele vulgarizzata et sposta* (1570,

1576).[28] In other words, in Shakespeare's lifetime the emphasis on the *three* unities of action, time and place was not a long-standing tradition, but a very recent innovation. In his efforts to establish *les règles* of dramatic poetry some 45 years after the death of Shakespeare, Corneille complains, 'our misfortune is that Aristotle and Horace after him have written so obscurely that they need to be interpreted'.[29] Dryden himself notes that the Greeks hardly conform to the strict rules of *les trois unités* and, perhaps for patriotic as much as artistic reasons, praises the 'incomparable' and 'irregular' English Shakespeare.[30]

Nonetheless, the critics from the eighteenth century were absolutely right: *The Winter's Tale* is a play *with* gaps; it does not follow Aristotle's guidelines in the *Poetics*. Many scholars from the twentieth century, on the other hand, have tended to read the entrance of TIME as an Aristotelian moment, a moment of good order, of good order for the whole. The best of plays, according to Aristotle, should 'represent one action, a complete whole, with its several incidents so closely connected that the transposition or withdrawal of any one of them will disjoin and dislocate the whole' (1451a). If, as Virginia Woolf had wished in *Orlando*, we could imagine Shakespeare as 'a rather fat, rather shabby man . . . sitting at the servants' table [in a country house] with a tankard beside him and paper in front of him', we could also imagine him wandering into the library of the country house and picking up a copy of Aristotle's *Poetics*.[31] We could imagine him objecting from the start to Aristotle's insistence that 'it is not appropriate in a female character to be manly, or clever' (1454a). And if he had taken Aristotle's judgement that the worst kind of play 'is when the personage is with full knowledge on the point of doing the deed, and leaves it undone', there would have been no *Hamlet* (1453b). If Shakespeare was a reader of Aristotle, he evidently decided not to follow the august and narrow guidelines of the *Poetics*.

We could also wonder whether Shakespeare would have accepted Aristotle's stark distinction in the *Poetics* between nouns (and names) and verbs. For Aristotle, 'a noun or name [*ónoma*] is a composite significant sound not involving the idea of time' while 'a verb [*rema*] is a composite significant involving the idea of time'. In other words, Aristotle explains, 'whereas the word "man" or "white" does not signify time, "he walks" and "he has walked" involve in addition to the idea of walking that of time present or time past' (1457a).

After Heidegger, it is difficult to think of 'man' without the complex relation of being and time, and *after* Derrida, it is hard to think of the proper name not marking the finitude, the mortality and the uncanny trace of what survives one's own death. Though perhaps more explicit in the nineteenth century in the anthropomorphic world of Balzac and Dickens, since at least Ovid animal-plant nouns have always been hard to distinguish from the human temporality of verbs.[32] We could also add that *after* Shakespeare, the names of things, of objects, have never stopped announcing the terrible fleeting passage of human life:

> That skull had a tongue in it and could sing once . . .
> Let me see.
> [*He takes the skull*]
> Alas, poor Yorick. I knew him, Horatio – a fellow of infinite jest,
> of most excellent fancy. He hath borne me on his back
> a thousand times; and now, how abhorred my imagination is!
> My gorge rises at it.[33]

When Shakespeare does *address* Greek philosophy, when he depicts a Greek philosopher in *The Life of Timon of Athens*, he describes Apemantus as a 'churlish philosopher'.[34] The word churlish has a very particular history in English. Prior to the Norman Conquest, a churl was a member of the lowest rank of freemen, but after 1066 a churl became a serf or bondsman. This traumatic fall in status developed into a more general sense of churlish as being of low birth (a peasant, a rustic) and eventually to acting *as if* one were of low birth. Whatever one's position in society, one could be described as *acting* churlish, as being surly, boorish, rude or ill bred. A 'churlish philosopher' is then a philosopher who performs, who acts as if they were of low birth: the philosopher as an *actor*.

> *First Lord*: What time o'day is't, Apemantus?
> *Apemantus*: Time to be honest.
> *First Lord*: That time serves still.
> *Apemantus*: The most accursèd thou, that still omitt'st it.[35]

When Apemantus the philosopher-actor laments that the time is not honest (that it 'is out of joint'), he is not that far from that other actor-philosopher, Hamlet.[36] Apemantus the philosopher charges that the time is dishonest, and that one can only reply to the *particular* question 'What time is it?' by answering with the *general* observation, the time is dishonest – Hamlet does much the same with women. Apemantus the actor, the churl-ish philosopher, the feigner of low birth, says that the time is *dishonest*. It is perhaps not by chance that Apemantus says this just as he is about to go to a banquet that Alcibiades is attending. Plato's *Symposium* (or *le Banquet*, as it is called in French) opens with Socrates arriving late for the banquet with Alcibiades: the philosopher is always getting the time wrong.[37]

Shakespeare plays with Greek philosophy, he turns the philosopher into a *player*. And whether or not Shakespeare read the *Poetics*, he did *play* with Aristotle. In Act Two of *Troilus and Cressida* Hector says:

> Paris and Troilus, you have both said well,
> But on the cause and question now in hand
> Have glossed but superficially – not much
> Unlike young men, whom Aristotle thought
> Unfit to hear moral philosophy.[38]

According to the editors of *The Norton Shakespeare* this is a reference to the *Nicomachean Ethics* in which Aristotle remarks:

> Each person judges well what he knows, and is a good judge of this. So, in any subject, the person educated in it is a good judge of that subject, and the person educated in all subjects is a good judge without qualification. This is why a young person is not fitted to hear lectures on political science, since our discussions begin from and concern the actions of life, and of these he has no experience.[39]

While some have responded to the passage in *Troilus and Cressida* by raising the possibility that Shakespeare didn't know that Aristotle came *after* Homer, others have used it as grounds for his acute reading of the *Ethics*.[40] Whether unintentionally or intentionally, in *Troilus and Cressida* Shakespeare treats Aristotle *anachronistically*: he confuses the proper order of the *before and after*.

As Nicholas Royle has shown, Shakespeare was preoccupied with anachronism, and the uncanniness of this anachronism is at the heart of Derrida's readings of Shakespeare.[41] As the unities of action, time and place, the question of anachronism, of 'how a text deals with its own datedness', was also a recent innovation in Shakespeare's lifetime.[42] Peter Burke has argued that the recognition of anachronism in the early modern period created a new 'sense of historical perspective'.[43] Anachronism, the problem of the date, of dating, becomes the origin of a new kind of historiography. How does one respond to this heightened sense of dating, of confronting what it is out of date, of the strange relation between the before and the after?

In *Troilus and Cressida* it appears that, like travellers to England after 1582, Aristotle arrives *before* he has departed. Let's imagine that Shakespeare knows what he is doing: he is making a joke, a very serious joke about *time* – Aristotle *before* Homer. He is playing with Aristotle, playing with Aristotelian time. As Hamlet suggests, it is all a question of *looking* before and after:

What is a man
If his chief good and market of his time
Be but to sleep and feed? – a beast, no more.
Sure, he that made us with such large discourse,
Looking before and after, gave us not
That capability and god-like reason
To fust in us unused.[44]

THE INADMISSABLE INSEPARABLITY OF TIME AND SPACE

Looking before *and* after, we must first turn to Aristotle's account of time (*khronos*) in Book IV of the *Physics*. Time, Aristotle argues, is 'a kind of number [*arithmós*]' (219b).[45] Number is always one *and* has the capability to be more than one. In other words, it is always the same and always different, which is what makes it the *same*. Time is *at once* 'continuous and divisible' (*sunekhē kai diairetà*) (220b). Time is *always* a dividing continuity, and this is what constitutes its nature (*phusis*).[46] This is how Aristotle resolves the problem of the apparent non-existence of time. It could seem that time 'either does not exist at all or barely, and in an obscure way. One part of it has been and is not, while the other is going to be and is not yet. Yet time . . . is made up of these' (218a). It is because time is 'a kind of number' that the past (*gégone*) and the future (*mellei*), the before (*próteron*) and the after (*hústeron*), do not threaten the existence of time.

'We apprehend time', Aristotle observes, 'only when we have marked motion, marking it by before and after' (219a). For *us*, it seems there is only time when there is the *movement* of before and after. The limitations of our perception of time could undermine the recognition that 'time is present equally everywhere and with all things' (218b). There is always time, but there are *gaps* in our perception of time. We notice time: 'if any movement takes place in the mind we at once suppose that some time has indeed elapsed'. We fail to notice time: 'we do not think time has elapsed', and 'when its difference escapes our notice the interval [*dià*] does not seem to be time' (218b). To get beyond this limited perspective, Aristotle accounts for the relation of movement (*kínesis*) to time through number. For Aristotle, as Derrida notes in '*Ousia* and *Grammē*' (1968), number 'is elsewhere'.[47]

'Time', Aristotle argues, 'is not motion, but number of motion' (221b). Number, as we have seen, is both the one and the more than one, a dividing continuity, and also accounts for what is counted, enumerated or measured. Time is 'what is counted'. It is 'number of motion in respect of "before" and "after"' (219b). Number, as the dividing continuity that counts and measures motion (the movement of before and after), is the *now* (*nun*). One and more than one, always the same and always different, time is 'both made continuous . . . and divided' by the now (220a). The now is divided into 'one before and one after' and *accounts for* the movement of before and after (219b). Time, or the *economy* of the now as number, is the now *as* the movement of before and after. For Aristotle, time becomes 'what is bounded by the "now"' (219a). Time is a kind of number, and the now is a kind of *boundary* (*hóros*). 'The "now", Aristotle writes, 'is the link of time . . . (for it connects past and future time), and it is a limit of time (for it is the beginning of the one and the end of the other)' (222a). The now divides and connects, terminates and unifies: it is 'the boundary of the past and the future' (*hóros tou parékontos kai tou méllontos*) (223a).

Book IV of the *Physics* is divided into three chapters. Aristotle's discussion of time is preceded by an examination of the arguments for and against the existence of a void and an account of place (*topos*). We cannot *start* anything without place. Place always precedes time. We have to *begin* with place, Aristotle argues, because 'things which exist are somewhere' (208a). Distinct from the sensible bodies that come and go in any given place, place is always there, place is always first (208b). For Aristotle, place is a *boundary*. It is 'the boundary of the containing body at which it is in contact with the contained body' (212a). It is a boundary of containment that can *at once* be separated from and be 'in contact with the contained body' (211a). It is this very delineation of *space* that Foucault challenges in *The Order of Things* (1966), when he writes that 'we shall never succeed in defining a stable relation of contained to container'.[48] As a boundary, place is not merely an external line around a body. It is the 'inner side', 'the innermost motionless boundary' (*tou periékhontos péras ákíneton*) of a body (212a).

Separated but in contact, marking a boundary and holding the inside, the place as boundary is also the *possibility* of movement. There can be no motion, no movement, without place (208a, 211a). It is only because there is place that bodies can change place (locomotion). Place is the 'motionless boundary' for bodies that move. It is *an inside that doesn't move*. Place is the boundary that always precedes time as number and the now as the *boundary* of the before and after.

As in his account of the *gaps* in our perception of time that require a standard beyond that of our own minds, Aristotle argues in his analysis of place and the void that there is *no* gap. Place is the boundary which is 'in contact with the movable body', it is not 'an interval' (*diástema*), a non-sensible gap 'which is other than the bodies which are moved' (212a–b). Nor is it 'an interval [*diástema*] in body', a 'corporeal interval' (212b). Similarly, those who are misguided into thinking about a void (and thus deny the ratio, the proportioned difference, of motion, speed and time) either mean 'an interval [*diástema*] in which there is *no* sensible body', or 'an interval in tangible body' (215a–b, 213a, 214a). For Aristotle, when it comes to place and time, boundary and number, there is no 'wide gap'.

In *Being and Time* (1927), Heidegger argues that our traditional relationship to time as 'that which is *counted*' (*Gezählte*) and defined by 'the use of clocks', has its origins in Aristotle's interpretation of time in the *Physics*. By '*following* the positions' of the hands or 'pointer' of a clock, Heidegger observes, one '*counts*' time. To count time, one always assumes that a '*travelling pointer*' (*wandernden Zeigers*) is *present*. For Heidegger, this positional accounting for time demonstrates that since Aristotle it has been accepted that '*time is what shows itself in . . . a making-present* [*gegenwärtigenden*]'. One counts time, one *retains* an earlier or before by '*making it present*', and one *awaits* a later or after by '*making it present*'. One always counts, accounts for and measures time from *the now*: the before is always the 'now-no-longer' (*Jetzt-nicht-mehr*) and the after always the 'now-not-yet' (*Jetzt-noch-nicht*). The before and after are always co-opted, put to work for 'making present'. This traditional ontological concept of time is founded on an assumption that begins with Aristotle, namely that *time is defined by space*. The '*travelling pointer*' that marks the *position*, the location and movement of the now . . . the now . . . and the now . . . is *spatial*.[49]

In *Of Grammatology* (1965–67), Derrida refers to Heidegger's reading of Aristotle and his description of 'a concept of time thought in terms of spatial movement or of the now' as 'intrinsic to the totality of the history of the Occident'.[50] This is what the West does: it thinks time in terms of space and in terms of the now. For Derrida, however, there is an important difference between thinking time in terms of *space* and thinking it in terms of the *now*. In his own reading of the *Physics*, in '*Ousia* and *Grammē*', Derrida emphasizes the differences between time as the *now* and time as *presence*. If one takes the now simply as the essence of time, time appears to be *incompatible* with being. As the *no longer* now (the before) and the *not yet* now (the after), the now 'accommodates nonbeingness' and therefore 'cannot participate in presence, in substance, in *beingness* itself (*ousia*)'.[51] Aristotle resolves this problem by arguing that time is a dividing continuity, or the now *as* presence.

According to Derrida, time in the *Physics* is not just the now *as* presence (as Heidegger implies). It is the now *working for* presence – and this makes all the difference.[52] Aristotle argues that the now as time can *only* be successive. It cannot – like a 'linear inscription in space' – 'coexist with an other (the same as itself), with an other now'. In other words, the now cannot endure two nows existing *at the same time*. But this is what time *as presence* does (the now as the *just* before coexisting with the now as the *soon* after). The *possibility* of presence presupposes, relies on, a *spatial* difference. As Derrida writes, 'The impossibility of coexistence can be posited as such only on the basis of a certain coexistence, of a certain simultaneity of the nonsimultaneous, in which the alterity and identity of the now are maintained together in the differentiated element of a certain same'.[53]

For Heidegger, time is inauthentic and fallen since Aristotle because it has been defined by and characterized as *a kind of space*. For Derrida, on the contrary, this reliance of time on space suggests that time (as presence) needs *spacing*. It *also* suggests that space (as presence) needs *temporalization*. Working *for* presence, the now cannot avoid *différance*. The differing *and* the deferring of the rhythms and speeds of space becoming time *and* of time becoming space, *différance* becomes both the only possibility *and* the unavoidable ruin of time (and space) as presence, as being.[54] For Derrida, Western philosophy has always relied on the inadmissible inseparability of time and space. In this instance, he questions Heidegger's denigration of space. In his earlier objections to structuralism, on the other hand, he challenges its privileging of space (as structure) to unify meaning and form at the expense of time.[55] This oscillating inseparability of time and space in Aristotle's *Physics* is the possibility of the history – of the senses that, as we shall see, Derrida reads in *De Anima*.

TIME SPEAKS

Differing and deferring, time can never be *itself*, can never *arrive* as itself. *Enter* TIME and we are always looking before *and* after. It would be far too easy to think that Shakespeare with all his verbal brilliance somehow just throws off the Aristotelian inheritance, and that he could simply stand 'outside' of the great ontological tradition of Western philosophy. But we can perhaps ask if Shakespeare merely remains the other *of* Aristotle.

For Hamlet, who may or may not be able to speak for William Shakespeare, part of what constitutes man is the capability to *look* 'before and after'. The editors of *The Norton Shakespeare* helpfully explain that 'looking before and after' can be read as 'able to see past and future', but I am not so certain of this Aristotelian interpretation. *Looking*, looking and searching for something, is not quite the same as *seeing* something that has been found. As we have seen, for Derrida what is *before* can always suggest both what is behind (in the past) *and* what is *in front* (in the future). The phrase, 'it is before us' can always be anachronistic, untimely.

Even Aristotle in the *Physics* admits to a certain indeterminacy of the before: ' "before" is used contrariwise with reference to past and to future time; for in the past we call "before" what is farther from the "now", and "after" what is nearer, but in the future we call the nearer "before" and the farther "after"' (223a). As Derrida notes, for Aristotle this *aporia* is part of the ordinary, commonplace, exoteric approach to the problem of time.[56] Aristotle starts with the *exoteric* (the outside): the exoteric is *first* (*proton*) (217b). In other words, from the moment he starts, Aristotle has *already* begun his account of time with a before that could be either behind or in front of the *esoteric* (the inside) – if there is an esoteric.[57] Aristotle starts, and startles himself, with the indeterminacy of the before and after. Whatever time 'is', whatever it does to the *is*, time perhaps arrives – without arriving itself – when we cannot decide if *before* is simply behind us or in front of us.

And if we take Shakespeare as an anachronistic, an untimely, reader of time in Aristotle, it is perhaps not fortuitous that in the opening of a play where TIME enters, Shakespeare gives us an instance of an indeterminate 'before and after'. Speaking to Hermione of his childhood friendship with Leontes, Polixenes says,

> We were, fair Queen,
> Two lads that thought there was no more behind
> But such a day tomorrow as today,
> And to be boy eternal.[58]

At first glance, this passage doesn't seem to make much sense. The two boys 'thought there was no more behind / But such a day tomorrow as today'. How can tomorrow be *behind*? As both the editors of the *Riverside* and *Norton* Shakespeare point out, the word *behind* means to be at the back, at the rear of something, but in a more archaic usage it *also* meant what was held in reserve, what remained *still to come*.[59] The 'two lads thought that there was no more behind [still to come] / But such a day tomorrow as today'. *Enter* TIME and we are caught in the strange dislocation, the hovering uncertainty of a 'behind' that can be *at once* behind us (at the back, in the past) *and* behind us (in the front, in the future). *Enter* TIME, and the now doesn't know whether it is coming or going, whether it has arrived *before* it has left. As Hamlet says: 'Thus bad begins and worse remains behind [still to come].'[60]

When TIME arrives in Act Four of *The Winter's Tale*, without the possibility of arriving as itself, wonder of wonders, TIME speaks. *Enter* TIME, the Chorus. TIME enters and speaks *as* the chorus. Speaking at the beginning of the Act, 'TIME, the Chorus' cites and repeats an Aristotelian scene from the *Poetics*. One of the recognized 'parts' of tragedy, the *parode* is 'the whole first statement of the Chorus' (1452b). The *parode* or *parodos* describes an entrance *from the side*. TIME enters from the side of the *Poetics*. It cites the *Poetics* and, as Derrida suggested, in citing it *re*-cites the *Poetics*, citing a part that becomes *greater* than the whole, a re-citation that is no longer simply inside (esoteric) nor outside (exoteric) of the work.[61] 'Enter TIME, the Chorus': a re-citation *from the side*.

As Jean-Pierre Vernant has suggested, when the Chorus *speaks* in ancient Greek tragedy, nothing is clear cut: 'The chorus, more often than not, hesitates and oscillates, rebounding from one meaning to the other, or sometimes dimly suspecting a meaning as yet unrevealed, or actually unconsciously formulating in a play on words an expression with a twofold meaning.'[62] When time enters and speaks from the side of Aristotle's text, its syntax is strange, and may echo a long tradition of pageantry and festival: of time as destruction; of time as the revelation and restitution of the truth; of time with a scythe, wings and hourglass, the symbol of rushing, imminent mortality.[63] But when TIME *speaks*, when it accounts for its own attributes, it claims among its first qualities the ability to make and unfold *error*, to be untimely, to be anachronistic:

> I that please some, try all; both joy and terror
> Of good and bad; that makes and unfolds error . . .

Like the Sphinx, TIME speaks in riddles. TIME begins, 'I that please some, try all.' I . . . *try* all. I examine, I submit to trial, I test the patience of everyone. I sift, strain and single out everyone. Time *singles* out *everyone*: an amazing *singular universal* that is worthy of Aristotle's definition of time as a *divided continuity*. Shakespeare's understanding of time initially seems very close to that of Aristotle. But TIME then says: I single out everyone *and* 'I please some.' I give some pleasure, but in the end I catch everyone. I single out *everyone and* I please *some*. What wondrous machine is it that can *universally* reach every individual and, at the same time, can also only touch *some*, can single out an indeterminate portion, an *indefinite* number? Shakespeare alludes to the possibility that there is an aspect of time that is unaccountable, that cannot be counted. This is what the theatre does: it *plays* with time. It ranges 'o'er sixteen years . . . in one self-born hour'.

THE MOVABLE JOINT: LOOKING BEFORE AND AFTER

For Aristotle, it is indispensable that time can be *counted* by the now (as the number of the movement of the before and after). The now is the *hinge* of time. The objections to Aristotle's association of time with movement are very old. Responding to Aristotle in the third century, Plotinus had asked: 'is Time the Measure of any and every Movement? Have we any means of calculating disconnected and lawless movement? What number or measure would apply?'[64] There is a footnote in '*Ousia* and *Grammē*' on Plotinus. For Derrida, the *trace* of and as *différance* constitutes presence without ever being reduced to the great ontological opposition of presence *or* absence.[65] Derrida suggests that Plotinus characterized presence as 'the trace of nonpresence', a trace 'which is neither absence nor presence'.[66] In another footnote to an earlier article on Husserl, 'Form and Meaning' (1967), Derrida refers to this reading of Plotinus, highlighting the relation between the trace that exceeds the *opposition* of presence and absence, of the *before* and *after*. He writes:

> The trace would not be the mixture, the transition between form and the amorphous, presence and absence, etc., but that which, by eluding the opposition, makes it possible in the irreducibility of its excess. Henceforth, the closure of metaphysics, the closure that the audaciousness of the *Enneads* (but one can credit other texts) seems to indicate by transgressing it, would not occur *around* a homogeneous and continuous field of metaphysics. Rather, it would fissure the structure and history of metaphysics, *organically* inscribing and systematically *articulating* from the inside the traces of the *before*, the *after* and the *outside* of metaphysics [*du dedans les traces de l'*avant, *de l'*après *et du* dehors *de la metaphysique*].[67]

Shakespeare offers what might be called an anachronistic variation on Plotinus' criticisms of Aristotle. Time may be a unique relation – singular universal, divided continuity, the other *of* being – but this does not necessarily suggest that time can always be counted or that the sequence and order of the before and after can be distinguished and measured by the now. When it comes to time, there is always a *some* that is incommensurable with the *all*.

It is from this incommensurability that time also appears indifferent to faith or morality, bringing 'both joy and terror / Of good and bad.' Time – rushing imminent mortality – delivers both 'joy and terror' to 'good and bad' *alike*. Time 'itself' is neither just nor unjust: it is the possibility of justice and injustice.[68] It is this unsettling time beyond measure (at once all and some) and beyond morality (at once just and unjust) 'that makes and unfolds error'. Time both creates *and* reveals error. One can easily imagine that the passage of time reveals error, but how does time *make* error? How does 'looking before and after' create error? Time *makes* mistakes, transgressions, flaws and malformations. Time *makes* wandering, digression and deviation. Time 'makes and unfolds error'. It makes and spreads out, unfurls, unwraps everything that is untimely and anachronistic when we are 'looking before and after' and, arriving before we have departed, only find the 'wide gap' of time.

Incommensurable, unequal, neither good nor bad and open to the *possibility* of the loss of direction, of the assured orderly sequence of the before and after, the behind and in front, TIME in *The Winter's Tale* is also, as critics have long pointed out, entirely *redundant* to the plot and narrative.[69] The information that TIME passes on to the audience – chiefly that 16 years have now elapsed – is immediately repeated at the start of Act Four scene two. In other words, Act Four scene one is a *detachable* scene. You can put it in, you can take it out – and the narrative of the play is unchanged. The entrance of time is not an integral part of the 'complete whole', and manifestly fails to follow Aristotle's criteria for a good play in the *Poetics*.

Act Four scene one is far closer to Aristotle's uncertainties in the *Physics* about whether time can be accounted for through the part–whole relation.[70] 'A part' (*méros*), he argues, is 'a measure of the whole, which must be made up of parts' (218a). The parts of a whole must be the *same* as the whole, and whatever time 'is', it is not 'made up' of only nows: time remains the strange relation between the now, the before and the after. If Shakespeare were playing with Aristotelian time, he might begin by saying that the problems of time as they are stated in the *Physics already* exceed the ideal qualities for the best kind of tragedy in the *Poetics*. How can there be a unity of time in the theatre, Shakespeare might ask the critics of the eighteenth century, when time *itself* cannot be unified?

This redundant, detachable scene in *The Winter's Tale* was described by William Blisset in 1971 as 'the hinge of the diptych' and by Frederick Kiefer in 1999 as 'the hinge, the joint that puts time back in order'.[71] The entrance of TIME is therefore 'the central principle, the cardinal or critical point, on which everything turns or relies' *and* a 'movable joint or mechanism by which a door is hung on its side post to permit opening and shutting' (*OED*). Following the suggestion of his friend Roger Laporte, in *Of Grammatology* Derrida associates 'the hinge' (*la brisure*) with the space becoming time and time becoming space of *différance* that challenges the traditional concept of time which conserves 'its homogeneity and its fundamental successivity by demonstrating . . . that the past present and future present constitute originarily, by dividing it, the form of the living present [*présent vivant*]'.[72] In other words, the before and after do not work for the now. The now is not, as Aristotle argues, the *measure* of the before and after. *For us*, time moves, time changes *and* we have no guarantee, no assurance that time 'itself' does not move, does not change. Derrida returns in *Specters of Marx* (1993) to the hinge in his extended reading of Hamlet's lament: 'The time is out of joint. O cursèd spite / That ever I was born to set it right!'[73] The entrance of TIME in *The Winter's Tale* can be seen as a remarkable personification or representation of that which is out of joint, of that which comes off its hinges, of that which always leaves us with a 'disjointed or disadjusted now'.[74]

Aristotle *before* Homer. If we accept that Shakespeare knew what he was doing in *Troilus and Cressida* and that he was playing anachronistically with Aristotelian time, we could see the beginning of Act Four of *The Winter's Tale* as an audacious and unprecedented disjointed hinge, as a 'movable joint' that permits not only the 'opening and shutting' of the 16-year gap between Act Three and Act Four, but also allows at least for the *possibility* of playing with the assured sequence of the before and after and the behind and in front. *Enter* TIME and there is no longer a fixed and certain order for the events in Sicily and Bohemia.

Aristotle *before* Homer? Bohemia *before* Sicily? *Enter* TIME, the 'movable joint', and *The Winter's Tale* could begin with *either* Act One *or* Act Four. This may not be so improbable and audacious as it sounds, and might even account for the strange echoes in these *two* openings:

Act One scene one. '*Enter* Camillo *and* Archidamus.' Archidamus and Camillo speak of the imminent visit of Leontes. Though

> separated for many years, they have remained in contact and 'have seemed to be together, though absent'. The two men talk of the King's son, Prince Mamillius, 'a gentleman of the greatest promise'.[75] *Act One scene two*. '*Enter* Leontes, Hermione, Mamillius, Polixenes, *and* Camillo.' Polixenes has been visiting his brother for nine months and, anxious about what may 'breed upon our absence', wishes to return to Bohemia.[76] First Leontes and then Hermione try to persuade him to stay and he relents. Leontes then reveals that he has adopted a disguise to hide his jealousy; a disguise that he will not be able to keep. Leontes then tries to convince Camillo to poison Polixenes, and the scene ends with Camillo and Polixenes leaving for Bohemia . . .
>
> *Act Four scene two*. '*Enter* Polixenes *and* Camillo.' It is sixteen years since Camillo has left Sicily and he now wishes to return. Polixenes pleads with him to stay and to not go back to Leontes, whose actions have led to the exile of Camillo and the 'loss of his most precious queen and children'. The two men talk of Polixenes's wayward son, Prince Florizel, whose absence from the court has been 'missingly noted' by his father.[77] The Prince spends most of his time at the house of an unaccountably wealthy shepherd who has a beautiful daughter 'of most rare note'.[78] Polixenes persuades Camillo to put aside his thoughts of going to Sicily and to visit in disguise the shepherd's house . . .

One could almost stage these opening scenes of Act Four and Act One *concurrently*, in the style of Tom Stoppard's *Arcadia* or *The Coasts of Utopia* with a revolving stage shifting back and forth, before and after: Camillo in Bohemia thinking of returning to Sicily; Polixenes in Sicily thinking of returning to Bohemia. Both kings adopting disguises; both kings (who have ostensibly overcome the absence between them) unable to respond to the real or imaginary absence (the betrayal) of those that they love most; both kings who, as children 'thought that there was no more behind / But such a day tomorrow as today', as adults making no sense, no order, of what comes behind and in front of them, before and after them.[79]

Enter TIME and Shakespeare is hinting at an unthinkable theatre *to come* where the unities of time, action and place are unhinged. Sicily *before* Bohemia. Is such an anachronism possible? The play *begins* with Camillo thinking of his 16-year absence from Sicily and his going with Polixenes to spy on Florizel and Perdita. Polixenes then forbids the marriage of his son to the shepherd's daughter and Camillo returns to Sicily with the young lovers. Off stage, Leontes discovers Perdita as his lost daughter and Polixenes blesses the wedding of the young prince and princess. On stage, the statue of the seemingly dead Hermione is revealed. It is a statue that has been aged 16 years, a statue that appears to take *account* of the 'wide gap' of time.[80] It is statue that moves, a living Queen that endures and overcomes the 'wide gap' of time.

And then, playing with Aristotle, Shakespeare's great and terrible insight: *Enter* TIME on the stage and the *future* of the past is always somehow still *to come*. Camillo finds himself talking to Archidamus about the king's planned visit to Bohemia. At the prompting of Leontes, Hermione pleads with Polixenes to stay a little longer in Sicily. Polixenes and Camillo leave in fear of their lives. Hermione is imprisoned and her newborn baby is taken away from her. Hermione is tried and collapses at the court. Her death is announced and the play *ends* with the first sight of Bohemia. Antigonus leaves the baby exposed to the elements and exits, '*pursued by a bear*'. An old shepherd and a clown find a baby . . .

> *Enter* TIME, the *Chorus*.
> I that please some, try all; both joy and terror
> Of good and bad; that makes and unfolds error
> Now take upon me in the name of Time
> To use my wings. Impute it not a crime
> To me or my swift passage that I slide
> O'er sixteen years and leave the growth untried
> Of that wide gap, since it is in my power
> To o'erthrow law, and in one self-born hour
> To plant and o'erwhelm custom.

PART TWO

HISTORIES – OF THE SENSES

CHAPTER 5

A 'NEW' HISTORY – OF THE SENSES

The longest tyranny that ever swayed
Was that wherein our ancestors betrayed
Their free-born reason to the Stagirite,
And made his torch their universal light.
So truth, while only one supplied the state,
Grew scarce and dear, and yet sophisticate;
Until 'twas bought, like emp'ric wares or charms,
Hard words sealed up with Aristotle's arms.

John Dryden[1]

THE DIAPHANOUS

If Derrida's early readings of Plato and Aristotle and his later retranslations of Heidegger suggest the possibility of a 'history – of literature' as a different way of starting again with metaphysics, one can see in his readings of Aristotle's *De Anima* what can be described as a 'new' history – of the senses. In Derrida's work, these two histories – *of* literature and *of* the senses – cannot simply be separated, and their relation is apparent in the *palintrope* of a turning back that does not start again *with* itself, but turns back again and startles itself. The 'fictionality' and the 'physicality' of this startling departure in the histories – of literature and in the histories – of the senses can be seen in the gaps and cuts, the blows and caresses of Derrida's readings of Aristotle and Hegel. These readings, over a span of forty years, are also part of Derrida's attempts to address the question of *thinking* through an affirmation of the resistance *of* thinking, of a thinking of that which remains – and remains to come.

It is appropriate that Derrida's first quotation of Aristotle, in his 1961–62 introduction to Husserl's *The Origin of Geometry*, is from *De Anima*, *On the Soul*.[2] Thirty years later Derrida will begin his most philosophical of late works, *On Touching – Jean-Luc Nancy* (1992–2000), with Aristotle's *De Anima*. As we have seen, in his introduction to *The Origin of Geometry*, Derrida argued that the 'Idea in the Kantian sense' provides Husserl with an infinite unifying idealization, the open horizon of a future that guarantees the erasure of the origin's own past. For Derrida, it is crucial to phenomenology that Husserl *excludes* the Idea itself from the phenomenological analysis. Phenomenology is concerned both with what *appears* and with 'the *possibility* of its appearing'.[3] The 'Idea in the Kantian sense' – '*Objectivity* itself', 'the regulative possibility of appearing' – is the standard, the guarantee and the goal of all phenomenology. What interests Derrida is that, as the 'origin' of phenomenology, which is so preoccupied with appearing and the possibility of appearing, the Idea itself 'can never appear as such'.[4] The Idea is invisible. It is to illustrate this point that Derrida first turns to Aristotle's *De Anima*:

> It is not by chance that there is no phenomenology of the Idea. The latter cannot be given in person, nor determined in an evidence, for it is only the possibility of evidence and the openness of 'seeing' itself; it is only *determinability* as the horizon for every intuition in general, the invisible milieu of seeing [*milieu invisible du voir*] analogous to the diaphaneity of the Aristotelian Diaphanous, an elemental third, but the one source of the seen and the visible: 'by diaphanous I mean what is visible, and yet not visible, and not yet visible in itself, but rather owing its visibility to the colour of something else'. It is thanks to this alone 'that the colour of a thing is seen'. (*De Anima*, 418b)[5]

The 'diaphanousness of pure ideality' is the invisible origin of the visible as a pure objective ideality, of a visible that has liberated itself from the sensible and the imaginary.[6] In 'Force and Signification' (1963), published the year after the *Introduction*, Derrida argues that 'diaphanousness is the supreme value' of phenomenology.[7] A decade later in *Glas* (1974), he will write of 'the diaphanous law of consciousness'.[8]

After having examined the previous and inadequate theories of the soul, Aristotle begins the second book of *On the Soul* (*De Anima*,

Peri psuchēs) with the fundamental distinction between *matter* (*húlen*), 'that which in itself is not a this', and *form* and *essence* (*morphen kai eidos*), 'that precisely in virtue of which a thing is called a this' (412a).[9] Matter is always *potentiality* (*dúnamis*), or that which is always ready, but never gets there on its own. Form is always *actuality* (*entelékheià*), or that which is always already there. It is from this grid of what is always *ready* (matter) to be there, and what is always already *there* (form), that Aristotle turns to the question of the soul. Soul, he argues, is the 'actuality of a body': it is the life, the organization and the unity of the body (412a–b). Soul cannot '*be* a body', but it can be '*in* a body' (414a). Aristotle doesn't so much say what the soul is, as describe the perfect operation of the seamless *concept* – the goal that Hegel will spend a lifetime trying to reach. The soul is actuality *working* with potentiality, form *working* with matter.

For Aristotle, it is 'the possession of sensation' that distinguishes the animal from the merely living and 'nothing except what has soul in it is capable of sensation' (413b, 415b). The soul is 'the cause or source' of sensation (415b). Without actuality working with potentiality, form working with matter, there can be no sensation. It is only by *starting* from the soul that one can then turn to the dependence of sensation 'on a process of movement or affection from without' (416b). Sensation is reliant on the 'stimulation of external objects', and this demonstrates that 'what is sensitive is so only potentially, not actually' (417a). 'The power of sense . . . never ignites *itself*, but requires an agent', Aristotle insists (my emphasis). But because it is only a living body, a body with a soul in it, that can be sensitive, the precedence of what is *inside* is in no way diminished by the dependence on what is *outside*. The soul (actuality working on potentiality) is the possibility of sensation (potentiality in need of an external agent).

It is from this basic architecture that Aristotle turns to the 'objects of sense' and the visible as the object of sight (418a). In defining the relationship between light and colour as the origin of the visible Aristotle turns to the diaphanous, the transparent, to a *seeing through*. 'By diaphanous', Aristotle writes, 'I mean what is visible, and yet not visible, and not yet visible in itself, but rather owing its visibility to the colour of something else' (418b). Light working with colour, actuality working with potentiality, form working with matter: the visible. Light 'exists whenever the potentially transparent is excited by actuality' and, as a mirror of the soul, it reflects what Derrida calls in the *Introduction* 'the invisible milieu of seeing', the unseen Idea as the origin of phenomenology, and the soul – non-sensibility *par excellence* – as the origin of the senses.

A year after the introduction to *The Origin of Geometry* was published, Derrida turns to the diaphanous at a critical moment in his reading of Foucault in his 1963 paper 'Cogito and the History of Madness'. The *mastery* of Foucault's project on the history of madness is measured by the assumption of a 'rational' language which provides *both* a necessary distance from and the greatest proximity to madness itself. This proximity, Derrida writes, 'this diaphaneity is nothing other than the language, meaning, possibility, and *elementary* discretion of a nothing that neutralizes everything'.[10] Derrida suggests that Foucault repeats an Aristotelian motif that leads him to 'a reappropriation of negativity'. In trying to avoid the Hegelian colonization of the negative, Foucault has evoked a *pure* negativity, an *absolute* difference. For Derrida, such a gesture only invites Hegelianism: 'to attempt to reintroduce a purity into the concept of difference', he argues, 'one returns it to nondifference and full presence'.[11] One can perhaps also see this legacy in Giorgio Agamben's attempts to *stop* with potentiality, with the potential of a *diaphanous* that can start – absolutely differently, like a darkness that absolutely resists the light of actuality – *with* itself.[12]

In this early period before *Of Grammatology* (1965–67) Derrida begins to make the *assumption* of the soul or psyche an explicit target in his work. In 'Violence and Metaphysics' (1964), he argues that Lévinas' absolutely *other* is the psyche: 'secret, separate, invisible . . . this is the very state, the very status of what is called the *psyche*'.[13] For the next forty years, Derrida will tirelessly question the unacknowledged presence of the psyche in contemporary philosophy and challenge the view that the psyche alone accounts for 'life as relation to self'.[14]

MATTER AND FORM

At the heart of the *De Anima* is the determination of *matter* as potentiality and *form* as actuality. If one adheres to Aristotle, the matter and form of the work become the *soul* of the work. When, from the late 1960s, Derrida began to bring attention to the style of philosophy, to the format and the layout of the philosophical work, this was not simply a heightened self-conscious textual playfulness: it was an attempt to challenge and to resist the Aristotelian inheritance. He had first touched on the question of matter and form in his early readings of Husserl in the 1950s. For Husserl, matter is real but not intentional. Form *animates* and brings intention to matter. This form–matter structure gives rise to a non-real ideal objectivity that oversees how consciousness relates to things.[15] Matter is a passive receptivity that facilitates and works for the active intentionality of consciousness.

Already in 1953–54 in *The Problem of Genesis in Husserl's Philosophy*, what interested Derrida was Husserl's reliance on matter as that which is real but not intentional – and 'constitutive of all perception'.[16] This non-intentional matter is characterized by Husserl as a *lived experience* (*vécu*), a lived experience before intentionality. How, Derrida asks, can there be a non-intentional lived experience *before* matter is animated by form?[17] Husserl is caught between the old traps of either starting with matter (empiricism) or starting with form (idealism). His only recourse is to treat the origin itself as a *synthesis* of matter and form, which already presupposes the existence of matter and form. Husserl cannot move beyond this impasse because he does not recognize an 'originary temporality'.[18] Derrida returns to this question of starting with matter (*hylē*) in his 1959 paper on Husserl, ' "Genesis and Structure" and Phenomenology':

> Now, at its greatest depth and in its pure specificity the *hylē* is primarily temporal matter. It is the possibility of genesis itself. Thus at these two poles of opening [matter and form] and from within the very transcendental structure of all consciousness there would arise the necessity for the transition to a genetic constitution and for the new 'transcendental aesthetic' which will be announced unceasingly but will be deferred always, and within which the themes of the Other and of Time were to have permitted their irreducible complicity to appear. It is that the constitution of the other and of time refers phenomenology to a zone in which its 'principles of principles' (as we see it, its metaphysical principles: the *original self-evidence* and *presence* of the thing itself in person) is radically put in question.[19]

One can already see Derrida moving away from Husserl through his analysis of the relation between matter and form as the *exclusion* of an original temporality and alterity. In his 1967 essay on Husserl, 'Form and Meaning', Derrida argues that for Husserl form 'is presence itself'. The question of formality, or 'whatever aspect of the thing in general presents itself', is the unavoidable and ceaseless restoration of being as presence. Form, even as an apparent limitation of ontology, always takes us back to being.[20]

For Derrida, in a palintropic genealogy, Husserl's use of *hylē* and *morphē* looks *back* to Kant looking *back* at Aristotle. As we have seen, in the *Physics* Aristotle argues that if one takes the now (as a part that divides the no longer now and the not yet now, the before and after) as the essence of time, time cannot be treated as being, as an unbroken presence.[21] As Derrida suggests in '*Ousia* and *Grammē*' (1968), the apparent incompatibility of time with being leads *both* to the unavoidable comparison of time to *space* and to the pervasive *idealization* of space: 'In effect, *as Aristotle says*, it is because time does not belong to beings, is no more a part of them than a determination of them, and because time is not of (phenomenal or noumenal) being in general, that it must be made into a pure form of sensibility (the nonsensuous sensuous)'.[22] As a '*pure* sensibility' that is 'free of all reference to sensation', Derrida argues, time will become an *inner sense* for Kant – and it has already become a form of the *soul* for Aristotle.[23]

In the *Critique of Pure Reason* (1781, 1787), the matter/form distinction *introduces* – and is the very *possibility* of – the *a priori*: 'Since that within which the sensations can alone be ordered and placed in a certain form cannot itself be in turn sensation, the matter of all appearance is only given to us *a posteriori*, but its form must all lie ready for it in the mind *a priori*, and therefore be considered separately from all sensation.'[24] For Kant, both time and space are 'pure *forms* of sensible intuition'.[25] Form is at once the *possibility* of all the appearances of outer sense (space) and of all the intuitions of inner sense (time), and the objectively valid guarantee of the subjective condition of sensibility. Kant will go on to describe 'the transcendental unity of the synthesis of the imagination' as 'the pure form of all possible cognition, through which . . . all objects of possible experience must be represented *a priori*'.[26] From the start, it is the *difference* between form and matter that orders the *a priori* relation between sensibility and understanding, intuition and concept, experience and reason.

The unassailable priority of form over matter may also explain why there is no memory in the *Critique of Pure Reason*. As the precondition of experience, the *a priori* synthetic unity of the transcendental imagination (which is later reinforced or steadied in the second edition by the transcendental unity of self-consciousness) in relation to the pure concepts of the categories provides the basic architecture of the understanding. Memory, it seems, has no explicit role in the understanding.[27] Kant will relegate the memory, 'the faculty of deliberately visualising the past', to the *Anthropology*.[28] No doubt this is a reaction on Kant's part to the British empiricists. Hobbes had argued that the imagination was itself a kind of memory, while Locke had suggested that consciousness and personal identity relied on the memory.[29] Hume had proposed that strength of feeling primarily distinguished the memory from the imagination.[30] For Kant, it is precisely this equivocal inheritance that threatens the primacy, the order and the sequence of form and matter. It is all a question of how one starts:

> Nevertheless, in the case of these concepts, as in the case of all cognition, we can search in experience, if not for the principle of their possibility [*das Principium ihrer Möglichkeit*], then for the occasional causes of their generation [*die Gelegenheitsursachen ihrer Erzeugung*], where the impressions of the senses provide the first occasion [*das ersten Anlaß*] for opening the entire power of cognition to them and for bringing about experience, which contains two very heterogeneous elements, namely a matter for cognition from the sense and a certain form for ordering it from the inner source of pure intuiting and thinking, which, on the occasion of the former, are first brought into use and bring forth concepts. Such a tracing of the first endeavours [*der ersten Bestrebungen*] of our power of cognition to ascend from individual perceptions to general concepts is without doubt of great utility, and the famous Locke is to be thanked for first having opened the way for this. Yet a deduction of the pure *a priori* concepts can never be achieved in this way.[31]

Eight pages after this assertion of the primacy of form over matter, Kant finds himself having to address a problem between form and content.[32] In a section comprising a single paragraph entitled 'Preliminary reminder' (*Vorläufige Erinnerung*), Kant acknowledges that because the deduction of the categories requires 'such deep penetration into the primary grounds of the possibility of our cognition in general', and 'in order to avoid the longwindedness of a complete theory [*die Weitläuftigkeit einer vollständigen Theorie zu vermeiden*] and nevertheless not to omit anything', he has had to include four introductory sections which 'prepare' rather than 'instruct' the reader, and 'only then to represent the exposition of these elements'. 'For this reason', Kant concludes, 'the reader should until then not be deterred by the obscurity [*die Dunkelheit*] that is initially unavoidable in a path that is thus far entirely unexplored.'[33] In order to 'avoid the longwindedness of a complete theory' Kant cannot avoid the initial obscurity of putting the cart before the horse.

This unavoidable disorder of form at the expense of content echoes Kant's own critique of empiricist philosophies. For the sake of the *a priori* transcendental deduction Kant must put four parts *before* the whole: the only way the transcendental deduction can begin is with an unavoidable and very material *induction*. Kant starts the *Critique of Pure Reason* itself by criticizing the incompleteness of a philosophy that begins with experience and thus lets reason run away with itself. Invoking the assurance of a pure 'unconditioned completeness' (*unbedingte Vollständigkeit*) in the preface (the first and the last word in the first edition), Kant begins his account of the transcendental deduction by avoiding 'the longwindedness of a complete theory'.[34] Given the absence of an analysis of memory from the *Critique of Pure Reason*, it is also fitting that this disorder of form and content is described as a 'Preliminary reminder' (*Vorläufige Erinnerung*), asking the reader to take note, but also to re-call, to be re-minded about what they have not even read yet. This temporal lapse only reinforces the initial lapse of an induction at the start of a deduction. At the start, it is always a problem of form and matter.

In the same year that Derrida explored the influence of Aristotle on the *Critique of Pure Reason*, in 'The Pit and the Pyramid' (1968) he turned to the role played by the *De Anima* in Hegel's work. Hegel, Derrida writes, 'takes us back . . . to Aristotle' (*nous reconduit . . . à Aristote*).[35] This turning back to Aristotle is a palintropic movement that takes us back again and – at once, once more, more than once – beyond Aristotle. In his reading of Hegel's theory of signs, Derrida quotes Hegel from the third part of the *Encyclopaedia of*

Philosophical Sciences, the *Philosophy of Spirit*, writing about the importance of Aristotle's treatise on the soul:

> Aristotle is the model claimed by Hegel for his philosophy of spirit, and specifically for his psychology [which contains his analysis of semiology]: 'The books of Aristotle on the Soul, along with his discussions on its special aspects and states, are for this reason still by far the most admirable, perhaps even the sole, work of philosophical value on this topic. The main aim of a philosophy of mind can only be to reintroduce unity of idea and principle into the theory of mind, and so reinterpret the lesson of those Aristotelian books.'[36]

THE BLOWS FROM OUTSIDE

Having distinguished form and matter and made the case for the soul as the *origin* of sensation and of the senses in general, Aristotle turns in *On the Soul* to sound, hearing and the voice. Things that make a sound (*phthóggos*) when they are struck are actual, things that do not make a sound when hit (like a sponge) are potential (419b). Actual sound requires that there is always *more than one* body: 'it is impossible for one body only to generate a sound – there must be a body impinging and a body impinged upon'. For sound to be *actual*, there must be more than one body and these bodies must strike and hit each other. There must be 'an impact' (*plegē*), something 'striking against something else' (*tinos prós ti kai én tini plegē*). Because the air dissipates sound, there can be no sound without a certain *violence*: a thing 'must be struck with a sudden sharp blow [*takhéos kai sphodrōs plegē*], if it is to sound' (419b). Without a *blow*, there can be no sound. Hearing contains this violence. The 'air chamber' inside the ear resists the dissipation of sound in the air and retains the 'sudden sharp blow' that has come from outside (420a). Relying on a concurrence of 'the air inside' and of 'the air outside', hearing is 'always the sounding of something else, not of the organ itself'. For there to be sound and hearing, there must always be 'something else' – more than one body, something 'striking against something else', something outside.

Voice, Aristotle writes, 'is a kind of sound characteristic of what has soul in it' (420b). Voice is sound *with soul*. Sound, 'the impact of something against something else, across a space filled with air', becomes voice when an animal breathes in. It is all a matter of inspiration. Voice is 'the impact of the inbreathed air against the windpipe' and, Aristotle adds, the soul is 'the agent that produces the impact'. In other words, the soul is the *author* of an internal violence that makes the voice possible. This is a very particular violence: 'what produces the impact [*túpton*] must have soul in it'. The violence of the soul must guarantee that the necessary 'something else' (the possibility of sound, hearing and voice) can lead only to an *articulate* voice, to a voice with *meaning*: 'what produces the impact must have soul in it and must be accompanied by an act of imagination [*phantasías*], for voice is a sound with meaning [*sēmantikos gàr dē tis phóphos estin ē phōnē*]' (420b).

Derrida argues in 'The Pit and the Pyramid' that this alliance of the soul and the imagination oversees Hegel's equation of the voice with meaning as the foundation, the starting point, of his theory of signs.[37] Hegel perpetuates the logic of 'the invisible ideality of a *logos* which-hears-itself-speak'.[38] Like Husserl, Hegel can only start again with Aristotle and the diaphanous. Already in his introduction to *The Origin of Geometry*, Derrida had argued that the Idea as the idealizing unseen origin of the seen is a *logos*, is speech:

> That a phenomenological determination of the Idea itself may be radically impossible from then on signifies perhaps that phenomenology cannot be reflected in a phenomenology of phenomenology, and that its *Logos* can never appear as such, can never be given in a philosophy of seeing, but (like all Speech) can only be heard or understood through the visible.[39]

In phenomenology, speech is the invisible idealizing origin of the visible.

Derrida later identifies this structure of idealization in the work of Lévinas in 'Violence and Metaphysics'. Like Hegel, Lévinas treats 'the sound of thought as intelligible speech' and *hearing* as an ideality that surpasses the sensibility of sound. Hearing is superior to seeing as a vehicle of ideality.[40] The diaphanous will always privilege the ear over the eye. In *Speech and Phenomena* (1967), Derrida argues that the presumption of *hearing oneself speak* is at the heart of Husserlian phenomenology.[41] He attempts to counteract this tradition of the diaphanous when he insists in 'Différance' (1968) that 'the difference marked in the "differ( )nce" between the *e* and the *a* eludes both vision and hearing'. Exceeding sight and sound, *différance* refers to 'an order which no longer belongs to sensibility', but it also no longer belongs 'to intelligibility, to the ideality which is not fortuitously affiliated with the objectivity of *theorein* or understanding'.[42]

In his account of hearing in *De Anima* Aristotle emphasizes the importance of 'the tympanic membrane' (420a), and it is appropriate that *Margins – of Philosophy* (1972), which is so concerned with Hegel starting again with Aristotle, opens with an introduction entitled 'Tympan'. From Aristotle to Hegel and beyond, the eardrum is at once an internal buffer that regulates and orders the sudden sharp blows of the outside on the inside and a membrane that cannot stop vibrating and registering something – always more than one body – 'striking against something else', something outside.[43] Resisting the 'frontal and symmetrical protest', the absolute exit, alterity or difference, Derrida starts by asking the question of the Aristotelian ear, that fabulous Greek machine designed 'to balance internal pressures and external pressures'.[44] 'How', Derrida asks, 'to unbalance [*déséquilibrer*] the pressures that correspond to each other on either side of the membrane? How to block [*enrayer*] this correspondence destined to weaken, muffle, forbid the blows from the outside [*les coups du dehors*]?'[45] The Aristotelian inheritance, which claims that philosophy can always maintain its grip on the *tympanum*, can be put under pressure by taking account of the *tympanum* not simply as the eardrum but also as a part of the printing press, of a writing machine in which – from the start – there is always more than one *tympan*. This writing machine is always trying to calculate the margins of a page: neither simply inside nor outside, it is always *on* and *from* the margins.[46]

TOUCH: EXACTNESS OF DISCRIMINATION

As we have seen, for Husserl, starting with Plato is to begin with *theoria* as the immaculate birth of *exactness*. For Aristotle in *On the Soul*, it is *touch* that gives the highest exactness to humans: 'While in respect of all the other senses we fall below many species of animals, in respect of touch [*aphén*] we far excel all other species in exactness of discrimination [*akriboi*]. This is why man is the most intelligent of animals' (421a). As a measure and expression of the uniquely human quality of exactness, touch is a sign of intelligence. Touch accounts for the human capacity for 'exactness of discrimination': an exactness in differentiation, in difference. First and foremost, touch describes the capacity to arrive at an exact – an ideal and pure – difference.

For Aristotle, the sense of touch as an ideal or pure difference is itself founded on the fundamental and exact distinction between form and matter. Concerned with the soul as the possibility of sensation and of the sense, Aristotle reiterates 'a sense is what has the power of receiving into itself the sensible forms of things without the matter [*ton aistheton eidon áneu tes húles*]' (424a). The senses – and there can *only* be five Aristotle insists – are always a question of sensible forms *without* matter. Sensible forms account for the impression of things on the senses, on us. Unlike plants, which cannot make a *distinction* between the form and matter of sensible objects, from the start *we* have made an exact discrimination, and not only separated but also excluded matter from the senses (424b). It is this absence of matter in sense that will make the imagination possible (425b). The five senses in general, Aristotle argues, form a *unified* apparatus of exact discrimination. Each sense is a ratio, a balancing mechanism that avoids the extremes (the too bright or too dark, the too loud or too quiet, the too hot or too cold) that leave one senseless. The senses are a unity that 'discriminates the differences' and avoids excess (426b). This wondrous machine, this five-in-one, is the work of the soul, the psyche.

The senses are always mediating between extremes, and this need for the *form* of a *medium* or *media* is inherent in each sense.[47] Poised between extremes (too bright, too loud) seeing and hearing require that there is *no* 'immediate contact' with an object. If something is lying on the eye or ear it cannot be seen or heard. For the senses to work, there must be '*something* in between [*metaksú*]' (419a). It is only through the medium of light that we can see colour, only through the medium of air that we can hear. 'The same, in spite of all appearances,' Aristotle adds, 'applies also to touch and taste' (419a). To avoid excess is to avoid *contact*. The senses can only work as a mediation between a 'pair of contraries' if they avoid touching – and this is the case with the sense of touch most of all (422b).

As one would expect, Aristotle begins by stating that 'the medium of touch' is flesh. 'Without touch it is impossible for an animal to be.' Touch is 'indispensable' (434b). The *possibility* of all the other senses, touch 'alone perceives by immediate contact' (435a). But both because there are a number of different kinds of tangible perceptions (taste and touch, the tongue and the skin) and because of the human capacity for 'exactness of discrimination', the *source* of touching and of its ability to mediate is more than the flesh and is 'situated farther inward' (422b). Aristotle warns that we *cannot* use 'contact with the flesh' to reach – to touch – the internal origins of touching, and he illustrates this by noting that if a kind of prosthetic skin were attached or even grafted to the body it would still tell us little about the fine discriminations of touching (422b–423a). Bodies, he reminds us, which are in the air or in the water 'cannot be in contact with one another', and because we are always either in the air or in the water if we are alive, touching cannot be described as the immediate contact of two bodies (423a). 'We perceive everything through a medium [*mesou*]' (423b).[48]

But the medium of touch is distinctive among the senses. Light and air, the medium of sight and sound, produces 'a certain effect on us' that leads to seeing and hearing. When it comes to touching, 'we are', Aristotle writes, 'affected not *by* but along *with* the medium' (423b). The medium is part of the message. Returning to the notion of a sudden sharp blow from the outside, Aristotle describes this unique inclusion of the medium (*metaksù*) in the sense as the violent reverberation of a shield being struck: 'it is as if a man were struck [*plegeis*] through his shield, where the shock [*plegeisa*] is not first given to the shield and passed on to the man, but the concussion [*plegenai*] of both is simultaneous'. When it comes to hearing, the 'air chamber' of the ear mediates the medium and the inside balances the force of the blow from the outside. When it comes to touch, there seems no time for such a natural homeostasis. Touching is what happens when the external blow hits the outside and the inside simultaneously. Touch is a simultaneous concussion of the external *and* the internal.

What interests Aristotle is the blow that reverberates beyond the surface, beyond the flesh, beyond the tangible. The flesh is the medium of touch, but the 'power of perceiving the tangible is seated inside [*entòs*]' (423b). It is only this power that is 'seated inside' that can mediate, discern and confirm the form–matter, actual–potential dynamic. At the same time, as Derrida observes in *On Touching*, the fact that sensation 'is only *potential*' means that sense cannot 'sense *itself*': sense 'does not auto-affect itself without the motion of an exterior object'.[49] The internal power of sensation, of touch, is in itself and to itself, *insufficient*. It is always in *need* of the other – the other that is outside, and the other that *moves*. For Derrida, when it comes to touch there is always the pre-cedence of a gap that moves.[50] For there to be place or touch, he argues, there 'must be *spacing* before it is space', there must be 'an interval' that is 'neither sensible nor intelligible'.[51] To touch, there must already be the *gap* of and as an irreducible *spacing* (*différance*), the gap of *and* as contact.[52] This is even the case when we try to touch ourselves: 'The *I* self-touches spacing itself out, losing contact with itself, precisely in touching itself' (*je se touché en s'espaçant, en perdant le contact avec soi, justement à se toucher*).[53] Touching, one is always touching the (moving gaps of the) other.

Aristotle tries to address the problem of the inescapable necessity of touching and the insufficiency of the internal power of sensation, by concluding that 'touch has for its object both what is tangible *and* what is intangible' (424a, my emphasis). Reaching for the sense of touch, Aristotle arrives where he started with the untouchable, the intangible – and the soul. For Derrida, this irreducible gap, this gaping – as spacing, as *différance*, as the elusive *possibility* of touching another or oneself, and the *ruin* of touching as a complete co-presence or self-presence – should not be confused with the long tradition of touch as an idealization, of the idealization of the 'other *as* untouchable'.[54] As he suggests in *On Touching*, in failing to touch the untouchable other, whatever is reaching out to the other, ultimately, only 'touches *itself and* loses contact – with itself.[55] Since Plato in the *Phaedo* described the truth as a touching on the soul *without* the body or *after* the body, and since Aristotle suggested that the true source of touch was the intangible, touch has been predicated on the assumption of a continuous, immediate and always exact intuition.[56] For Derrida, the constitution – the idealization – of philosophy itself *starts* with 'retaining the sense of touch within sight so as to ensure for the glancing eye the fullness of immediate presence required by every ontology or metaphysics'.[57] Starting with Plato and Aristotle, philosophy starts with the diaphanous – and with itself.

Intuition is an inviolate inside that always *anticipates* the sudden sharp blows of the outside. As Kant argues over and over again in the *Critique of Pure Reason*, mediation with the outside is possible only because we can start with and from the inside. The *a priori* conditions for a possible experience, Kant writes in the first edition of 1781, are founded on the transcendental faculty of the imagination. Without the *a priori* and *formal* synthetic unity of the imagination, there can be no experience.[58] In the second edition of 1787, Kant tries to reinforce and shore up this inviolate internal anticipation by moving the emphasis away from the reliance on the imagination to the authority of the transcendental unity of self-consciousness, and comes up against the limits of the *form* of inner sense which, as we have seen, again following Aristotle, he describes as time, or 'the intuition of our self and of our inner state'.[59]

EXACTITUDE: STARTING AGAIN

Derrida begins *On Touching* by noting Jean-Luc Nancy's preoccupation with 'exactitude' and the exact.[60] Since his early readings of Husserl, Derrida had associated exactitude with Husserlian idealization – with an 'exact and nonsensible ideality' that arises *from* 'a sensible ideality'.[61] For Husserl, this exactitude is nothing less than the *beginning* of Western philosophy. In 'Le facteur de la vérité' (1971–75), Derrida notes Lacan's evocation of an '*exactitude*' that treats literature as 'something that stages and makes visible, with no specific intervention of its own, like a transparent element, a general diaphanousness [*une diaphanéité générale*]'.[62] It is perhaps not fortuitous that a few pages before this Derrida makes one of his earliest references to Jean-Luc Nancy.[63] For Derrida, Nancy seems to at once echo the Aristotelian tradition of exactness *and* to exceed it: 'Nancy is the thinker of the *exorbitant* and *exactitude* at the same time.' He is concerned with an 'exorbitant exactitude', an exactitude that remains 'faithful to the excess of the exorbitant'. Derrida will later call this Nancy's 'exact hyperbole'.[64]

As Derrida points out in *On Touching*, for Aristotle, touch as discrimination, as mediation, as life, is predicated on resisting and refusing the destructive force of all 'tangible excess'. 'In the beginning,' Derrida argues, 'there is abstinence', but this abstinence is already founded on the *possibility* of touching the untouchable. Starting *with* Aristotle, touch cannot avoid the *aporia*, the 'hyper-dialectical' (touching without touching, contact without contact) *and*, beyond this, the disturbing hyperbole of touching (the blows *and* caresses) that exceed *both* the exact and the inexact.[65] As we have seen, for Aristotle the 'sudden sharp blow' (420a) from the outside is indispensable for the sense of hearing, and the sense of touch is distinguished by a reverberating blow from the outside that concusses *both* the outside and the inside (423b). Even in the midst of insisting on the life-preserving mediation of the senses, of the unseen and unfelt work of the soul as the 'exactness of discrimination' in all the senses, Aristotle cannot avoid what Derrida had first called in 1972 in 'Tympan', 'the blows from the outside' (*les coups du dehors*).

For Aristotle, the 'exactness of discrimination' defines the uniquely human capacity of touch. Taking up Aristotle's admission that the tangible seems to entail a multiplicity of senses (422b), Derrida treats the tangible indeterminacy of the blow and the caress as a touch that is not 'necessarily human'. The blow and the caress exceed the Aristotelian classifications. 'A blow', Derrida suggests, 'is perhaps not a kind of destructive touching, indeed, of the excessive tangibility that, as Aristotle already noted, can have devastating effects.' The caress is also 'not only a species of soothing, beneficial, and pleasant touch, pleasure enjoyed by contact'. Beyond good and evil, beyond the exact and the inexact, 'a caress may be a blow and *vice versa*'.[66]

For Derrida, the philosophies of touch, in particular those post-war French philosophies that responded to the work of Husserl, while never straying that far from the questions *of* Christianity, are always starting again with Aristotle, with *Peri psuchēs*:

> But they already know that this thinking of touch, this thought of what 'touching' means, must touch on the untouchable. Aristotle's *Peri psuchēs* had already insisted on this: both the tangible and the intangible are the objects of touch (*hē haphē tou haptou kai anaptou*) (*Peri psuchēs* 424a). Once this incredible 'truth' has been uttered, it will resonate down to the twentieth century, even within discourses apparently utterly foreign to any Aristotelianism.[67]

What distinguishes Jean-Luc Nancy, Derrida argues, is an emphasis on *prosthetics* that attempts to resist the traditional association of the soul, and of the touching the untouchable, with 'the pure life of the living' and the 'immediate continuity' of intuition.[68] At the same time, while Nancy links the possibility of exactitude to the spacing and *tekhnē* of a prosthetics that exceeds the *phusis* of touch as the natural, living continuity of the soul, he also associates it with a certain beginning or *starting again*, with an untouchable resurrection or salvation that Derrida sees as a *repetition* of Aristotelianism that is still prevalent, even – and perhaps most of all – in Nancy's call for a 'deconstruction of Christianity'.[69]

Derrida links Nancy's description of Psyche as a dead woman lying in her coffin with a group standing around her (around psyche, *Peri psuchēs*, being also the title of Aristotle's treatise) to Nancy's reading of Caravaggio's *The Death of the Virgin*: psyche becomes Mary, the mother and virgin. Psyche as Mary becomes 'Christianity's indeconstructable', the inadmissible ideality of the *immaculate conception* that Derrida sees at the heart of the sexual difference in his readings of Hegel and Genet in *Glas*.[70] The 'deconstruction of Christianity' *begins with* 'the Christian body', a seemingly intact and unique body *to be* deconstructed.[71] It also presupposes that there is an *outside* of Christianity, an outside or 'passage beyond itself' that, precisely, Christianity *par excellence* has always taken account of. Christianity has always had the 'ability to part without parting'. This is an exactitude that always takes account of its *own* hyperbole: 'For a certain Christianity will always take charge of the most exacting, the most *exact*, and the most eschatological hyperbole of deconstruction.' In this sense, 'dechristianization will be a Christian victory'.[72]

BOTTOM'S DREAM

'Aristotle has not left us for a moment.'[73] For Derrida, the exact is never far away from Aristotle's *Peri psuchēs*, and the enduring tradition of the idealization of the diaphanous and of touch as 'the exactness of discrimination.' 'This treatise', Derrida notes, 'begins by explaining to us, at the very outset, what one is to begin with.'[74] For Aristotle, the dynamic of matter as what is always *ready* and form as what is always *there* resolves any apparent problems of precedence. Passive matter can be *first*, because it is always *potential* matter. What is always ready is *always* on its way to what is always there. As Aristotle observes, 'in the individual, potential knowledge is in time prior [*protéra*] to actual knowledge, but absolutely it is not prior even in time' (430a). 'All things', he insists, 'that come into being arise from what actually is [*entelekheia óntos*]' (431a). Potential matter can be first, because to *be* potential, it must *already* start with and start from 'what actually is'. This is the ontology of Aristotle. As Derrida remarks, 'the fullness of immediate presence signifies above all the *actuality* of what gives itself effectively, energetically, *actually*'.[75] It is because potential knowledge is *not* prior 'even in time' to actual knowledge that 'actual knowledge is identical with its object' (430a). *Thought* – which is always of and from the soul – is always thinkable, always 'becoming all things', always 'separable, impassible, unmixed', always separable from matter, body and sensation, because 'when separated it is alone just what it is': 'immortal and eternal'. It is the soul. This is where Hegel begins and ends: *with a thought that only thinks itself.*

For Derrida, as for Hegel, it all starts with Aristotle's *On the Soul.* As he had suggested in 1968 in '*Ousia* and *Grammē*', the matter–form, potential–actual relation starts with Aristotle, with Aristotle starting again, and again and again. Potentiality – force, dynamics – is always an eschatology and a teleology *on its way* (back) to an archaeology. Aristotle is always starting (again) with matter on its *way back* to form, and has kept all of us '*going around in circles*' (à tourner en rond).[76] In his fifty years of reading *On the Soul*, Derrida offered what amounts to a 'new' history of the senses (a history that is always *à venir*, to come), tracing the gaps of and as *différance in* each of the senses, *and* the gaps of and as *différance between* each of the senses: *plus de cinq* – not only five, more than five, never five-in-one. Derrida's reading of Aristotle suggests that we still have yet to interpret 'Bottom's Dream': 'The eye of man hath not heard, the ear of man hath not seen, man's hand is not able to taste, his tongue to conceive, nor his heart to report what my dream was.'[77]

CHAPTER 6

LEAPING TO PLATO

> But truly to escape Hegel involves an exact appreciation of the price we have to pay to detach ourselves from him. It assumes that we are aware of the extent to which Hegel, insidiously perhaps, is close to us; it implies a knowledge in that which permits us to think against Hegel, of that which remains Hegelian. We have to determine the extent to which our anti-Hegelianism is possibly one of his tricks directed against us, at the end of which he stands, motionless, waiting for us.
>
> Foucault, 'The Discourse on Language'[1]

A HISTORY – OF PHILOSOPHY

While in his readings of Aristotle Derrida gestures to the possibility of a 'new' history – of the senses, he also insists that such a history cannot avoid the 'mighty shadow' (*ombre immense*) of Hegel.[2] The first part of Hegel's *Lectures on the Philosophy of History*, the often disputed and always unstable collection of loose papers and student notes from Hegel's 1805–31 lectures, offers a remarkable history of Hegel's own attempts to begin philosophy by having to start again and again to escape an inaugural and idealized *sensible certainty* that, as we shall see, both opens the *Phenomenology of Spirit* (1807) and begins Derrida's own rereading of Hegel, which culminated in the publication of *Glas* in 1974.

After no less than three attempts to introduce the *Lectures on the History of Philosophy* (the Inaugural Address, the Prefatory Note and the Introduction), Hegel adds yet one more introduction before he begins his history with Greek philosophy.[3] To no more than gesture to these repeated introductions, for Hegel a *history* of philosophy is indispensable just as a body is indispensable to the spirit or time indispensable to the truth. A *history* of philosophy demonstrates the journey that spirit must take on its way to absolute knowledge and to the *end* of history. At the same time, if truth is to be found in time or the spirit in the body, a philosophy of history must *begin* and must *maintain* itself as a history of 'the living present' (*gegenwärtig Lebendigen*), as a history *of* truth. You can only *start* a history of philosophy with philosophy, with *thought thinking itself thinking the truth*, with thought using difference to make its *own* outside to reach its *own* inside. You cannot start a history of philosophy, Hegel warns, by relying on the external representation of writing (on 'canvas, paper, marble'), nor can you entirely avoid anachronisms, alterations, deviations or gaps.[4]

ORIENTAL PHILOSOPHY

After the trinity of introductions and before starting with Greek philosophy, there is a section in the *Lectures* devoted to 'Oriental Philosophy'. *After* the introduction and *before* the start of the book, this quasi-introductory and quasi-opening section appears to be detachable. Oriental philosophy: take it or leave it – it is a leftover, an editorial remainder at the beginning.

Orientalische Philosophie: Hegel starts again and immediately has a problem with the *order* of the beginning. 'The first [*erste*] Philosophy in order is the so-called Oriental', he writes (117; 138). The Oriental is at once before *and* in front, behind and ahead of Greek philosophy. Hegel overcomes and circumvents the problem of what precedes and exceeds Greek philosophy by insisting that 'its position is preliminary [*vorläufiges*], and we deal with it at all in order to account for not treating of it at greater length'. What is first (*erste*) is not really first, it is only the first as that which is preliminary and provisional (*vorläufiges*). It is a beginning with a time limit, a starting point that will be replaced and displaced by what is really and truly first. The history of philosophy begins with a *temporary* first philosophy.

How does one respond to what is only temporary at the start? Hegel says 'we deal with it', we only *speak* of it (*nur sprechen*) to escape, to get away from giving an account of it (*um davon Rechenschaft zu geben*), and not be extensively occupied with it (*nicht weitläufiger damit bechäftigen*). This is a strange speaking indeed. We shall speak of this first and temporary philosophy, but only in a manner where we will give no account of it and not get caught up or occupied with it. We shall speak of it, and not let it remain with us: we shall avoid the remainders of *Orientalische Philosophie*.

In the introduction to the *Lectures*, Hegel acknowledged both the precedence of religion and the necessity for a history of philosophy to begin *without* religion: 'Inasmuch as in the progress of culture in time the manifestation of Religion precedes [*vorangeht*] the appearance of Philosophy, this circumstance must really be taken account of, and the conditions requisite for beginning the History of Philosophy have to depend on this, because it has to be shown how far what pertains to Religion is to be excluded from it [*auszuschließen*], and that a commencement [*Anfang*] must not be made with Religion' (61; 82). Religion comes *first*, and we cannot *begin* with it. Hegel uses the quasi-introductory section on oriental philosophy to resolve this problem and to delineate what aspects of religion must be excluded from a history of philosophy. Hegel can only begin with what must be *excluded*, with the remainders that are before (and in front of) the commencement (*der Anfang*). He can also only *begin* with what must *not* begin a history of philosophy.

Oriental philosophy should be understood as a 'religious philosophy' (117). The 'religious ideas' of oriental philosophy are 'not individualized' (118). The history of philosophy begins (and does not begin) with an almost static universality. God is taken as 'only one substance', and the individual is only registered 'through an identification with this substance in which he ceases to exist as subject and disappears into unconsciousness [*worin es dann aufhört, als Subjekt zu sein, verschwindet ins Bewußtlose*]' (118; 140). Everything starts 'in the absence of individual consciousness [*Bewußtlosigkeit*]' (119; 140). This universal unconsciousness in turn gives rise to a bad infinite and a bad finite that perpetually announce at the outset 'the destruction of all that is particular'. The individual can either only find itself irrevocably disappearing into 'an illimitable . . . exaltitude' (*ein Maßloses . . . Erhabenheit*), or in a finitude that is cut off from the 'one substance' and can be no more than 'a dry, dead [*Geistloses*] understanding, which cannot take up the speculative Notion [*Begriff*] into itself' (119; 140–1). In other words, the only individuality that is possible in oriental philosophy cannot reach – cannot begin and end with – the concept.

Making his way *through* Chinese and Indian philosophy, Hegel argues in the *Lectures* that the more one knows of these philosophies the more 'diminished' (*herabgesetzt*), they become (119; 141). He attempts to reduce, to cut-down, to de-pose or deposit the *remainders* at the beginning. As Derrida suggests in *Glas*, for Hegel what is posited (*gesetzt*) is always de-posed by the *Aufhebung*, which (despite itself) leaves deposits, remainders that resist (*restance*) any determined or absolute position, that *remain* – and remain to come.[5] As Derrida writes, for Hegel, 'the beginning [*le commencement*] – before it the *déjà*, the already – befalls, as always, by the instance of the result. The rebound [*ressaut*] of the *already* should not leave any remain(s). In speculative dialectics, the result is not a remain(s), the remain(s) does not result'.[6] The beginning should – *already* – reflect and lead *to* the end, *to* the result and it should do this *without* any mad precipitation or anticipation. 'This anticipation cannot be insignificant', Derrida observes.[7] We have to get the speeds right. For Derrida, from the start it is all about the traces of speeds that are always going too fast or too slow for the already (*déjà*) of the *Aufhebung* to take care of its leftovers, to keep the remains away from the beginning and the end.

One should not begin with Chinese philosophy, Hegel argues, because it is merely an exercise in 'universal abstraction' (123). It is so preoccupied with the 'forms of representation' that it begins and ends with *nothing*: 'the origin of things is nothing [*der Ursprung aller Dinge ist das Nichts*], emptiness, the altogether undetermined, the abstract universal' (125; 147). And one should not begin with Indian philosophy because 'nothing can be more confused, nothing more imperfect than the chronology of the Indians' (126). The 'unsystematic' (*unordentlichen*) nature of Indian philosophy is apparent in that while recognizing that 'the negation of the object which is contained in thought is necessary in order to comprehend', it offers a bad trinity, a trinity with an 'imperfect' chronology (132; 153). The first principle of *unity* is followed by *difference*, but the third principle is *negation*. 'As far as we are concerned', Hegel writes, 'the important distinction is that the third principle is not the return to the first which Mind [*Geist*] and Idea demand, and which is effected by the removal of the negation [*Aufhebens der Negation*] in order to effect a reconciliation with itself and to go back within itself. With the Indians the third is still [*bleibt*, remains] change and negation [*Veränderung, Vernichtung*]' (135–6; 158).

A formal universality that begins and ends in negation, and a mad trinity that ends not in the enhanced return to itself but in 'change and negation': these are the unavoidable remainders at the beginning that one should not begin with. To begin, Hegel must negate the negations that end in negation, because he can only start the history of spirit with negation. In Hegelianism 'the beginning is negated at the beginning, in order for it to begin'.[8]

AT HOME WITH THE GREEKS

The remainder to be excluded at the outset of the *Lectures* is the *exclusion* of individual consciousness. In contrast to oriental philosophy, Greek philosophy will start not with the universal unconsciousness of religion but with the proto-philosophical dilemma of 'individual freedom' (*der Freiheit der Individualität*) (117; 138). 'In the Greek and Christian religion', Hegel writes, 'the subject knows himself to be free', and it is this individual consciousness that *begins* the speculative dynamics of Greek philosophy. Starting *with* individuality it is 'much more difficult for thought to free itself' and to begin 'the work of Thought [*dem Gedanken seine Arbeit*], which is to give due value to the universal [*Allgemeinheit*]'. To begin a history of philosophy, one must start with *thought* finding its difficult 'independence' from the freedom of individual consciousness (118–19; 140).

How does one begin with a beginning that is not one's own? Greek philosophy, Hegel insists, begins *from* Indian philosophy. Indian philosophy ends in the separation of nature and thought when the soul separates itself from the body and draws 'itself within itself' (143–4). The mind has separated itself from nature and philosophy is finished. Thought is defined merely by the emptiness of what it has escaped: objectivity has been discarded and all that remains is a weak and vain subjectivity that must be transcended (145). For Hegel, this is yet again a philosophy that does not begin with negation, but ends in negation: 'Just as in empty vanity [*Eitelkeit*], where the subjective power of negation alone remains [*Macht des Verneinens das Bleibende*], everything disappears [*untergeht*], this abstraction of intellectual substantiality only signifies an escape into what is empty and without determination [*Leere und Bestimmungslose*], wherein everything vanishes' (145; 168).

But this empty vanishing at the end is also the *true beginning* of Western philosophy: 'Intellectual substantiality is in India the end [*ist das Ziel*], while in Philosophy it is in general the true commencement [*die wesentliche Grundlage, der Anfang*, the essential foundation, the beginning]' (145; 167). Philosophy must begin with this dubious separation of nature and thought, because 'to philosophize is the idealism of making thought [*Denken*], in its own right, the principle of truth [*die Grundlage der Wahrheit*]' – and this separation is only the beginning (145; 167). Philosophy – which has still not started – will be about thought becoming *objective*, of thought thinking itself thinking the truth by putting difference to work with the help of the *Aufhebung*. Philosophy must begin by giving birth to the *Aufhebung*, which is itself the *possibility* of the birth of philosophy. It is from this impossible conception that we must start.

Extricating himself from oriental philosophy, Hegel still cannot begin with the Greeks. To leave what is at once *before* (in front of) Greek philosophy and *behind* it (in every sense of the word), Hegel must gesture to what is ahead of and *after* the Greeks. Descartes is the quiet hinge between oriental and Greek philosophy. At the end of Indian philosophy, 'what remains to be done is to force forward the real ground of the inwardly self-forming and determining objectivity' and one has to begin 'in the first place' (*erstens*) with the recognition that thought 'as subjective, is mine, because I think' (*als subjektiv das meinige* (*Ich, meine Seele denkt*)) (145; 168). This is only the first stage, and is followed by universality and culminates in 'forming activity, the principle of determination' (146). But it is from this starting point that thought becomes objective, and having the freedom *to think itself thinking the truth* gives rise to – or, *already*, at the start takes us *back* towards – the presiding Greek concern with the universality of individual freedom.

For Hegel, because individual thought can be objective the universal has 'actual presence' (*Gegenwart*). Throughout the history of philosophy this 'actual presence' is always with us – implicitly. The universal is always 'implicit' (*Ansich*), and is 'the truth of present objects' (*die Wahrheit der Gegenstände sei*). It is this 'principle that we find in the Greek world' (146–7; 169–70). Philosophy can only begin when presence is – already – implicit.

'When man began to be at home with himself [*da hat der Mensch angefangen, in seiner Heimat zu sein*], he turned to the Greeks', Hegel writes. At the proper starting point of the history of philosophy, 'the common spirit of homeliness [*Heimatlichkeit*] unites us'. From the start, Greek philosophy brings *us* (European man) together; it brings *us* home to ourselves (*chez nous*). Greek philosophy gathers us to ourselves, at the beginning. The ancient Greeks have *already* brought European man home to himself because they have made *their* origin their *own*:

> They certainly received the substantial beginnings [*Anfänge*] of their religion, culture, their common bonds of fellowship, more or less, from Asia, Syria and Egypt; but they have so greatly obliterated [*getilgt*] the foreign nature of this origin [*das Fremde dieses Ursprungs*], and it is so much changed, worked upon, turned round, and altogether made so different, that what they, as we, prize, know, and love in it, is essentially their own [*wesentlich das Ihrige ist*].

The Greeks have appropriated themselves *from* the origin; they have named themselves in the aftermath of the origin – and made a home for all of us. They have gathered us *and* kept us from the origin – the 'foreign derivation' (*fremden Hineingelegte*) – that is not our own. They have called us back (to ourselves) so that we can *go back* and *still* be at home: 'For this reason, in the history of Greek life, when we go further back and seem constrained so to go back [*zurückgeht und zurückgehen muß*], we find we may do without this retrogression [*Rückgang*] and follow within the world and manners of the Greeks' (150; 173–4). As Derrida suggests in *Glas*, for Hegel to begin a history of philosophy he can only start with 'the not-yet-there of the already-there' (*pas-encore-là du déjà-là*) and, Derrida adds, 'one must interrogate this circular and teleological structure of the before and after [*de l'avant et de l'après*]'.[9]

The Greeks make us feel at home, *and* they never stop announcing that the origin is uncanny (*unheimlich*).[10] That's their secret, and 'the *Heimliche* of the *Geheimnis* [the secret] presents itself as the most foreign, the most disquieting (*unheimliche*)'.[11] The beauty of the Greeks, for Hegel, is that they celebrate their 'spiritual rebirth' (*geistige Wiedergeburt*) – their separation from their foreign origin – as their 'real birth' (*eigentliche Geburt*). They have built a home for their at-homeness (and ours) by forgetting and burying the foreign origin. From the start, the history of philosophy begins as a re-birth *and* as the burial of a secret:

> The foreign origin [*fremden Ursprung*] they have so to speak thanklessly forgotten [*vergessen*], putting it in the background

> [*Hintergrund*] – perhaps burying [*vergraben*] it in the darkness of the mysteries which they have kept secret [*geheim*] from themselves. They have not only done this, that is they have not only used and enjoyed all that they brought forth and formed, but they have become aware of and thankfully and joyfully placed before themselves this at-homeness [*diese Heimatlichkeit*] in their whole existence, the ground and origin of themselves [*den Anfang und den Ursprung ihrer Selbst*], not merely existing in it, possessing and making use of it. (151; 174–5)

How do the Greeks forget and bury their foreign origin so that they start philosophy, and so we can start the history of philosophy? It is all a question of representation, of the self-consciousness of a self-representation that comes from the spiritual re-birth of the origin:

> For their mind [*Geist*], when transformed in this spiritual new birth [*geistiger Wiedergeburt*], is just the living in their life, and also the becoming conscious of that life as it has become actual. They represent [*stellen*] their existence as an object apart from themselves, which manifests itself independently and which in its independence is of value to them; thence they have made for themselves a history [*eine Geschichte*] of everything which they have possessed and have been. (151; 175)

They begin history by *making* their own history and *showing* it to themselves. Like a film. History begins with me showing myself my *own* history. So I cannot help but be at home: it is the only film in the house.

Hegel describes this cinematic erasure of the foreign origin of the Greeks as 'making what they are to be also a sort of Mnemosyne' (151). The burial and forgetting of the foreign origin is also the *beginning* of memory, of thinking *as* memory. As Heidegger reminds us in *What is Called Thinking?* (1951–52):

> Mnemosyne, daughter of Sky and Earth and bride of Zeus, in nine nights becomes the mother of the nine Muses. Drama and music, dance and poetry are of the womb of Mnemosyne, Memory [*der Gedächtnis*]. It is plain that the word means something else than merely the psychologically demonstrable ability to

> retain a mental representation of something that is past. Memory thinks back to something thought [*Gedächtnis denkt an das Gedachte*]. But when it is the name of the Mother of the Muses, 'Memory' does not mean just any thought of anything that can be thought. Memory is the gathering of thought [*Gedächtnis ist die Versammlung*] upon what everywhere demands to be thought about first of all. Memory is the gathering of recollection, thinking back [*Gedächtnis ist die Versammlung des Andenkens*]. It safely keeps and keeps concealed within it that to which at any given time thought must first be given in everything that essentially unfolds, appealing to us as what has being and has been in being.[12]

Mnemosyne: the beginning, *die Versammlung*, the gathering or re collection *to* the beginning of the history of philosophy when, as Hegel argues, 'philosophy is being at home with self, just like the homeliness of the Greek; it is man's being at home in his mind, at home with himself' (*Wie die Griechen bei sich zu Hause, so ist die Philosophie eben dies: bei sich zu Hause zu sein – daß der Mensch in seinem Geiste zu Hause sei, heimatlich bei sich*) (152; 175).

The Greeks were able to begin with their own memory, a memory that could only be-at-home-with-itself by forgetting a (history of the) foreign origin, but they still cannot escape their starting point: 'The Greeks have a starting-point [*Voraussetzung*] in history as truly as they have arisen from out of themselves: this starting-point, comprehended in thought [*in Gedanken aufgefaßt*], is the oriental substantiality of the natural unity between the spiritual and the natural' (152; 176). And they never quite get over this starting point. Despite evoking *beauty* as the always more spiritual 'happy medium' (*der schönen Mitte*) between nature and spirit, despite avoiding the oriental 'extreme of formal subjectivity', and being 'in unity with themselves' (*im Einen bei sich*), they are never entirely able to shake off the natural element of their foreign element (152–3; 176). The (foreign) origin, the inescapable starting point, *remains* with them, it leaves remainders, till the end: 'In the Greek world what is potentially and actually eternal is realized and brought to consciousness [*Bewußtsein*] through Thought; but in such a way that subjectivity confronts it in a determination which is still accidental, because it is still essentially related to what is natural' (153; 177).

BEGINNING WITH WATER

Before turning to Solon and, finally, beginning philosophy properly with Thales, Hegel reassures his audience. Don't worry, he says, the Greeks' beautiful spiritualizing mediation with nature may not have freed them from their own dubious beginnings, but it went far enough for *us* to begin, for the *process* to start, for Greece and Rome and Christianity to bring us – always at-home – to this moment of German philosophy. It was enough, just enough. Be of good cheer, because 'it is not Thought in its commencement [*der anfangende Gedanke*] that constitutes the first principle [*die Grundlage*] from which all culture must be grasped' (154; 178). To start a history of philosophy, *we* must 'have always two things to distinguish, the universal or the Notion [*den Begriff*, the concept], and the reality of this universal'. We must start *with* the concept and it is from the concept that we can judge whether 'the reality [of the universal] is itself Thought or Nature'. We start with Greece because it allows us to begin *with* the distinctions *of* the concept, and 'we find in fact [in Greece] that reality at first has still the immediate form and is only Thought potentially' (155; 178).

Bringing his last of many introductions to the history of philosophy to an end, Hegel *begins* philosophy with a collapse of a patriarchy, a patriarchy that was also to some extent foreign. The (foreign) fathers are dying and philosophy is beginning. This collapse of patriarchy also produced the *historia* of Herodotus as that which cannot start with the origin (*arkhē*) and must contend with the chance of the before *and* after:

> Greek philosophy commences [*Anfang*] in the sixth century before Christ in the time of Cyrus, and in the period of decline in the Ionic republics in Asia Minor. Just because this world of beauty which raised itself into a higher kind of culture went to pieces, Philosophy arose. Croesus and the Lydians first brought Ionic freedom into jeopardy; later on the Persians were those who destroyed it altogether so that the greater part of the inhabitants sought other spots and created colonies, more particularly in the West. At the time of the decline in Ionic towns, the other Greece ceased to be under its ancient lines of kings; the Pelopideans and the other, and for the most part foreign, princely races had passed away. Greece had in many ways come into touch with the outside

> world and the Greek inhabitants likewise sought within themselves for a bond of fellowship. The patriarchal life was past [*das patriarchalische Leben war vorbei*]. (155; 179)

'With Thales we, properly speaking [*eigentlich*], first begin the history of philosophy' (171; 195). But we have still not quite begun. Solon, the law-giver and man of understanding (*sunetous*) is not quite a philosopher, and before 'we, properly speaking, first begin the history of philosophy' he leaves us with a gap. At the start, there is a gap that he cannot close between the laws that he gives, and making these laws 'effectual in the manners, habits and life of a people' (120). If he could have closed this gap between abstract law and concrete actuality, Athens could have avoided the tyranny of Pisistratus: the gap and the tyranny before the beginning of philosophy.

This tyranny of a gap in Athens is important because for philosophy to get started, Athens will need to take 'a middle place' (*der Mitte*) and become the 'centre' (*Hauptsitz*) (169; 193). Philosophy begins, but it does not begin at home, it does not find its centre, until it gets to Athens. It starts in the East on the coast of Asia Minor before 'Philosophy plants itself in Greece proper, and there makes its home [*im eigentlichen Griechenland sich aufpflanzt und heimisch wird*]'. It also starts in the West in Italy, and this separation goes on until Anaxagoras moves to Athens and the gap is *bridged*. Athens is the axis, the pivot, the point of equilibrium, in a 'geographical distinction [*Unterschied*] [that] makes its appearance in the manifestation of thought [*Darstellung des Gedankens*]'. The East *tends* towards sensuous materiality, the West *tends* towards 'the form of thought' and 'the ideal determination of the absolute' (169–70; 192–3).

At the same time, Hegel acknowledges that Athens' irreplaceable role as centre and clear point of separation between East and West was undermined by Sicily. Though in the West, Sicily produced both Gorgias ('the Sicilian sophist' who 'remains faithful to the ideal side') *and* Empedocles (who is 'somewhat of a natural philosopher') (170). Sicily could do *both* natural and ideal philosophy, a philosophy somewhere *in between* the East and the West. For Hegel, though the history of philosophy begins with Thales of Miletus, philosophy only really begins when Anaxagoras moves to Athens: 'with Anaxagoras it is the moving [*der Bewegende*], self-determining thought itself [*sich selbst bestimmende Gedanke*] that is then known as existence, and this is a great step forward [*ein großer Fortschritt*]' (170; 194). Thinking begins not in Sicily, but in Athens.

We have begun the history *of* philosophy, but 'properly speaking' we have still not started *with* philosophy. Hegel must first wade his way through the natural philosophers, who take 'something material as the principle and substance of all that is' (175). Thales begins with *water*: 'water is the god over all' (*der Gott von allem*) (175; 199). And how is a speculative philosopher to respond to this? *If* water is 'the universal substance' (and since it is in proximity to other elements, this is unlikely), it can only be understood as a speculative universal concept if 'what is sensuous [is] removed' (177). Hegel will later write, 'as soon as men speak, there is a Notion [a concept] present' (*wie der Mensch spricht, so ist ein Begriff darin*), and if we begin not with water, but with men *speaking* about water, if we begin with the *logos*, it is possible to find 'pure thought' in the water: 'Now since, by way of confirmation, men swear [*der Eid aussprechen*] by what is best, by what is absolutely certain, and the gods swore by the subterranean water, it follows that the essence of pure thought [*das Wesen des Gedankens*], the inmost being, the reality in which consciousness finds its truth, is water [*die Wahrheit, Realität ist das Wasser*]' (292 [336]; 177 [202]). As if this was already a baptism of the concept as thought thinking itself thinking the truth. 'But why', Derrida asks in *Glas*, as he follows Hegel through the Christian story, 'why is John fond . . . of immersing the body in water? Why did he baptize Jesus in the Jordan?' For Hegel, 'in the water's fullness, there is no lacuna' (*dans la plénitude liquide il n'y a aucune lacune*).[13] Jesus leaves the water and goes from the mother to the father, from nature to spirit, to rebirth and resurrection.[14] Cleansing oneself from the gaps, at the start – to start again.

Derrida writes in *Glas*: 'There is a *not yet* [pas encore] of philosophy. Philosophy – already [*déjà*] – is announced in it. Now, reason's and thus Hegelian philosophy's essential proposition: philosophy has its beginning only in itself [*n'a son commencement qu'en elle-même*]. Philosophy is the beginning, as the beginning of (it)self, the posit(ion)ing by it(self) of the beginning.'[15] So when, if ever, does philosophy begin in the history of philosophy? 'Spirit will always have been nature's essence; nature is within spirit as its being-outside-self', Derrida writes. 'In freeing itself from the natural limits that were imprisoning it, the spirit returns to itself but without ever having left itself [*il revient à lui mais sans s'être jamais quitté*].'[16] For Hegel, this is how – at last, some two hundred pages into the book – philosophy *begins. Spirit is already taking nature towards thinking*, and so that philosophy can therefore start with Thales: 'The real essence of nature has to be defined, that is, nature has to be expressed as the simple essence of thought . . . The proposition of Thales, that water is the Absolute, or as the ancients say, the principle, is the beginning of Philosophy, because with it the consciousness is arrived at that essence, truth, that which is alone in and for itself, are one' (178).

But at the very moment of this long-awaited beginning Hegel turns back again and wanders into a *palintrope*. The beginning is the departure from the sensuous and material particularity. Water can just about pass as 'the simple essence of thought', as the concept of the universal (spirit). Philosophy *needs* this water as the first glimmerings of spirit at work to look back from Thales to *counteract* the Homeric tradition. The first thing philosophy does when it has started is to turn backwards: 'What there is besides, like the conceptions of Homer, for instance, is something in which thought could not find satisfaction; it produces mere images of the imagination, endlessly endowed with animation and form but destitute of simple unity' (179). Philosophy begins with Thales so water as the first glimpse of spirit can flow backwards and, like a calm and tranquil sea, still the restless imagination: 'this wild, endless varied imagination of Homer is set at rest by the proposition that existence is water' (179). Philosophy begins by drowning Homer.

WAITING FOR ANAXAGORAS

Hegel is always going to have a problem with chronology and progression as he works his way *towards* Plato. Thales starts with water. Anaximander follows with the infinite, and we can see that 'absolute essence no longer is a simple universal' (187). But Anaximenes then goes back to 'a definite natural element', to the air (189). Hegel gets around this – and what else is this history of philosophy before Plato but a history of Hegel having to *get around* what he can't quite digest (pre-Socratic philosophy would be the raw before the cooked) – he gets around this by deciding that air is the soul: 'Anaximenes shows very clearly the nature of his essence in the soul, and he thus points out what may be called the transition [*den Übergang*] of natural philosophy into the philosophy of consciousness, or the surrender of [*Aufgeben*] the objective form of principle' (190; 214). Just after the beginning, Hegel surrenders the air to the soul, nature to consciousness. But to make this great leap forward he must invest everything in the master–pupil, father–son relation. We must *wait* for Anaximenes' pupil, Anaxagoras. If we wait for him, he will come. Anaxagoras will take us to the Sophists, who always pre-cede Socrates, but this can only happen if we take a very long detour from Hegel announcing the coming of Anaximenes' pupil (page 190) to the arrival of Anaxagoras (page 319). To get to Plato, Hegel must leap, from gap to gap.

'There I leap' (*là je saute*), Derrida writes in *Glas*.[17] As he remarks, Hegel loves to leap. 'The epoch here is unanimous: the leap is good [*le saut c'est bien*]. But it is always necessary to ask oneself why and on top of what one presses to leap [*sauter*].'[18] Derrida warns against what I have called elsewhere the leap *over* the text, but he never stopped marking the leaps *of* the text.[19] In the midst of writing on Antigone, and of the sister as the immaculate concept and inadmissible figure in the Hegelian family, Derrida marks the leap *of* the text:

> The effect of focusing, in a text, around an impossible place. Fascination by a figure inadmissible in the system. Vertiginous insistence on an unclassable. And what if what cannot be assimilated, the absolute indigestible, played a fundamental role in the system, as abyssal role rather, the abyss playing and almost tran-
>
> [this is on page 151a, and the text leaps to page 162a, cutting the word and marking the possibility of the leap, the inadmissible, unclassable, indigestible gap as the immaculate concept, as ruin of a system destined for virginity.]
>
> scendental role and allowing to be formed above it, as a kind of effluvium, a dream of appeasement? Isn't there always an element excluded from a system that assures the system's space of possibility?[20]

THE SILENCE OF PYTHAGORAS

The problem with the beginning of philosophy (Thales, Anaximenes, Anaxagoras) is that there is no *Aufhebung* (193). This is what a *history* of philosophy does to you: it makes you start without the *Aufhebung*. Turning away from this impossible beginning, Hegel turns towards Pygathoras as 'thought breaking away from what is sensuous' by treating 'numbers as ideas' (194–5). But Hegel is more interested in the life of Pythagoras. He was the first philosopher *to move*, and his wanderings indicated 'the abandonment [*das Verlassen*] of sensuous consciousness' (197; 223). This abandonment of nature was also reflected in Pythagoras' insistence that the novices in his school were to remain *silent* (*Schweigen*). Once again, like the men who swore by the water, at the origin of philosophy Hegel latches on to how one speaks. Pythagoras' injunction that those who have just started to study philosophy should be silent is testament to the 'formal elements' in his thought and a resistance to what was merely 'present in the nature of things' (203).

There is no *Aufhebung* at the beginning of philosophy, and the only way that we can start is with a kind of *aphasia*. Hegel writes: 'Pythagoras may be regarded as the first instructor in Greece who introduced the teachings of science' (203). When I first read this, I thought Hegel had said that Pythagoras was the first instructor in Greece who introduced the teachings of *silence*. There's no *Aufhebung*: quiet!

Hegel just keeps extricating everything he can from the progressive withdrawal from what is merely sensuous and keeps taking the beginning of philosophy back to some impossible, unthinkable state of mere matter, to an *immaculate matter*. The *Aufhebung* almost starts up with Pythagoras' recognition of 'the ideality of differences', of the 'principles of number' as 'rational differences' (210; 212). But Pythagoras' sense of the relation between an original unity and a subsequent duality is still 'destitute of process or dialectic' (212). Pythagoras 'has not yet [*noch nicht*] got the speculative form of expression for the Notion' (239; 275). Without the *not yet*, there could be no narrative, no history of philosophy.

ALMOST THERE

With the Eleatic school, we at last see 'Thought grasp itself in purity' (*den Gedanken sich selbst rein ergreifen*) (239; 275). In arguing that 'the one as the immediate product of pure thought' is Being, Xenophanes and Parmenides made 'a wonderful advance' (243). 'Thought', Hegel comments, 'thus becomes for the first time [*das erste Mal*] free for itself' (243; 279). For Hegel, everything depends on all these *first* moments, all of them, one before another, one after another. With each of these *first* moments, we have to keep *starting again*. Keep leaping.

By arguing that thought *is* being and there can be no not-being, Parmenides – once again – 'began Philosophy proper' (*hat das eigentliche Philosophieren angefangen*) (254; 290). The 'advance into the reign of the ideal is observable', but not yet (254). Xenophanes and Parmenides have made the mistake of arguing that change or negation (not-being) does not exist, that the other is 'inconceivable' (246). Zeno is 'the master of the Eleatic school' and 'the originator of the true objective dialectic', because he announces the birth of the *other* (*das Andere*), the advent of the negative (261; 263; 240). He colonizes the other, he starts up the *Aufhebung*, he puts the negative to work in the service of the truth of being, of the truth as being (278). In conceiving the other, Zeno is the first to start the dialectic, the first to get the concept *moving*. At last, 'pure thought arrives at the movement of the Notion in itself' (*das reine Denken derselben zur Bewegung das Begriffs in sich selbst*) (261; 295).

The dialectic has begun, but starting and ending in 'pure Being alone', it is subjective and abstract (278). With Heraclitus, we turn 'from Being [*Sein*] as the first [*das Erste*] immediate thought, to the category of becoming [*Werden*]'. The dialectic is objective, and 'the first concrete' (*das erste Konkrete*) and 'speculative form' has arrived (279; 320). Speculating on Parmenides and Zeno, it is apparent that 'since everything is and is not', the 'first truth' of being is that 'everything is Becoming' (*alles ist Werden*) (283; 324). Heraclitus has harnessed negativity as an immanent moment in the dialectic, and we see 'a perfecting of the Ideas into a totality, which is' – once again – 'the beginning of Philosophy [*der Anfang der Philosophie*], since it expresses the essence of the Idea . . . as the unity of opposites' (284; 282 [323]). With Heraclitus, there is the 'first appearance' of 'the unity of the principle of consciousness', of 'absolute mediation' as 'Thought itself' (*der Gedanke*) (293–4; 338). We have been at sea, but now 'we see land' (*sehen wir Land*) (279; 320). It is not the river (which Heraclitus says 'we step into and do not step into'), but the sight of land, of the grounding of philosophy, that has begun.[21] The speculative dialectic will soon make landfall: it is on its way to Athens (282).

We are almost there. While recognizing the principle of becoming, Heraclitus does not appreciate the 'permanence' of the 'universal Notion'. For Heraclitus, the unity of the Notion 'only exists in opposition' and is not 'reflected within itself'. This is why we have had to wait for Anaxagoras. Philosophy will reach 'new ground', will be on its own ground, its home ground, when the speculative dialectic *returns* to itself as itself and the Idea is seen as the universal concept (320; 292–3). Treating Democritus and Empedocles as the 'transition to the universal', in which the Heraclitean motion of the dialectic begins to gather itself together into a synthetic unity, Hegel places Anaxagoras on the threshold of the *dawn* (320; 298). The day has almost started: 'With Anaxagoras a light, if still a weak one, begins to dawn' (*ein Licht aufzugehen* (*es ist zwar noch schwach*)) (319; 369). This weak light, which appears just before the sun rises, is the light of reason (*nous*), the light which recognizes 'that pure thought is the actually existent universal and true' (320).

Before Anaxagoras, even when being and becoming are taken as 'universal thoughts', they were still seen to have *started* from the sensuous. With Anaxagoras, this induction comes to an end. Now we can *begin* with 'the Universal, Thought itself, in and for itself, without opposition' as 'the substance or principle' (320). We can start with thought as the *arkhē*, the origin. But at the same time, this beginning is *already* a returning from what pre-cedes the origin as thought thinking itself: 'the unity as universal, returns from the opposition into itself'. What makes all the difference, is that this return is thought determining *itself* as a 'self determining universal' (320). Thought displays itself in the motion of dialectic *and* it 'retains itself as the universal self-identical [*Sichselbstgleiche*]' (331; 382). At last, thought can do the *Aufhebung* (333). Nonetheless, it still cannot think itself thinking the truth as absolute knowledge, it still cannot comprehend the concept – we will have to wait for Hegel for philosophy to not only begin, but also to end (329). With Anaxagoras we 'find Philosophy in Greece proper . . . and coming, indeed, as far as Athens' (*nach Athen wandern*) (322; 370).

Before *and* in front of Plato, there are the Sophists and there is Socrates. It is still only the dawn of philosophy because Anaxagoras' notion of reason remained formal: it did not offer a comprehension of the world (340). And the Sophists appear in this disjunction between universal reason and reality (349). With the rise of subjective reason comes the Peloponnesian war and the fall of the Athenian empire (350). The empire is collapsing, and the Sophists revel in this subjectivity as their own, while Socrates tries to think this subjectivity as 'in and for itself' (351). Socrates will be killed in this war of subjectivity and Hegel will only have Plato, the philosopher who 'in his writings never himself appeared as teacher, but always represented other people in his dialogues as the philosophers' (*in seinen Schriften nie selbst als Lehrer auftritt, sondern immer andere Personen in seinen Dialogen als philosophierend darstellt*) (166; 190). It is with the philosopher who never appeared that Hegel must start again and leap into the first day of philosophy.

CHAPTER 7

SENSE CERTAINTY, OR

> The difficulty of representing thoughts as thoughts always attaches to the expedient of expression in sensuous form
>
> Hegel, *Lectures on the History of Philosophy*[1]

WITH AND WITHOUT HEGEL

Behind the papers, the lectures and the fragments are the seminars that Derrida delivered for forty years, first at the École Normale Supérieure and later at the École des Hautes Études en Sciences Sociales. There were times when the publications gave glimpses of the rhythm and scope of these seminars, in such works as 'The Double Session', *Glas*, 'Parergon', 'To Speculate – on "Freud"', *Politics of Friendship*, and *Of Hospitality*, to only name the most obvious. Derrida often made a point of publishing *fragments* of his seminars, and one must be careful not to see them as a monolithic continuity, an inexhaustible background resource. As with many of Derrida's publications, they were highly wrought and prepared texts that displayed all the demands of their place and time of delivery. There are only traces, and the seminars (even after they are eventually all published) can only offer us traces of Derrida's pedagogical practice and his ongoing institutional and academic negotiations.[2]

In 1967 Derrida gave a seminar on the *Phenomenology of Spirit*, concentrating on the opening section on sense certainty (*Sinnliche Gewißheit*). As he says in an interview from 1975, this 1967 seminar marks the start of Derrida's palintropic reading of Hegel in *Glas*:

> And how could a here-now [*un ici-maintenant*] pass through writing unscathed [*indemne*]? Perhaps we interpret today more

> effectively, with or without Hegel, the intervention of a written trace (in the ordinary sense) in the chapter of the *Phenomenology* on sense certainty and its here-now. In 1967, I believe it was, we fit a whole [*arrimé tout*] seminar within this question, and the 'first' line of *Glas* is divided on it or cuts across [*divise ou recoupe*] it as well.[3]

When Derrida says that he 'fit a whole seminar within' the chapter in the *Phenomenology* on sense certainty – which is only nine pages or twenty paragraphs – he echoes his argument in *Dissemination* (1972) for a literature, or 'history – of literature', that exceeds the traditional determination of literature in philosophy as *doxa* and *mimesis*. As we have seen, in 'Outwork' (1972), he argues, ' "Literature" is a part, that, within *and* without the whole [*dans* et *hors le tout*], marks the wholly other, the other incommensurate with the whole.' Beyond its characterization by Plato and Hegel, 'literature' becomes a part that is bigger than a whole and treats the whole itself as a part, as 'a *totality-effect*'.[4] Looking back in 1975 on his 1967 seminar, Derrida says that he 'fit a whole seminar' into nine pages of the *Phenomenology*. This is not only an indication of Derrida's remarkable capacity for close and concentrated reading, it is also an oblique reference to re-inscribing a whole within a part, a part that 'within and without the whole, marks the wholly other', a part that interprets the question of the written trace and the here-now 'with or without [*avec ou sans*] Hegel'.

STARTING A PHENOMENOLOGY OF SPIRIT

Before or after the celebrated preface, which can be read *at once* as the first word or as the last word, the *Phenomenology of Spirit* begins with the 'Introduction', and Hegel's first words are about the problem of starting. 'It is a natural assumption', Hegel writes, 'that in philosophy, before [*ehe*] we start to deal with its proper subject matter, viz. the actual cognition of what truly is, one must first of all [*vorher*] come to an understanding about cognition'.[5] 'Before we start,' Hegel begins, 'one must first . . .' He starts the *Phenomenology* by saying that to start we must deal with what comes 'before we start'. There is a 'first of all' that somehow precedes our proper beginning: a first before the start. This 'first of all' is perhaps both the possibility of starting properly and something that does not belong to or at least cannot be confused with our starting. It is first, but it is not how we start a *Phänomenologie des Geistes*.

We have still not started – we have already started.

For Hegel, what is at stake is the problem of how consciousness can reach and represent 'what exists in itself'. How, with the help of cognition, can consciousness (subjectivity) reflect the absolute (objectivity, or thought thinking itself thinking the truth)? The question at the beginning of the 'first of all' – 'before we start' – is about the *assistance* of cognition in the journey of consciousness to the absolute. It is a problem with the assistant or servant, with the hired help. If cognition is a kind of 'instrument' or 'medium' for consciousness to reach the absolute, cognition will *contaminate* and *change* the absolute, and 'not let it be what it is for itself' (§73). 'It is a natural assumption', Hegel warns, that we must deal with this 'first of all' 'before we start'. This is the first lesson of a *Phenomenology of Spirit*: *don't* assume that there is something prior to starting a *Phenomenology of Spirit*. There is only something before *and* in front of starting a *Phenomenology of Spirit*, some palintropic turning back that also turns again and always more than once, if we pre suppose that there is an *absolute difference* between cognition and the absolute, and that cognition is somehow *at once* true and 'outside of the truth' (§74). There can be no *absolute* difference with the absolute.

This is how Hegel begins. He pre-empts what appears to be first and outside by characterizing it is as an absolute difference. As Derrida had noted in 'Violence and Metaphysics' (1964), 'Hegel's critique of the concept of pure difference is for us here, doubtless, the most uncircumventable theme'.[6] The claim that there is something outside, something first before we start, is *already* inside, *already* assisting the journey of consciousness to absolute knowledge, to 'the point where knowledge no longer needs to go beyond itself' (§80). Hegel starts by *anticipating* absolute difference and this is how, after the 'Introduction', he will start the *Phenomenology of Spirit* with sense certainty.

Derrida refers to Hegel's chapter on sense certainty twice in works published or delivered in 1968. There are only traces, and these traces – along with the 1975 interview – will be our only guides to Derrida's 1967 seminar on the *Phenomenology of Spirit*. The earliest reference is probably in '*Ousia* and *Grammē*', which Derrida described in 1967 in *Of Grammatology* as a forthcoming work.[7]

In '*Ousia* and *Grammē*', as we have seen, Derrida challenges Heidegger's argument in *Being and Time* that Hegel simply repeats wholesale Aristotle's concept of time in the *Physics* as an unbroken series of nows. For Heidegger, the fundamental problem with the *Physics* is that it defines time in spatial terms: it reduces time to space. For Derrida, in contrast, this suggests precisely that time cannot simply be separated from space. And while Aristotle and Hegel rely on the now as, respectively, the number and the *Aufhebung* of time, they also both *mark* the inescapable not-now, the before and after, of time – of time becoming space *and* space becoming time.[8]

In a brief reading of the *Philosophy of Spirit*, the third part of the *Encyclopaedia*, Derrida suggests that while Hegel concludes that time is the *Aufhebung* of space, he *begins* this process with space '*itself* negating itself'. This 'negation *of* space *by* space' leads to the *point* – 'the space that does not take up space, the place that does not take place [*ce lieu qui n'a pas lieu*]' – which in turn 'spatializes or *spaces* itself' into the *line* and, finally, into the *plane*. Time is 'the truth of space', because it is 'the negation at work in space', the *spacing* of space that *temporalizes* itself.[9] For Hegel, this process ends in the *Aufhebung*, the idealization of space as time. For Derrida, on the contrary, it marks Hegel's reliance on a *différance* that threatens all the beginnings and all the ends of a history of spirit on its way to absolute knowledge. It is in questioning how Hegel 'repeats' Aristotle's concept of time in a footnote that Derrida first refers the reader to 'the entire problematic of sensible certitude'.[10]

FORM AND MEANING

As Derrida observed in early 1968 in 'The Pit and the Pyramid', in the *Philosophy of Spirit* Hegel had also acknowledged the profound influence of Aristotle's *On the Soul* on his own work, writing: 'The main aim of a philosophy of mind [spirit] can only be to reintroduce unity of idea and principle into the theory of mind, and so reinterpret the lesson of those Aristotelian books.'[11] For Hegel, the journey of consciousness to absolute knowledge, of appearance (phenomenal knowledge) to truth in the *Phenomenology*

> can be regarded as the path of the natural consciousness which presses forward to true knowledge; or as the way of the Soul which journeys through the series of its configurations as though

> they were the stations appointed for it by its own nature, so that it may purify itself for the life of the Spirit, and achieve finally, through a completed experience of itself, the awareness of what it really is in itself. (§77)

To start a phenomenology of spirit is to start again with Aristotle's *Peri psuchēs*, with an Aristotle who is *already* on his way to Christ and following the Stations of the Cross. Christ before Aristotle: Hegel's anachronism.

In *De Anima*, Aristotle addresses the question that will preoccupy Hegel at the beginning of the *Phenomenology*: how does one get *from* the senses *to* thinking? As we have seen, form working with matter, actuality working with potentiality, the soul is the *possibility* of sensation and of the senses in general. One can only begin with the soul to start with the senses. Having described vision, hearing (and the voice), smell, taste and touch, Aristotle concludes his account of the five senses with a definition of sense as 'the power of receiving into itself the sensible forms of things without the matter [*áneu tes húles*]' (424a).[12] When we hear the ear is not touched by what we hear, when we see the eye is not touched by what it sees – such contact could only lead to deafness and blindness. The senses only register the reception of 'the sensible forms of things' (*ton aistheton eidon*). To start with *sense* certainty, Aristotle will tell Hegel, is already to start 'without matter', and the progression from the senses to thinking is facilitated by 'the sensible *forms* of things' (my emphasis).

As we have seen, to make a 'completely fresh start' in answering the question 'what is soul?', in *De Anima* Aristotle makes a fundamental and dynamic distinction:

> We say that substance is one kind of what is, and that in several senses: in the sense of matter [*húlēn*] or that which in itself is not a this, and in the sense of form or essence [*morphēn kai eidos*], which is that precisely in virtue of which a thing is called a this, and thirdly in the sense of that which is compounded of both. Now matter is potentiality [*dúnamis*], form actuality [*entelékheia*]; and actuality is of two kinds, one as e.g. knowledge, the other as e.g. reflecting. (412a)

'He who *is* anything cannot want to be that which he *is*', Socrates had argued in the *Symposium* and, from the start, all of Aristotle's progressive distinctions from matter to reflecting are founded on 'what is'.[13] Hegel's *reinterpretation* of the lessons from Aristotle's books on the soul will not only focus on 'what merely is', but also admit the assistance, the service of 'the seriousness, the suffering, the patience, and the labour of the negative' in speculative dialectics (§76, §19). At the same time, Hegel entitles the opening chapter of the *Phenomenology*, 'Sense-certainty: or the This and Meaning (*Die sinnliche Geißheit oder das Diese und das Meinen*), and one can see the lasting influence of Aristotle in the distinction between 'the This and Meaning'.

For Aristotle, the sense of matter is 'that which in itself is not a this'. A plant, for example – and this example of the plant will resonate through both Hegel and Derrida's work – is only 'affected' by matter and has 'no principle' no 'mean' (no mediating, no discriminating power), and is therefore incapable of 'taking on the forms of sensible objects' (424b). A 'this' is both that which has a discernible form (as opposed to amorphous matter), and that which can separate, discriminate and mediate *between* matter and form. Matter alone cannot distinguish itself from itself, cannot treat itself as matter *and* form. Without the work of the soul, matter cannot see its *own* form. And in *seeing itself*, matter is *already* 'without matter', is already the *form* of a sensible object. Form 'or essence . . . is that precisely in virtue of which a thing is called a this'. Hegel's subtitle, 'This and Meaning' (*das Diese und das Meinen*) can be read as 'Form and Meaning', and it is hardly surprising that in the year in which he gave his seminar on the first chapter of the *Phenomenology*, Derrida published an article on Husserl entitled 'Form and Meaning' ('La forme et le vouloir-dire') (1967) in which, as we have seen, he argued that form – or how a thing *presents itself* as present – has always, ultimately, been concerned with the reaffirmation of being as presence.[14]

In his second reference to the first chapter of the *Phenomenology*, in 'The Ends of Man', written in the spring of 1968, Derrida situates the *Phenomenology* within the wider context of Hegel's other works and, once again, emphasizes that the work of the *soul* precedes the sense certainty of a *Phenomenology of Spirit*:

> The *Phenomenology of Spirit* succeeds the Anthropology and precedes the Psychology. The Anthropology treats the spirit – which is the 'truth of nature' – as soul or as natural-spirit (*Seele*

> or *Naturgeist*). The development of the soul, such as it is retraced by the anthropology, passes through the natural soul (*natürliche Seele*), through the sensible soul (*fühlende Seele*), and through the real or effective soul (*wirkliche Seele*). This development accomplishes and completes itself, and then opens onto consciousness. The last section of the *Anthropology* defines the general form of consciousness, the very one from which the *Phenomenology of Spirit* will depart, in the first chapter on 'Sensuous Certitude'. Consciousness, i.e. the phenomenological, therefore, is the *truth* of the soul, that is, precisely the truth of that which was the object of the anthropology.[15]

Starting with sense certainty, Hegel has *already* started with 'the *truth* of the soul' as 'the general form of consciousness' or, as Derrida writes, 'objectivity in general, the relation of an "I" in general with a being-object in general'.[16]

ODER

In his *Lectures on the History of Philosophy* (1805–31), Hegel notes that for Heraclitus, 'sensuous certainty has no truth; for it is the certainty for which something exists as actual, which is not so in fact. Not this immediate Being, but absolute mediation, Being as thought of, Thought itself, is the true Being.'[17] Hegel starts the *Phenomenology* with Heraclitus. From the start, sensuous certainty has no truth. But at the same time, Hegel begins the *Phenomenology* with the *assumption* that a sensuous certainty *as* immediate being is *possible*. It has no truth, but it is possible. But how can one *start* with *immediate* being? Consciousness (*Bewußtsein*) *begins* with sensuous or sensible certainty (*sinnliche Geißheit*), with a stable, steady and assured (*gewiß*) concept of sense (*Sinn*). Hegel immediately *qualifies* this absolute confidence in the stability of sense by adding a second title: *oder das Diese und das Meinen* (58; 82). This second title not only suggests that sensible certainty can be characterized and demonstrated by 'the This and Meaning' – by the relation between form and meaning – but also that, from the start, there is an 'or' (*oder*) when it comes to beginning with consciousness: sensible certainty *or* the this and meaning. From the start, there is an 'or'.

This possibly equivocal *oder* – this or, or else, otherwise (*autrement*, this difference) – is repeated in the first sentence: 'The knowledge or knowing which is at the start or is immediately our object cannot be anything else but immediate knowledge itself, a knowledge of the immediate or of what simply *is*' (§90; 82). We have to begin, Hegel says, with 'what simply *is*' (Seienden *ist*), with the immediate knowledge (*unmittelbares Wissen*) of the immediate. But in simply starting with the immediate, we have also started with the qualification *or* equivocation of the 'or'. When Hegel writes, 'a knowledge of the immediate or [*oder*] of what simply *is*', he suggests that *already* – before we have even begun – there may be a difference between 'what simply *is*' and 'a knowledge of the immediate'. Perhaps more significantly, the 'or' in the opening words of a chapter on sensible certainty raises the question of starting with sensible certainty. What we start with, Hegel argues, 'cannot be anything else [*kann kein anderes sein*] but immediate knowledge'. Hegel begins with a statement of certainty about beginning with the insufficiency of sensible certainty.

Translation could be defined as an unavoidable proliferation of 'ors', and in his translation of the opening words A. V. Miller has added his own 'or': 'The knowledge *or* knowing' (*Das Wissen*). But Hegel also adds his own 'or': 'The knowledge, which first *or* immediately is our object [*Das Wissen, welches zuerst oder unmittelbar*], cannot be anything else but immediate knowledge.' Before his statement of certainty about beginning sensible certainty with immediate knowledge, Hegel *starts* with the difference between what is *first* and what is immediate (*zuerst oder unmittelbar*). First *or* immediate: what comes first, what comes before the immediate, what comes before *and* in front of the immediate? What is faster than the immediate? What trace of speed could get in just before the immediate? Having asserted that we can only begin with the immediate knowledge of the immediate, Hegel can only add another qualification or equivocation, which seems less than a restatement of certainty about starting with the immediate, than an injunction, a *call* to certainty that is not yet assured: 'Our approach to the object must also be *immediate* or *receptive* [unmittelbar *oder* aufnehmend]; we must alter nothing in the object as it presents itself' (§90; 82).

STARTING WITH PURE BEING

In the second paragraph, Hegel will argue why sensible certainty *appears* to be the '*richest*' and '*truest*' kind of knowledge. He will deflate and curtail the claims for sensible certainty as the best kind of knowledge, but he in no way questions the unavoidable necessity (or the injunction) of starting *with* immediate knowledge of the immediate (§91; 82–3). Sensible certainty seems to give us the *whole* object, but in truth 'its truth [*ihre Wahrheit*] contains nothing but the sheer *being* of the thing [*das* Sein *der Sache*]', and its '*certainty* [Gewißheit] proves itself to be the most abstract and poorest *truth* [Wahrheit]'. Having been asked ostensibly to start only with the immediate, the truth is *already* on hand to show up the shortcomings of sensible certainty. These delusive shortcomings have their origin in the 'concrete content' (*der konkrete Inhalt*) of sensible certainty. It is a problem with content (*Inhalt*).

Starting from sensible certainty we can *only* start with – or be startled by – what *is*. We can discern no more about the object than 'that it *is*', we can learn nothing more than the bare '*being* of the thing' (*das* Sein *der Sache*). 'The thing *is* [ist], and it *is*, merely because it *is*. It *is*; this is the essential point for sense-knowledge [*sinnlichen Wissen*], and this pure *being*, or this simple immediacy [*dieses reine* Sein *oder diese einfache Unmittelbarheit*], constitutes its *truth* [Wahrheit].' For Hegel, divested of its pretensions, sensible knowledge can only tell us – again and again – that the thing *is*. This is the poverty of sensible knowledge: it can only start with the '*is*', with 'pure being', and can offer no explanation, no *account* of the 'being of the thing'. For Heidegger in *Being and Time*, this could be taken as the definition *par excellence* of the ontological tradition: 'We do not know what "Being" means. But even if we ask, "What *is* Being"?', we keep within an understanding of the "is", though we are unable to fix conceptionally what this "is" signifies.'[18] Beginning a phenomenology of spirit with consciousness, and beginning consciousness with sensible certainty, we can *only* begin with ontology.

For Hegel, the limit of sense-knowledge not only gives us nothing more (but isn't this already everything?) than the *pure* being of the thing, it also *confines* consciousness to 'a pure "I" ' (reines *Ich*). In relation to the thing, I have not 'developed myself or thought about it in various ways' (*mich entwickelte und mannigfaltig den Gedanken bewegte*) (§91; 83). The thing just *is*, and *I* cannot think about the thing and, consequently, 'the "I" does not have the significance of a manifold imagining or thinking [*Vorstellens oder Denkens*]'. The thing just is – and I cannot *think*. From this perspective, the mere '*being* of the thing' becomes perhaps more startling than just a confirmation of starting with ontology. The thing that is 'merely because it *is*' somehow arrests and precludes the pure 'I' thinking. It holds thinking back, and most of all the thinking about being.[19] From the start, there is being and 'I' am startled, and cannot think about it. Hegel describes this limited and limiting state as the relation – without any mediation – between a particular 'I' and a particular object. In such a state, both consciousness and its object are only 'a pure "This" '. But as Aristotle had shown in *De Anima*, and as Hegel had anticipated by placing phenomenology after anthropology, a 'This' *already has form*, and the alliance of form and meaning will facilitate the generation of what Derrida had called 'objectivity in general, the relation of an "I" in general with a being-object in general', an objectivity in which thought *thinks itself* thinking the *truth* about objects.

THE FORM OF SENSIBLE CERTAINTY

The problem, Hegel goes on to say, with pure being as the truth of sensible certainty is that it presupposes that the *form* of the I and of the object (the 'this' and the 'this') does not have *meaning*. Meaning is 'the significance [*Bedeutung*] of a complex process of mediation [*Vermittlung*]' that gives rise to 'the significance [*Bedeutung*] of a manifold imagining or thinking' (§91; 83). Form *with* meaning is mediation, is *thinking*. Hegel notes that 'in sense-certainty, pure being at once splits up into [*herausfallen*, falls out or cuts into] what we have called the two "Thises", one "This" as "I", and the other "This" as object. When *we* reflect on this difference [*diesen Unterschied*], we find that neither one nor the other is only *immediately* present [*unmittelbar*] in sense-certainty, but each is at the same time *mediated* [zugleich als *vermittelt*]' (§92; 83). For Hegel, this differentiation and mediation suggests that sensible certainty must complicate and exceed pure being: both the I and the thing must pass '*through* something else' (*durch* ein Anderes). It is through *meaning*, the meaning *of* form that Hegel exceeds pure being and what simply is.

The meaning of form acknowledges and puts difference to work (as 'this difference', a difference of the form of 'this' I and 'this' thing), and passes *through* the other on its way to its destination. At the moment of first evoking the dialectic, Hegel reiterates the Aristotelian inheritance (form is actuality) by describing this sensible certainty beyond pure being as 'actual sense-certainty' (*wirkliche sinnliche Gewißheit*). To make his case for the insufficiency of a sense certainty without meaning, Hegel also turns to *us* at the start of the *Phenomenology*, to the 'we' (*wir*) that *already* knows, that already has the capacity to recognize that this meaning is obvious and necessary: 'When *we* reflect on this difference [*Reflektieren* wir *diesen Unterschied*], we find that neither one nor the other is only *immediately* present in sense-certainty, but each is at the same time *mediated*.'

'*Mais qui, nous?*', Derrida famously asks a year after his 1967 seminar at the end of 'The Ends of Man'.[20] As Derrida suggests, much as the 'Idea in the Kantian sense', which is both indispensable to Husserlian phenomenology and always stands *outside* of any phenomenology, the 'we' of the *Phenomenology of Spirit* is the *seemingly* blind assurance of the small presence of the end at the beginning, of the end of the history of spirit already lending a helping hand on the way, of absolute knowledge or thought thinking itself thinking the truth when one starts with sensible certainty. In his essay 'From Restricted to General Economy', published in May 1967, Derrida writes:

> The 'we' ['*nous*'] of the *Phenomenology of Spirit* has the beauty of presenting itself as the knowledge that does not know [*le savoir de ce que ne sait pas*] the naïve consciousness sunk [*enfoncée*] in its history and in the determinations of its figures, it remains natural and vulgar since it only thinks of the *passage*, the *truth* as the circulation of meaning or of value. It develops the meaning [*sens*] or the desire for meaning of natural consciousness, the consciousness that encloses itself in the circle to know the meaning [*savoir le sens*, sense or direction]: always where it comes from and where it is going [*toujours d'où ça vient et où ça va*].[21]

As he observes in 'The Ends of Man', 'the *we* is the unity of absolute knowledge and anthropology, of God and man, of onto-theo-teleology and humanism'.[22] In the midst of dismissing pure *being*, Hegel reasserts the most pervasive ontology.

For Hegel, the *form* of sensible certainty confirms what 'we' have already discerned: 'It is not just we [*wir*] who make this distinction . . . between immediacy and mediation; on the contrary, we find it within sense-certainty itself [*sinnlichen Gewißheit selbst*], and it is to be taken up in the form [*der Form*] in which it is present there, not as we have just defined it' (§93; 83). The form of sensible certainty treats the object – the object that *is*, because Hegel still needs pure being as the independence, the 'essence' (*Wessen*) and truth of the object – 'in the form of a simple, immediate being', while it recognizes the mediated 'I' as 'something which in sense-certainty is not *in itself* but through an other' (*nicht* an sich, *sondern durch ein Anderes*). The meaning of the form of sensible certainty is the genesis of an *I* that exceeds sensible knowledge, of an I that *knows* and *thinks* about objects. It is the birth of the concept (*Begriff*) (§94; 84). Derrida will return to this genesis and birth in *Glas*.

WRITING THE TRUTH

The meaning of the form of sensible certainty facilitates a new configuration in which the question – because now the I can ask the object questions – 'What is *This*?' (*Was ist das Diese?*) is no longer about the I as 'this' and the object as 'this', but the ' "This" in the twofold shape [*gedoppelten Gestalt*] of its being, as "Now" and "Here" ' (§95; 84). The dialectic between the *now* (Jetzt) and the *here* (Hier) will, Hegel promises, give an intelligible form (*verständliche Form*) to sensible certainty itself. It is at this moment, *after* the genesis of the I that knows about objects, and *before* sensible certainty is elevated to an intelligible form, that Hegel turns to what Derrida calls the 'written trace' and, as he asked in his 1975 interview, raises the problem of 'how could a here-now pass through writing unscathed?' Hegel writes:

> To the question: 'What is Now?' [*was ist das Jetzt?*], let us answer, e.g. 'Now is Night' [*das Jetzt ist die Nacht*]. In order to test [*prüfen*] the truth of this sense-certainty a simple experiment [*Versuch*] will suffice. We write down this truth; a truth cannot lose anything by being written down, any more than it can lose anything through our preserving it [*Wir schreiben diese Wahrheit auf; eine Wahrheit kann durch Aufschreiben nicht verlieren; ebensowenig dadurch, daß wir sie aufbewahren*]. If *now*, this *noon*, we look again at the written truth we shall have to say that it has become stale [*Sehen wir* jetzt, diesen Mittag, *die aufgeschriebene Wahrheit wieder an, so werden wir sagen müssen, daß sie schal geworden ist*]. (§95; 84)

To 'test' the question 'what is now?', to push sensible certainty towards self-consciousness, Hegel turns to the 'experiment' of *writing* the truth. From the start, this experiment is very strange. To the question 'what is now?' there is the answer 'now is night'. But Hegel does not actually state that it *is* night when the answer is given 'now is night'. It is as if someone – who doesn't know if it is day *or* night, someone who might be blind – asks 'what is now?', and someone else *says*, 'now is night'. Hegel takes it for granted that this question (*Frage*) and answer (*Antwort*), this blind dialogue, this speech that precedes writing, is the *truth*. It can be written down as the truth because it has *already* been *spoken* as the truth, as Derrida suggested in *Of Grammatology*, published in the year of his seminar on Hegel.[23] This speech is the possibility and the limit of 'written truth' (*aufgeschriebene Wahrheit*).

In his translation of this moment of speech A. V. Miller abbreviates a short but significant phrase. Hegel writes: 'To the question: "What is Now?", let us answer, e.g. [*zum Beispiel*, for example] "Now is Night".' Since at least his introduction to Husserl's *The Origin of Geometry*, Derrida had been interested in the example – the part, fragment or trace that is brought in to *represent* something in general, to illustrate the particular that *stands in for* the general, the extraordinary as the typical.[24] Hegel uses the answer 'Now is Night' and the writing down of this spoken truth as examples to illustrate the truth that *exceeds* mere sensible certainty. Hegel has incorporated this part as whole, this particular as general, into the actuality, form and meaning that constitutes a dialectical sensible certainty. 'Actual sense-certainty', he writes, 'is not merely this pure immediacy, but an *instance* [*eine* Beispiel] of it' (§92; 83). In other words, when sensible certainty becomes actual, the immediate pure being (of the object) becomes only a *part*, and becomes *part of* the mediation between the object and the I. Sensible certainty makes an example *of* itself, *from* itself: in a phenomenology of spirit, sensible certainty cannot help exceeding itself – and giving itself to consciousness.[25] For Hegel, this is why 'it is not just we who make this distinction between essence and instance [*des Beispiels*], between immediacy and mediation; on the contrary, we find it within sense-certainty itself' (§93; 83).

Hegel's strange and strained experiment – saying it is *now* night, writing this truth down and finding this truth has 'become stale' (*schal geworden*) when it is *now* noon – appears, as Heidegger had argued in *Being and Time*, to follow Aristotle and treat time as a succession of nows.[26] But Hegel's experiment (*Versuch*), his attempt or trial, seems at first sight even more stark than Aristotle's troubled account of time in the *Physics*. As we have seen, for Aristotle the now is the number (the dividing continuity) that counts and accounts for time as the movement of the before and the after. Hegel's trial describes the implicit passage of time as an unavoidable movement *from* the now (night) *to* the now (noon) that takes no account of the before and after. It is the 'written truth' (*aufgeschriebene Wahrheit*) alone which appears to register the *traces* of the before and after. Moving from the now of night to the now of noon, the written truth alone has 'become stale' (*schal geworden*) or, in an almost oxymoron, *grown* stale, *grown* spiritless. *Before*, it represented, carried and preserved the spoken truth (the now of night). *After*, with the spoken truth seemingly untouched, the written truth has lost its freshness, its spirit of the truth. Writing marks and pays the price for the movement of the before and after.

As Derrida often noted, when I write *today*, this very day, this here and now, and when you read this singular *today*, it will always be *another* today, the other of today. When I write *today*, even when I date this today and mark its finitude (20 January, or 20 January 2006), it will repeat itself, it will give itself to the other, to a today that is beyond my writing today, here and now.[27] This can be seen as the trial or test, the ordeal, that Hegel's 'experiment' describes: the would-be repetition of the now that puts writing to work and exceeds its own destination.

'The Now that is Night is *preserved*' (aufbewahrt), Hegel writes (§96; 84). What does writing do? It preserves the spoken truth and illustrates the work of the *negative* on its way to the *universal*. The truth (now is night) is a truth (at night) that preserves itself (in the day) as 'something that is *not*' (*Nichtseiendes*). The truth of the now is something that is *preserved* in virtue of being neither night nor day. It is a mediated, 'self-preserving' (*sich erhaltende*) truth. Neither this nor that, at once this and that, the now passes intact and untouched '*through*' (*dadurch*) night and day (the before and after) (§96; 84). The now needs the before and after, but only to *announce* its universal truth – and for Hegel this is a journey from speech (via the written truth) to speech: 'it is as a universal too that we *utter* [sprechen] what the sensuous is. What we say *is* [*was wir sagen*, ist]: "This", i.e. the *universal This* [das allgemeine Diese]; or, "it is", i.e. *Being in general* [das Sein überhaupt]' (§97; 85).

Hegel immediately qualifies this announcement of the universal truth and being in general of sensible certitude: at this stage in the *Phenomenology* we do not yet '*envisage*' this universal, we only '*utter*' it. We speak *from* or *out of* (sprache . . . aus) the universal. We are not placed *before* or in *advance* of (stellen . . . vor) it. Having just argued that when the truth of sensible certainty reaches a *universal* truth the now is untouched by night or day (the before or after), Hegel insists that this spoken truth can only arise *after* this universal, not *before* it. Writing has preserved the truth regardless or in spite of the night and day, but when it comes to *speaking* this truth, it can *only* be spoken in the daylight, *after* the night, *after* writing. As we have seen, when Thales was asked, 'what comes first – day or night?', he had replied 'night – by a day'. As Derrida suggested throughout his work, with the question of writing and speech, philosophy has always been haunted not only by what comes before, by what comes first, comes in front, but also by what comes at once before *and* after, behind *and* in front, *avant et devant*, by the *palintrope* of what turns back and turns again, startling itself *from the start*.[28]

LANGUAGE SAVES US

It is this order of precedence, this insistence on the distinction between from (*aus*) and ahead of (*vor*) the universal that introduces the other key concept in Hegel's title: *das Diese* (Form) and *das Meinen* (Meaning). Hegel goes on to explain:

> Of course, we do not *envisage* the universal This or Being in general, but we *utter* the universal; in other words, we do not strictly say [*wir sprechen schlechthin nicht*] what in this sense-certainty we *mean* to say [meinen]. But language [*Sprache*], as we see, is the more truthful; in it, we ourselves directly refute what we *mean* to say [*in ihr widerlegen wir selbst unmittelbar unsere* Meinung], and since the universal is the true of sense-certainty and language expresses [*ausdrückt*] this true alone, it is just not possible for us ever to say a sensuous being [*ein sinnliches Sein*] that we *mean* [meinen]. (§97; 85, trans. modified)

Language (*Sprache*) saves us from what we *mean* to say (*meinen*), from the spoken truth *of* 'sensuous being' that arises from the example of the written truth. Language saves us from the meaning to say, from the *vouloir-dire*, the translation Derrida proposed for *Bedeutung* in the year that he was reading this passage from the *Phenomenology*. In *Speech and Phenomena* (1967), Derrida suggested that meaning to say (*vouloir-dire*) reinforces the traditional link in philosophy between 'speaking' and 'meaning', but *also* marks a limit of a meaning that is both *reliant* on speaking and that can *never* draw a pure and absolute distinction in language between indication (*Anzeichen*) and expression (*Ausdruck*).[29] For Hegel, not *ahead of* but coming *out of* the truth of sensible certainty, we can never actually say what we mean. We can never speak simply, can never simply say what we aim or intend, and can even say what we didn't mean to say. There is something holding us back, there is a disproportion, a limit or time lag, an elusive oscillation between what we indicate and what we express, between what we *mean* to say and what we *say*.

For Hegel, this gap between meaning to say and truth – which language overcomes – indicates that even as a universal, pure being 'remains' (*bleibt*) the essence of the truth of sensible certainty. But as a universal, this pure being is also 'something to which negation and mediation are essential'. Once sensible certainty is universalized, we can no longer say what *we* mean about pure being: the universal truth of pure being speaks *for itself*. There is a gap between 'what we *mean* by being' (*Sein meinen*) and a '*das Sein mit der* Bestimmung', a determined being, a being with its own destination, a being that knows where it is going. We have become like the changing night or day which leaves the now and the here untouched and unmoved (§99; 85–6).

Hegel treats this gap as the pivot for the next stage of the progression from sensible certainty. The universal object has become 'empty and indifferent', and now 'all that is left over' (*bleibt allein*), all that remains, is 'our meaning' (*unsere Meinung*) (§99; 86). All we can do now is to turn away from the object and go back to the *I*. The limitation of the spoken truth that follows the written truth and leaves a gap between truth and speech, the *meaning* to say that can never fully or entirely say what it wants to say (the truth) or reach its destination (the object), Hegel argues, can *only* take us towards the enhancement, the amplification and generalization of the *I*. Language leads us to self-consciousness. The truth of sensible certainty 'is now [*ist jetzt*] to be found', Hegel writes, in 'the object as *my* object, or in its being *mine*; it is because *I* know it' (*dem Gegenstande als* meinem *Gegenstande oder im* Meinen; *er ist, weil* Ich *von ihm weiß*) (§100; 86). Before *meinen* was what we *mean* to say, now *meinen* is mine. Hegel loved words in the German language with a 'twofold meaning', and what could *mean* more than the *meaning* of the meaning *to say* that becomes *mine*.[30]

PUNCTUALITY: THE ARRIVAL OF THE I

As with the genesis of the object in general, the birth of the I in general is of course only a station on the way, and it has its own limitations (it is a universal that can only *mean* to speak of the particular), but the *I* (the *Aufhebung of* the I and *as* the I, always with the assistance of the *we*) – that will carry consciousness through to self-consciousness, reason, spirit and reach its epiphany in absolute knowledge – has *arrived* (§102–3, 105; 86, 88). Already looking towards the next stage of consciousness, looking beyond the generalization of the object and the I of sensible certainty, Hegel argues 'I am a pure intuiting' (*Ich bin reines Anschauen*) and 'I stick firmly [*Ich halte . . . fest*] to *one* immediate relation: the Now is day [*das Jetzt ist Tag*]' (§104; 88). Faced with such a situation, *we* can only work with and become one with this I: *we* must become *punctual*. For now, we must *point* to the truth of sensible certainty, of the now as night, we must point *blindly* into the darkness as one in time and space.[31] Hegel writes:

> Since, then, this certainty will no longer come forth to us, when we direct its attention to a Now that is night, or to an 'I' to whom it is night [*ein Jetzt, das Nacht ist, oder auf einen Ich, dem es Nacht ist*], we will approach it and let ourselves point to the Now [*das Jetzt zeigen*] that is asserted [*behauptet*, maintained, retained, preserved]. We must let ourselves point *to it* [zeigen]; for the truth of this immediate relation is the truth of this 'I' which confines itself to one 'Now' or one 'Here' . . . We must therefore enter the same point of time or space [*in denselben Punkt der Zeit oder des Raums eintreten*], point them out to ourselves [*sie uns zeigen*], i.e. make ourselves into the same singular 'I' [*demselben diesen Ich*] which is the one who knows with certainty. (§105; 88)

Everything is due, everything is owed, to this *now*, this now that is retained (*behauptet*) and that makes us punctual – but only for a moment, and already, we are *too late* to point at anything else but a universal now that *has been*, at a now that is caught up in the *Aufhebung*. *Now*, pointing at the here we can *recognize* the not-being of the 'before and behind' (*Vorn und Hinten*), but now it is *already* just part of the one in the many, the many in the one: the number of the *Aufhebung* (§107–8; 89). Everything is due, everything is owed to this now that might be spoken *or* (*oder*) even written. For Hegel, in the end this indeterminacy between speaking *or* writing the truth of sensible certainty doesn't matter, because language is *safe*, language *saves*. The 'divine nature' of language *preserves* the truth of consciousness in a phenomenology of spirit (§110; 92).

THIS BIT OF PAPER

But, at the same time, Hegel can only *maintain* (retain) this, only speak of this truth through a palintrope, by *turning back, again*, to the example of writing: They who 'assert [*behaupten*] the truth and the certainty of the reality of sense-objects' (§109; 91), they who 'speak [*sprechen*] of the existence of *external* objects [äußerer *Gegenstände*]',

> they mean *this* bit of paper [dieses *Stück Papier*] on which I am writing [*schreibe*] – or rather have written [*geschrieben*] – 'this'; but what they mean is not what they say [*aber was sie meinen, sagen sie nicht*]. If they actually wanted to *say* [sagen] 'this' bit of paper [*dieses Stück Papier*] which they mean, if they wanted to *say* [*sie* wollten sagen] it, then this is impossible [*unmöglich*], because the sensuous This that is meant *cannot be reached* [unerreichbar *ist*] by language [*Sprache*], which belongs to consciousness, i.e. to that which is inherently universal. (§110; 91–2, trans. modified)

Despite Hegel's attempts to elevate a phenomenology of the spirit away from the bits and parts of sensible certainty through a language 'which belongs to consciousness', the *example* of the written truth retains the *or* (*oder*) that precedes, that is at once before *and* in front of, starting *with* sensible certainty. The written truth retains the *or* (speaking *or* writing, now *or* not-now) and marks a part that *exceeds* and *limits* the truth of sensible certainty as the launching of a phenomenology of spirit. As Derrida would later remark in a reading of the introduction to Hegel's lectures on aesthetics in

'Parergon' (1973–78): 'The totality of philosophy, the encyclopaedic corpus is described *as* [comme] a living organism *or as* [ou comme] a work of art. It is represented on the model of one of its parts which thus becomes greater than the whole of which it forms a part, which it makes into a part [*elle fait (une) partie*]'.[32]

For Hegel, in contrast, this first spoken then written now of night is the *origin* and the *genesis* of the senses. Tested by the now of noon, it became the consciousness of the mediating, negating universal truth of a pure and sensuous being. It describes the *passage* of preservation from the written truth to the truth, the punctuality, of the *universal I*: 'The force of its truth thus lies now in the "I" [*Die Kraft ihrer Wahrheit liegt also nun im* Ich], in the immediacy of my *seeing, hearing* [Sehens, Hörens], and so on; the vanishing of the single Now and Here that we mean [*meinen*] is prevented by the fact that *I* hold them fast [*festhalte*]. *Now is day*, because I see it [Das Jetzt ist Tag, *weil Ich ihn sehe*]' (§101; 86, trans. modified).

Now is day, because I see it – and the *Phenomenology* can begin.

DARKNESS AT NOON

Das Jetzt ist die Nacht . . . But everything begins with the example of writing at night. Phenomenology begins in the dark.[33] Writing preserved (*aufbewahrt*) the truth of the now to illustrate the harnessing of negativity in the first articulation of the universal truth of sensible certainty. Writing is a kind of night storage (*Aufbewahrung*), a depository (*Aufbewahrungsort*) in the dark. In 'The Pit and the Pyramid', on the same page where he first alludes to *Glas* as a work in preparation, Derrida describes the role played by what is preserved (*aufbewahrt*) in the Hegelian process of idealization:

> In this movement of representation, intelligence *recalls itself* [se rappelle] to itself in becoming objective. *Erinnerung*, thus, is decisive here. By means of *Erinnerung* the content of sensible intuition becomes an image, freeing itself from immediacy and singularity in order to permit the passage to conceptuality. The image thus interiorised in memory (*erinnert*) is no longer *there* [là], no longer existent or present, but preserved [*gardée*] in an unconscious dwelling, conserved without consciousness (*bewusstlos, aufbewahrt*). Intelligence keeps [*tient*] these images in reserve, submerged [*enfouies*] at the bottom of a very dark shelter,

> like water in a nightlike or unconscious pit (*nächtliche Schacht, bewusstlose Schacht*), or rather like a precious vein at the bottom of the mine.[34]

As the 'written truth' in the *Phenomenology*, this pit retains 'all the powers of the voice which it holds in reserve [*tient en réserve*] . . . like truth speaking to itself [*une vérité parlant toute seule*] from the bottom of a well'. We are blind and we are pointing blindly – and we keep on speaking, keep on meaning to speak.

As Derrida suggests in 1968 in both 'The Pit and the Pyramid' and 'Plato's Pharmacy', *Glas* starts with the problem of writing as the reserve, as the remainder that still *remains – and remains to come*, as the depository (*Aufbewahrungsort*) of truth. While struggling with the many names of the *pharmakon*, Plato dismisses writing as a danger to memory. Derrida writes: 'if one takes the king's word for it, then, it is this life of the memory that the *pharmakon* of writing would come to hypnotize: fascinating it, taking it out of itself by putting it to sleep in a monument'. This is what the Sophist applauds: 'not memory but memorials'.[35] In the *Phenomenology*, without forgetting that he precedes the written truth with the speech that *makes* truth, Hegel emphasizes that writing can preserve the truth. 'A truth cannot lose anything by being written down', he writes, 'any more than it can lose anything through our preserving [*aufbewahren*] it.' *After* speech and *on the way to* the idealization of and as the truth, Hegel allows for monuments (written truths) that in the end efface themselves and grow spiritless as the history of spirit goes on its way to absolute knowledge.

. . . oder *das Jetzt ist Mittag* (§109; 90). But it is also worth recalling that this moment of monumental inscription in the *Phenomenology* takes place *after* the assertion of an actual, formal and meaningful sensible certainty, and *before* the presentation of the intelligible form and universal truth of sensible certainty. Written truth is just before, already part of, the transformation of sensible certainty into intelligible form. As we have seen, for Derrida Plato's association of the sun with the unseen intelligible origin of the visible ties the ideality of the intelligible to a blinding sun.[36] What makes us see, also makes us blind: it is unseen and unseeable. The intelligible origin of the sensible, of the sensible that is always talking its way back to the intelligible, is as blinding, as deadly, as looking on the face of God.

Like Oedipus before him, Derrida writes, 'Hegel has blinded himself' (*Hegel s'est aveuglé*).[37] 'The opposition of noon and midnight resolves itself into noon', Derrida would write in *Glas*.[38] Hegel's trial takes the spoken now of night preserved as written truth to the now of *noon*: to the blinding light of the midday sun. Writing the truth at night blinded by the sun. Darkness at noon. Now: not-now, but now. Night *or* noon: or. Starting with sensible certitude, we can only be startled again by the oscillation of the *or*:

> what, after all, of the remain(s), today, for us, here, now [*quoi du reste aujourd'hui, pour nous, ici, maintenant*], of a Hegel?
>
> For us, here, now [*Pour nous, ici, maintenant*]: from now on that is what one will not have been able to think [*penser*] without him.
>
> For us, here, now [*Pour nous, ici, maintenant*]: these words are citations, already, always, we will have learned that from him.[39]

CHAPTER 8

CUT *GLAS*

R(EST)E

'*quoi du reste aujourd'hui*'?[1] What remains today (*reste aujourd'hui*) Derrida asks in the first line of *Glas*, what remains of *today*, this today, that is at once a singular and unique today (this very day, the day 'today' was written), and a today in general, a today that always gives itself to *another* today (any and every day, the day you are reading this 'today')? From the start, what remains – remains to come: remains 'between its *before* and *after*'.[2] *Glas*: resistance of the remainder, of the leftover to come.

With its echoes of Derrida's 1967 seminar on sensible certainty at the opening of the *Phenomenology of Spirit*, *Glas starts* with this remainder, 'this bit of paper' (*dieses Stück Papier*), this writing that cannot be reached (*unerreichbar*), that cannot be touched by language, that keeps language safe, and saves us for consciousness.[3] Hegel is always trying to make use of, to use up and finish with, the sensuous to take phenomenology on its way from anthropology to logic, to bring thought to a stage where, with the help of the *Aufhebung*, it can think difference and *think itself thinking the truth*. But for Derrida, there are already the palintropic remainders, *dieses Stück Papier* for example, that remain and remain to come, the remainders that we turn back to, again, once more and find that they are already more than one.

Derrida begins with 'two unequal columns', 'two passages' and 'two functions' on and around the work of Hegel and Jean Genet, and as part of his interest in the possibility of a 'new' history – of the senses and the palintropic turn from Hegel back to Aristotle, one could say that *Glas* starts – and startles – with at least two tracks that cross and re-cross from left to right and back again (1a–b; 7a–b). First, there is the track of the generation of the *concept* and the giving of the *name* according to Hegel and Genet, of the genesis and sexual difference of the (immaculate) *conception* of the concept, of thought thinking itself. For Derrida, this track begins with the 'thought of the remain(s)' (*la pensée du reste*) and what still 'remain(s) to be thought' (*reste à penser*). Second, there is the track of *les coups* (stokes, blows, leaps, cuts, gaps) that *recoupent* (overlap, recut). This is also the question of a marked conception, of a generation that marks and re-marks *itself*. As Derrida writes in introducing his column on Genet, 'the incalculable of *what remained* calculates itself, [and] elaborates all the *coups*'. '*What remained*' (*ce qui est resté*) is already a quote, a re-citation, and one should not simply equate what remains (*le reste*) with what remained (*est resté*): the *est* of *être* always has an agenda to be more than what remains. But the text '*r(est)e*'. It resists and remains, both the possibility *and* the limit of the *est* (4b; 10b).

The 'incalculable of *what remained*' is always attempting to calculate *itself* (*se calcule*), and, as we have seen, in Derrida's rereading of Aristotle's account of the sense of hearing in *De Anima*, in trying to calculate (or to hear) itself, it 'elaborates all the *coups*', it tries to organize, to gather all the details, all the parts, all the remainders, all *les coups du dehors*, all the *blows* from the outside. It elaborates: it tries to organize the remainders *and* it *works on* the remainders, and makes them even more complex or ornate. In trying to gather the details, it *overworks* them. The incalculable *est resté* calculates itself, elaborates its *coups* – and *se recoupe*, overlaps itself, recuts itself from itself and gives itself *to* the other, *to* the other unequal column. Reading – with the *gaps*: 'at the outset – but as a setting out that already departed from itself [*au départ – mais comme un départ de lui-même se départit déjà*]', Hegel recognizes the cuts and blows, the breaching from the start (*entamaient*) that leaves gaps (*Öffnungen*) (3a; 9a).

THE GAPS AND CUTS OF NAMING

'Socrates feigns to take part' (235b). Since Socrates had mocked and somewhat ambivalently mimicked etymology in the *Cratylus*, the dizzying derivation of words and the unceasing attempt to establish the *etymon* (the truth of the name, the name as the truth) has haunted philosophy.[4] As Derrida suggests, the derived conception of a word that gains the authority of a concept 'would be inconceivable to Kant' (7a). But as he remarked in the *Science of Logic*, Hegel took great delight in the fact that the German language 'has come to use one and the same word for two opposite meanings'. *Aufheben*, he notes, 'has a twofold meaning in language: on the one hand it means to preserve, to maintain, and equally it also means to cause to cease, to put an end to'.[5] Hegel puts great weight on this capacity of language: the *Aufhebung* with its 'twofold meaning' will become the engine of the history of spirit as it progresses towards absolute knowledge (10a). For Derrida, the relentless Hegelian question of starting again is always a problem of conception, of conceiving words *and* concepts.

What interests Derrida is Hegel's recognition that there are words (in this case *Sittlichkeit* and *Moralität*) that 'are difficult to translate and even as words, if not concepts, difficult to distinguish' (6a). From the outset, *au départ*, Hegel tries to maintain a clear separation (a gap) between words and concepts. Having acknowledged his difficulties, he insists that he does not 'entrust to etymology the right to regulate a concept's content' (6–7a). The concept will always exceed the word, cut itself clearly and cleanly from the word like an immaculate caesarean.

For Hegel, that the 'same word' can have 'two conceptually different, verily opposite, significations proves that a word is never a concept' (7a). As Derrida observes, in Hegelianism there is an 'auto-differentiation as auto-determination' and the 'auto-production of the concept' (7a). [6] Thanks to the work of the *Aufhebung* (one word, two concepts), 'natural language . . . ceases to be what it is the moment it posits itself as such'. Positing itself 'as a system of natural signs, as existing in exteriority, language raises itself to the concept (ideal interior signification)' (8a). The concept is the *Aufhebung* of a language that 'vomits a natural remain(s)' (*un reste naturel*) (9a; 15a). Natural language raises 'its natural corpse to the height of the concept' (10a). The concept *brings* life and *gives* life to language by *marking* the death of the body of natural language. The passage from the word to the concept is impossible without this re-marking of what remains. Language endures 'the conception of the concept', and becomes a 'living language [that] hears and understands itself', a language that has the capacity to conceive, to grasp and to possess itself (9a). In the end and at the outset, the concept gives birth to itself – and leaves a remainder.

The concept gives birth to itself, like the 'immaculate choice' of giving a name. When Genet names his characters, and 'erects the attribute, the adjective, the epithet' ('Mimosa, Querelle, Divine, Green-Eyes, Culafroy, Our-Lady-of-the-Flowers, Divers'), it produces 'what is not yet even the name of the thing but the supervening accident [*l'accident survenu*] that unnecessarily adds itself to the substance and can always detach itself from the substance, in order to fall (to the tomb)'. The name in Genet's work first appears as a 'supervening accident', as an addition that can always be detached, an unnecessary supplement that can never be considered as an *etymon*. But in the end, like Hegel before him, Genet finds a 'nominal singleness' (*unicité nominale*) in this process that 'tightens the name', and 'reduces the classifying gap [*l'écart*] between the name and the first name'. This reduction of the *gaps* of naming delivers and gathers up the body into speech: 'one's own proper, sublime, glorious body is gathered into an organless vocable [*un vocable, sans organe*]'. For Genet, naming becomes a kind of *glory* (*la gloire*), a speaking without the body (7b–8b; 13–14b).

For Derrida, there is always more than one gap, no one gap. Genet does not only reduce the gap in the *glory* of naming, he also celebrates the gaps of the *gallery*.[7] There is another gap, a gap on the side (*à l'écart*), a gap that Genet wants to keep open: 'Why . . . is he so fond of galleries?' Derrida asks. 'Not only those that keep you, orient you . . . but those for which one lays oneself open [*s'expose*] to the theatre, those that architecture associates with boxes, homes, balconies, all the galleries of language, all the constructions of simulacra to one side [*toutes les constructions de simulacres à l'écart*], all the dissimulated shelters, more or less fake, in the corners' (9b; 15b). At the outset, there are gaps – the gaps that must be filled and bridged, and made into the column of a name. But, *before* the glory of the single unity of the name in Genet's work, there is also 'the supervening accident [*l'accident survenu*] that . . . can always detach itself' *and* 'all the constructions of simulacra to one side [*à l'écart*]'. The name is a gap that moves, that steps aside, and wanders in *and* out of 'the galleries of language'.[8]

According to Hegel, Derrida argues, gaps (*Öffnungen*) would be 'like accidents coming over [*comme survenues*] the phallic columns at first unperforated or apparently unperforatable' (3a; 9a). Gaps come *after* the immaculate conception of the column and names come *after*, follow on *and* return to, the truth (the *etymon*). But, as with Genet, both gaps and names are also *surprising* (*survenue*): they are events that arrive unexpectedly, unforeseeable interruptions that are always *before* us, behind us *and* ahead of us.

For Hegel, in the end, love bridges or binds the gap. Love is 'a unity that feels itself' (14a). Love will oversee, order and bridge the sexual difference and the human copulation that produces the immaculate conception of the concept (as absolute knowledge). 'Love plays . . . in the gap [*l'écart*] between understanding and reason' (18a; 25a). For Hegel, the gap *between* X and Y *always* works to *surpass* X and to *resolve* itself into Y: love as the *Aufhebung*. The 'dialectical contradiction' of love 'surpasses understanding [*passe l'entendement*] only in order to resolve itself [*se résoudre*] in actual rationality' (18a; 25–6a). The Hegelian gap moves. It moves on from station to station, from blow to blow (*coup*), 'but only in order to announce or prepare another stroke [*coup*]; the resolving is already in the act of producing another unheard-of contradiction in which the *zugleich* [the at-once] will separate [*se dissociera*] from itself in order to reason against understanding' (19a; 26a). It is a programmed gap: *gap* (surpass, resolve), *gap* (surpass, resolve), *gap* (surpass, resolve) – and so on, until the end of history, when the programme stops, when it knows to turn itself off, when it knows that there are no more gaps.

But for the Hegelian programme to work, for the leap upwards from one station to the next, *the* gap and *the* cut must *move*, must not only separate and divide, but also deviate and re-cut, and *exceed* – if only for a moment – the programme: 'The *zugleich* [the *du-même-coup*]', Derrida writes, 'is immediately divided, unbalanced, breaking the symmetry, the *même coup* worked (over) by two unequal forces: the resolving – also the dissolving – outmatches production [*l'emporte sur la production*]. But only in order to announce or prepare another stroke [*un autre coup*]' (19a; 26a).[9] Hegel needs the separation and the division: he cannot do without *the* gaps and *the* cuts that move, and then bridge and heal themselves.

The law of the *Aufhebung*: it 'appropriates itself only in expropriation' (20a). Like an apotheosis of the *Aufhebung*, the glory (of the name) arises from decapitation: 'the given proper (sur) name relieves [*relève*] the head that falls (to the tomb) of the scaffold'. Genet makes himself, makes his proper name into a flower (*genêt*, broom), and Derrida is caught in an impossible decision when it comes to responding to this *etymon* of flowers, a decision *from* the impossible – 'dissemination or recapitulation, recapitalization?' (12b). He begins with erection as decapitation: 'the phallic flower . . . *appears* only on the scaffold', 'in letting itself fall, the head was already relieved [déjà *relevée*] . . . To be decapitated is to appear – banded, erect.' And within this fall-as-rising-to-greater-heights, the gap that *moves* is also *put to work*: 'When a flower opens up, "blows", the petals part [*s'écartent*], and then there rises up [*se dresse*] what is called the *style*' (21–2b; 28–9b).

The giving of a name 'consecrates and glorifies the fall, cuts one more time [*coupe une fois de plus*], and engraves – on a literary monument' (9b; 16b). Like *the* gap, the history of spirit puts *the* cut (*coupe*) to work: 'what denies and cuts [*coupe*] subjectivity from itself is also what raises and accomplishes it [*l'élève et l'accomplit*]' (13a; 19a). The glory as *Aufhebung* cuts or inscribes the name into a *monu-memorialization*, a mourning as interiorization and idealization, a monument as subject and the subject as monument (9b; 15–16b).[10] For Derrida, as soon as there is a name, mourning has *already* begun: 'when I sign, I am already dead' (*quand je signe, je suis déjà mort*) (19b; 26b). The name that will *survive* my death announces a finitude, from the start (133a). It also *re-marks* (marks itself and re-marks or exceeds itself, gives itself over to the other) a *sur-vivre*, a living-on, a living over that overflows (*recouper*) the opposition of life and death. After *Glas*, Derrida will call this *la vie la mort*: the excessive alternations and alterations beyond the idealization of life *as* death or death *as* life.[11]

The name is at once behind *and* in front of opposition of life and death. And for Derrida, because the name cannot merely be reduced to life as presence or death as absence (to the great ontological economy of presence *or* absence), it is indicative of an *already* (*déjà*) that exceeds the Hegelian determination of the already as the *result* that is already *present* at the beginning (11a). For Hegel, the already is always already an *Aufhebung* of the beginning: it precedes and anticipates the beginning and puts it on the right road. For Derrida, the *déjà* is already at once before *and* ahead of (*avant* et *devant*) the beginning as the (result) of the presence of the present:

> When I sign, I am already dead. I hardly have time to sign than I am already dead, that I am already dead [*que je suis déjà mort*]. I have to abridge the writing, hence the siglum, because the

> structure of the 'signature' event carries my death in that event. For which it is not an 'event' [*un 'événement'*] and perhaps signifies nothing, writes out of a past that has never been present and out of a death that has never been alive . . . it imparts a stroke of writing (or of *already*) [*coup d'écriture* (*ou de* déjà)] to all the forces that cling to the present, to the truth as presence. The past is no longer a past present, nor the future a present to come (19b; 26b).

Before *and* in front: 'a stroke of writing (or of *already*)'.

DER SPRUNG

In the midst of this impossible monu-memorialization of naming, Derrida emphasizes again and again that the gap moves (*écart, écarter*) and that the leap (*saut*) can always explode, blow up in mid-air (*sauter*). As Derrida suggests, Hegel never stops leaping: 'The leap from [*le saut de*] animality to humanity, as the leap from [*saut du*] feeling to thinking, takes its impulse [*élan*] in a suppression of the pressure' (26a; 33–4a). The leap *from* the animal is a leap *towards* the concept. 'Man passes from feeling to conceiving' through the *Aufhebung* of the natural pressure of animality (25a). Man pushes down and leaps to thinking, and the arc of the leap describes an idealization, 'the constitution of ideality as the milieu of thought [*milieu de la pensée*]' (26a; 34a). For Hegel, the leap is always 'the qualitative leap' (*le saut qualitatif*) of and as the *Aufhebung* (29a). The qualitative leap can *only* jump over and cross the gap of the animal, and it can *only* land 'with the human individual', with the human individual that divides itself and 'is conscious of itself as the other'. *From* the leap, the human individual 'conceives itself' (*se conçoit lui-même*) and 'names itself' (*s'est appelé lui-même*) (29a; 37a).

As in the later *Identity and Difference* (1957), in *What is Called Thinking?* (1951–52), Heidegger also evokes the leap (*der Sprung*).[12] 'The leap alone takes us into the neighbourhood where thinking resides' (*bringt uns in die Ortschaft des Denkens*), he writes, and adds, 'we therefore shall take a few practice leaps right at the start' (*darum lernen wir Schon zum Beginn des Weges einige Vorübungen im Springen*).[13] But how does one *practise* a leap? How does one practise a leap *right at the start*? From the start, one cannot *practise* a leap, one can only leap. And from the start, there is always more than one leap (no one leap), and the leap repeats and doubles itself, gives itself over to another leap, to the other leap, the leap of the other. Heidegger attempts to draw a line when it comes to leaping. He contrasts the leap to 'a steady progress [*einem stetigen Fortgang*], where we move unawares from one thing to the next and everything remains alike'. But can a leap not have steady progress? And can a leap not be described as moving 'unawares from one thing to the next'?

The leap (which can be practised), Heidegger argues, 'takes us abruptly to a place where everything is different [*jäh dorthin, wo alles anders ist*], so different that it strikes us as strange'. We can perhaps practise leaping because we can be assured even *before we leap* that it will take 'us abruptly to a place where everything is different'. The abruptness of this leap is assured by the *sublimity* of the gap: 'abrupt means the sudden sheer descent or rise that marks the chasm's edge [*den Rand der Kluft*]'. This is a Caspar David Friedrich leap. The leap and its destination seemed assured right from the start: 'Though we may not founder in such a leap, what the leap takes us to will confound us [*be-stürtzt uns*]'. The assurance of such a leap – even if it will 'confound us' when we land – is that we can jump over, that we can cross and span a gap. 'The matter of thinking', Heidegger concludes, 'is always confounding.'[14]

For Hegel, the qualitative leap (*saut*) is always the rebound (*ressaut*) of a resource for the history of spirit on its way to absolute knowledge.[15] 'A father without a son is not a father', and in the leap *from* Judaism, Christianity evokes the Son as the 'proper result' *of* the Father, 'of the relation of infinite spirit freely relating to itself as its own rebound, its own resource [*son propre ressaut, sa propre ressource*]' (31a, 29a [37a]). In Christianity, the speculative religion *par excellence*, the 'dialectical leap' always jumps *again* – *back* to itself. As the Father is the Son, so 'self-conception' is a leap that jumps back to itself (31–2a). And what does Genet do, Derrida asks? Genet 'leaps wherever that explodes in the world [*il saute partout où ça saute dans le monde*], wherever the absolute knowledge of Europe takes a blow [*prend un coup*]' (36–7b; 45b). 'Yes, he is wherever that explodes' (*Oui, il est partout où ça saute*) (207b; 232b).

A HISTORY OF BOMBING

'The speechform is a mere sorrogate', Joyce writes.[16] In *Glas*, Derrida begins his own *Finnegans Wake* on Hegel's history of the world, from the Flood to the Resurrection and beyond. And on the way, he traces the gaps, the leaps, the cuts and blows to the *immaculate conception* of the concept. Hegel confers 'a rigorous status on the gap [*à l'écart*]', and founds the history of the world on the assured opposition of the sexual difference (43a; 52a). The qualitative and dialectical leap jumps back to itself. It starts again *with itself*. This is what (God) the Father does with his Son, and 'the essence of speculative marriage . . . consecrates the union of father and son' (36a). The leap rebounds and unifies the father and son. For Hegel, women don't jump. In speculative marriage the wife is only 'a short detour' (*un bref détour*) (36a). But at the same time, for both Hegel and Genet, everything rests on the immaculate conception.

For Derrida, the *name*, hidden and disseminated in the text, is not an origin or first principle (*arkhē*) to end or to start with. The text is not the return to or the return of the proper name (the *etymon*). This is the dangerous – impossible and unavoidable – dream of writer and reader, living on after death, despite death: 'he is no longer there, but you live in his mausoleum', and everything works towards the name that lives on (his, yours and mine), 'capitalized in the depths of the crypt' (41b).[17]

Genet erects 'a funerary hymen to nomination' and, despite the Hegelian leaps that blow up in mid-air, at the heart of this preservation and resurrection of the name is an *immaculate conception*, the erection of (and as) the Virgin Mary (30b, 34b, 47b). Hegel also works his way, mourns his way, towards the (immaculate) concept of absolute knowledge through the Christian *Aufhebung* of Judaism, with a little help from the Greeks.

Things do not start very well. The concept begins with the cut and the gap. The Flood 'tears man from nature'. It opens a gaping wound between man and nature. Mother Nature 'turns against man', and what else can man do but begin to conceive for himself? 'Noah is concept': he is the first concept that tries to think, to master, 'to control maternal nature's hostility'. He is the first concept that tries to close the gap. But from the start, 'the concept busies itself around a wound' (*le concept s'affaire autour d'une blessure*), around a gap that it can neither close nor bridge (37–8a; 46–7a). From the start, it can only keep dreaming of conceiving itself.

If Noah is the first concept, Abraham is first and last cut of Judaism, and Moses is the man who cannot close the gap. Abraham, the man of circumcision and sacrifice, remains 'attached to the cut'

(41a). Unable to reconcile himself with nature, Abraham embodies the cut *into* materialization, the gap that cannot be spiritualized. The *Aufhebung* – what the Jews cannot do (39a–47a, 54a). Moses can do nothing about this because everything is addressed to the absence of an abstract infinite. He strikes a blow (*Schlag*), but it is not enough to 'reduce the gap' that Abraham had opened (54a, 45a). The God of Moses is a god in need of incarnation (48a). The Jewish home and the Jewish temple 'opens onto nothing, confines nothing, contains as its treasure only nothingness: a hole, an empty spacing, a death [*un trou, un espacement vide, une mort*]' (49a; 59a). Judaism leaves remainders, leaves the traces of a gap that *cannot be closed*. It 'parts the curtains [*écarte les rideaux*]', and it leaves 'nothing behind the curtains' (*rien derrière les rideaux*) (49a; 59–60a).[18]

For Hegel, when it comes to the Jews, there is always a gap in their propriety, in their ownership of and proximity to an essence (50a, 53a). The Jew has 'no concept of freedom', no (immaculate) conception of the concept (52a). A Jew cannot reach the concept: 'he signifies what does not let itself be raised . . . to the height of the *Begriff*' (55a). When it comes to Christianity, Jesus *is* the *Aufhebung*, the *Aufhebung* of and as the *is* (58a). Christianity is the copula of love, the essential link or ligature of the 'is' that brings copulation to the level of the concept: 'the father *is* the son, the son *is* the father', and 'the spirit of Christianity is . . . the essentiality of the essence that permits in general copulating in the *is*, saying *is* [*de copuler dans l'*est, *de dire* est]' (56a; 67a). Incarnating and reconciling 'the infinite with itself', Christianity is the true birth of onto-theology. And it is *from* this essential binding together, Derrida argues, that the *women* of Christianity (the Virgin Mary, Mary Magdalene and the three Marys in Hegel's life, his mother, his wife and his daughter) come to signify a copulation that is 'destined for virginity' (*promise à la virginité*) (61–3a; 74a). Christian copulation and Hegelian sexual difference on the road to the immaculate concept of absolute knowledge: copulation destined for virginity.

This conception destined for virginity reaches its first apotheosis in the scene of the Last Supper. Jesus speaks to his disciples at the table, and Derrida asks, 'What then is Jesus doing when he says while breaking the bread: take this, this is my body given for you, do this in memory of me [*c'est mon corps qui est donné pour vous, faites-le en mémoire de moi*]? Why already memory in the present feeling? Why does he present himself, in the present, before the hour [*avant l'heure*], as cut off [*retranché*] from his very own body and following his obsequy?' (65a; 77a). When difference is put to work by the *Aufhebung* in the name of the history of spirit, when copulation is destined for virginity and conception for the immaculate concept, thought thinking itself thinking the truth becomes thinking *as memory*.

In Hegelianism, there is a proximity, and economy even, between *Erinnerung* (recollection, remembrance), *Gedächtnis* (recollection, memory, remembrance, monument) and *Denken* (thought).[19] As Derrida had already noted in 'The Pit and the Pyramid' (1968), this is first and foremost an economy *of* the concept: 'by means of *Erinnerung* the content of sensible intuition becomes an image, freeing itself from immediacy and singularity in order to permit the passage to conceptuality'.[20] 'Memory', he writes in *Glas*, 'here is *Gedächtnis*; Hegel often insisted on the kinship [*la parenté*] between memory and thought (*Denken*). Think me, Jesus says to his friends while burdening their arms, in advance, with a bloody corpse [*Pensez-moi, dit Jésus à ses amis en leur mettant sur les bras, d'avance, un cadavre sanglant*]' (65–6a; 77a). This is how it all starts for *thinking*: in advance, with the body of Christ as the *burden* of thought, as the weight (*pèse*) of thought (*penser*), of thinking *as* the interiorization, the idealization, the transubstantiation of the (dead) body, the weight (lessness) of thought: think me – *pe(n)sez moi*.

Pe(n)sez moi – and thinking destined for the terrible weight(lessness) of the virgin conception is always already gathering up the morsels, the bits from the Last Supper in the never-ending *Aufhebung* of the cut, and is always looking to a coupling that is to come, that is to rise again to its own virgin birth (67–8a).[21] And 'all these morsels, cannot, naturally, be bound' (118b).

'What I am (following) [*ce que je suis*] is always the Immaculate Conception' (74b; 87b). And, Derrida argues, there is 'this strange *already* (déjà)' (79b). This strange already: like death, 'as a past that has never been present, has never taken place', 'as a past we have not yet [*pas encore*] lived'. 'What I am (following) is always the Immaculate Conception' and I am already at once before *and* in front of the concept that I am following, the concept that I am *turning back to, again*, once more, more than once – without the consolation or redemption of thinking *as* memory. Derrida writes: 'We do not await death, we only desire it as a past we have not yet lived, that we have forgotten, but with a forgetfulness that has not come to cover over an experience, with a memory more ample, more capable, older than any perception. That is why there are only traces here [*n'y a ici que des traces*]' (79b; 92b). 'I am always (following) the dead man' (*je suis toujours le mort*) (255b; 284b).

'*Au commencement était le logos*, in the beginning was the *logos . . . Im Anfang war der Logos*' (75a). The Resurrection takes us from thinking to the *logos* and *beyond* the concept. The Son *is* (always) God the Father, and 'this immortality, the glorious resurrection of his body, consists in letting itself be thought [*se laisser penser*]. To think is to think being [*penser c'est penser l'être*], and to think being as immortal is to think its life. To think being as life [*penser l'être comme vie*] in the mouth that is the *logos*. Being, life, father, and son are equal in the infinite unity of the *logos*' (72a; 84a). In the Resurrection, the Son is the Son and, at the same time, is the Father: 'his father goes through him and beyond him [*le traverse et le dépasse*]' and establishes an infinite induction (72a; 85a). The son (the part) is always taken back, recollected in the father (the whole). When thinking is taken as *memory*, the son is always *taken back* by the father, by the father who always goes *beyond* the son: 'The bond [*le lien*] (*Band*) holds God and Jesus together, the infinite and the finite; of this life Jesus is a part, a member (*Glied*), but a member in which the infinite whole is integrally regrouped, remembered [*se remembre, se rappelle intégralement*]. Such is life's secret (*Geheimnis*), the remembrance, the inner recollection of the whole in the morsel [*la recollection intérieure du tout dans le morceau*]' (72a; 85a).

This infinite induction of the *logos* is always a question of *life*: 'each living part is the whole. Life is that strange division producing wholes': a Hegelian proposition that Aristotle would have appreciated (77a). It is the *logos* as life that *exceeds* the concept, but *only* to announce that *in the beginning* was the immaculate concept, the 'nonconceptual conception'. Derrida writes: 'The unity of son and father is not conceptual, for every conceptual unity lives on opposition, is finite. Now life is infinite. If the living relation of father to son is life as a nonconceptual unity, every conceptual unity presupposes that relation, implies that nonconcept as the concept's production, the concept's nonconceptual conception' (80a). In the beginning, beyond the concept is the immaculate conception of the concept.

'How does one distinguish philosophically a before from an after [*un avant d'un après*], if the circularity of the movement makes the beginning the end of an end [*du commencement la fin de la fin*]?' Derrida asks (84a; 97a). The concept begins with what exceeds its own end: from the start the conception of the (living) concept is a non-conceptual conception, an immaculate conception. But as Genet shows to Hegel and as Hegel shows to Genet, one can never start with the gap (between two columns) as a pure division or absolute separation. The part *écarte*, deviates, diverges and has already become the trace of a gap (*écart*) that exceeds the whole, from the start. In the midst of all this virginal conception, Derrida argues, no one can avoid the *he* or *she* (*il* or *elle*), the sexual *différance* of the he becoming she *and* the she becoming he.[22] Oscillating, not drowning, resisting the conceptual assurance of *either* castration *or* virginity (125–7b). The possibility *and* the limit, the ruin of ideality: 'indecision, oscillation, the trembling vibration where ideality is announced' (132b).

And 'so he strangles himself by saying, "I am the Immaculate Conception"' (103b). This is a constriction, a stricture or strangulation that does *not* simply raise itself to the next level, (back) to virginity (105a, 107a). The sexual *différance* is always the *irreducible* gap that moves, that oscillates 'on the (representative) threshold of absolute knowledge [*savoir absolu*] where the *glas* [the death knell] finally returns (close) by self, resounds, reflects itself for (it) self, admires its glory and is equal to itself' (106b; 122b). In the end, the immaculate conception undoes absolute knowledge. 'We are still on the threshold.'[23]

We are still on the threshold, and as Christianity is the *Aufhebung* of Judaism, for Hegel philosophy is the *Aufhebung* – the truth – of Christianity (70a, 92a). Christ has departed from the world and left the Christians much like the Jews, *struck* by the resonating absence of the master. 'The spirit never raises itself high enough', and we are drawn down by 'a kind of weight' (*une sorte de pesanteur*) (91a; 106a). The spiritual world has been separated from the political world and the immaculate conception of the concept must still make its way from station to station towards *absolute knowledge* (94a). And for Derrida, 'the nearly total silence on the woman, the daughter, the sister, the mother [on this journey] probably points to something other than a lacuna to be filled' (93a).[24]

And this impasse, this snag of sexual *différance*, is unavoidable because philosophy *needs* the gap. What Hegel calls 'The Need of Philosophy' (*Bedürfnis der Philosophie*), 'upsurges in the *between* [entre], the narrow gap of a split [*l'écart étroit d'une scission*], a cleavage, a separation, a division in two' (95a; 109a). Without the gap that is waiting-to-be-filled, the separation and division that are waiting-to-be-bridged, philosophy cannot progress to absolute knowledge. The gap gets speculative thinking going, it feeds the combustible engine of the *Aufhebung* as it works for history as spirit, and 'reason proceeds to busy itself thinking the wound [*s'affaire à penser la blessure*], to reduce the division' (95a; 109a). The 'interest of reason' (*Interesse der Vernunft*), Derrida writes, evoking both Kant and Hegel, is in (closing) the gap.

From the beginning, there is a split, a gap, and philosophy has a problem: 'philosophy only proceeds from/by itself, and yet it is the daughter of a need or an interest [*un intérêt*] that are not yet [*ne sont pas encore*] philosophy' (95a; 110a). Philosophy starts by *preceding itself*. Philosophy goes out ahead, goes out in front, in advance *and* it gives up its place, it yields its place – *to itself*: 'In its own proper position, philosophy presupposes. It precedes and replaces itself in its own proper thesis. It comes before itself and substitutes for itself' (95a). Precedence always pre-cedes itself: going first, going out ahead it cannot avoid also *giving up* its place, giving up *the* place. The pre-cedant cannot avoid being at once behind *and* ahead, before *and* in front of its proper position, of the position of the proper. It is a 'pro-position' that always relies on and is replaced by a 'pros-thesis' (96a, 199b, 138b).

Hegelianism – the incessant labour of the *Aufhebung* taking the history of spirit to its end in absolute knowledge – cannot avoid the structure of the re-presentation of a reconciliation to come. This is the very promise and limitation *of* the *Aufhebung*: 'the reconciliation has produced itself, and yet it has *not yet* taken place [n'*a* pas encore lieu], is *not present*, only represented or present as remaining in front of, ahead of, to come [*comme restant devant, devancée, à venir*], present as not-yet-there and not as presence of the present' (220a; 246a). The unavoidable not yet (*noch nicht*), Derrida writes, marks 'a next-to-nothing that parts [*écarte*] the present from its presentation', marks an irreducible gap, a gap that moves (222a; 248a). Precedence is a 'forestroke' (*avant-coup*) that is always struck by the blows from outside (*les coups du dehors*) (96a).[25]

For Hegel, 'above all, the division, the split . . . will be conceived [*sera conçue*]'. The concept(ion) of the gap will fill the gaps on the way to absolute knowledge. The gap 'will actually produce itself and will be consum(mat)ed [*sera consommée*]' (99a; 114a). And everything will proceed as if philosophy can make the gap its own, make its own gap. Hegel will say much the same about the leap. The leap is indispensable. It is the only way for philosophy to move up, to make use of the gaps. Leaping – from gap to gap to absolute knowledge, to the end of all the gaps. This is how Hegel 'meant to be read': 'What Hegel says of the structure of *Potenz* [power] – and this will be true of the dialectical moment – explains for us how he, Hegel, meant to be read. What he states on each *Potenz* can be transposed to each organized totality of his text, which at once repeats and anticipates, yet marks a jump, a leap [*un bond, un saut*], a rupture in the repetition, and all the while ensures the continuity of passage and the homogeneity of a development' (105a; 121a).

Hegel takes care of, anticipates all the gaps and the leaps on the way, but he also announces that philosophy *cannot get ahead, cannot move*, without the gap and the leap: 'this history, although it unfolds the divinity of the *telos*, develops by discontinuous and painful jumps [*se fait par bonds discontinus et douloureux*]' (106a; 122a). Everything rests on the confidence that the gaps and leaps always know where they are going, that they do not wander (*écarter*) or explode (*sauter*). And Hegel cannot avoid the 'metaphor, of course, of the bomb [*la bombe*], time of the explosive bomb [*temps de la bombe explosive*]' (106a; 122–3a). The history of the spirit of philosophy is a history of the 'discontinuous jump' (*bond discontinu*), of the springing up of a gap, of a cutting blow (*coup*) that explodes *as* a controlled explosion, again and again: a history of bombing (107a [123a], 141a).

STARTING WITH THE GAP

One can't just throw a bomb at Hegel. Hegelianism anticipates and exploits (absolute) rupture and displacement. 'The event cannot be as noisy as a bomb' (107a). As Derrida keeps saying over and over again, what strangles *itself* only comes to life again, starts again. So Derrida turns to what is *at once* most natural *and* most spiritual in Hegelianism: the sexual difference. Overseen by the philosophy of spirit (by that which goes out and always returns, always comes back to itself), the generation through sexual difference begins with a *gap*. Needing to divide or double itself to reassemble itself more closely to itself, the genus opens a gap for the individual: 'The lack [*le manque*] is opened with the inadequation of the individual to the genus. The genus is in the individual as a gap, a tension (*Spannung*). Whence lack, need, pressure: the movement to reduce the wound of the gap [*réduire la blessure de l'écart*], to close the cut [*fermer la plaie*], to draw together its lips.' The genus opens this gap and it closes it: 'this operation consists of filling in the gap [*à combler l'écart*]' through '*copulation*' (110a; 126a). For Hegel, this is what *Geschlecht* is all about: opening *and* closing a gap.[26]

From nature *to* spirit: this (should be) how philosophy starts and how it overcomes 'the gap [*l'écart*] of the sexual difference'. The gap of the sexual difference in nature is akin to 'the *germ of death*' (germe de mort). It is *the* gap *as* death: the gap that *works* for Hegel. It is a gap of nature that kills itself, that commits suicide, a gap that lets itself be closed in the *name* of spirit: 'there the spirit calls itself, names itself [*s'appelle*]'. And in naming itself, spirit brings, recollects and liberates the concept. Spirit 'recalls, recollects itself to itself [*se rappelle à lui*]', and it sets free 'the concept that wants to reassemble itself close by itself' (116–17a; 134–5a). This is what Hegel teaches us, Derrida warns over and over again: *the* gap is always ready to kill itself for thought thinking itself thinking the truth. 'Speculative dialectics thinks this death in its structural necessity' (132a). Hegelianism anticipates death *as* the gap, the death *of* the gap. *From* nature *to* spirit, consciousness (as 'mediation, middle, medium') fills the gap, and mourning, 'as idealizing consum(mat)ing', begins (118a, 122a).

'Neither a definite whole nor a part detached from a whole', 'the trace of deviation [*trace d'écart*]' cannot be reduced to an induction or deduction *and* it *remains* the possibility – the possibility and the ruin – of the part whole relation (119b; 203b [228b]).[27] For Hegel, the copulation of the gap of the sexual difference rests on the unity, the totality of the part–whole relation. And yet, copulation cannot avoid an *overlap*, a trace that exceeds the totality, the oscillation of a gap that moves somewhere between the traditional conception of the sexes: 'Each one is, as the party taking part, as the receiving party, at once a part and a whole; this general structure recuts and overlaps [*recoupe*] them both, passes as bisexuality in each of them' (110a). 'One cannot cut through [*trancher*] to a decision . . . between the sexes' (229b; 256b).

Hegel will never stop insisting that this overlapping is restrained and determined in a clear hierarchy of the sexes and the loving union of marriage and parenting (125a, 131a, 147a). Kant had already argued that when it comes to the sexual difference, 'the gap has been calculated for all time' *and*, Derrida adds, 'all this is played out in the gap [*tout se joue dans l'écart*] of a sign that is almost nothing [*presque rien*] and necessarily describes itself in the subtlety of nuances and of wordplays [*jeux de mots*]' (127a, 131a [149a]). The gap of the sexual difference *moves*, it 'strays' (*écartant*), 'diverges' (*s'écarte*) and 'deviates itself from itself' (*s'écarte d'elle-même*) (131a [149a], 159b [179b], 251b [279b]).

From the plant *to* the animal, *from* matter *to* spirit, *from* animal *to* human, *from* woman *to* man: this is where the *Aufhebung should* stop. The *Aufhebung* should 'leave no remain(s)' (*laisser aucun reste*) (137a; 156a). But Hegel cannot stop thinking about Antigone and the conflict between the divine law and the human law, the female and male, the night and day, over the burial of the *remains* – and 'the feminine work' of preserving the *name* as the work of mourning (142–4a, 166a). When it comes to Antigone the sister, mourning and dying for her unburied brothers, for her brothers without a monument, the *Aufhebung* becomes the mourning *for* an impossible mourning. 'Is that the inconceivable?' Derrida asks (150a). The sister appears as the 'unique example in the system', the inconceivable example in Hegelianism of a relation that is 'without desire' (149a). Neither the mother, nor the wife, nor the daughter, the sister is 'a kind of holy Virgin': an *inconceivable* immaculate concept (151a).

For a moment, it almost seems as if the sister needs no *Aufhebung*. The dream of the immaculate concept (the sister, absolute knowledge) leaves the *Aufhebung* in tatters – and, from the start, it cuts the concept with the inconceivable: 'Like Hegel, we have been fascinated by Antigone, by this unbelievable relationship, this powerful liaison without desire [*sans désir*], this immense impossible desire that could not live, capable only of overturning, paralyzing, or exceeding any system and history, of interrupting the life of the concept, of cutting off its breath [*couper le souffle*]' (166a; 187a). 'And what if the *Aufhebung* were a Christian mother?' (201a). Everything is done for 'the virginity of the mother' (223a). The *Aufhebung* marks and *re-marks* itself in the gaps of the sexual difference and 'the overlap goes over itself indefinitely' (*la recoupe repasse indéfiniment sur elle-même*) (111–14a, 130b [148b]). It leaves a remainder, the trace of a gap (226a).

For Hegel, everything falls (back) to absolute knowledge through a trinitarian speculation, 'a triangulo-circular structure' (227a). For a long time, since Pythagoras, 'the triad (*triás*) has been 'held to be the first perfect form in the universal'.[28] But what happens, Derrida asks,

> if one deviates [*s'écarte*] from the three, the *écart*, as its name indicates [gap, quarter] cutting the [*découpant*] text up into squares or squaring it, dividing it into quarters more or less regular . . . What about the text as remain(s) – ensemble of morsels that no longer proceed from the whole and that will never form altogether one [*n'en formeront jamais tout à fait un*]? (227a; 254a)

There is always more than one gap, there is no one gap: *plus d'un écart*.

Always not-quite there, always tied to the promise of what is just out ahead, just in front, absolute knowledge 'empties itself with a view to determining itself, *it gives itself time* [il se donne le temps]. It imposes on itself a gap [*un écart*] in signing itself' (229a; 256a). It gives itself time (as a gap that moves). It gives itself the time of a gap, of a *gaping*, and exposes the concept to the chance of not returning to itself as an immaculate concept (229a). The concept's possibility and its ruin, is a saturnalia of gaping, *from* nature *to* spirit, *from* spirit *to* nature, to the spirits of nature, the rhythm of the seasons, the fermentation and drunkenness of the harvest: 'to play with the four seasons: this play, this evil of *Sa* [*savoir absolu*, absolute knowledge], opens this play with a gap [*l'ouvre d'un écart*] that no longer assures it of being able to reappropriate itself in the trinitarian circle. This season disorder [*mal de saison*] neither destroys nor paralyses absolutely the infinite concept. If it formed only the negative of this concept, it would yet confirm that concept dialectically. Rather, it puts that concept out of order, stops it, jams it [*il le détraque . . . l'enraye, le grippe*] inconceivably. Also scratches it [*le griffe*] with writing. The *etymon* of *Begriff* looks forward to that. As soon as it is grasped by writing, the concept is drunk, cooked [*cuit*]' (233a; 260a).

Starting with the gap, 'there is – always – already – more than one [*plus d'un*] – *glas*' (150b; 170b). *From* column *to* column, starting with the concept, starting with the name, Hegel can only *start again*: 'in genealogies of a structure such that the crossings, couplings, switchings, detours, and branchings never simply come under a semantic or formal law. No absolute idiom, no signature. The idiom or signature effect does nothing but restart [*ne fait que relancer*] – reverberate – the *glas*' (149b; 169b).

THE GAPS OF THINKING

Between two notches or gaps in the right-hand column of *Glas*, Derrida gestures to a palintropic reading of Heidegger's *What is Called Thinking?* Heidegger approaches the question *Was heisst Denken?* through a turning *towards* and turning *away*. 'We are still not thinking' (*wir noch nicht denken*) Heidegger insists, and thinking begins 'only when we are so inclined toward what in itself is to be thought about [*zu-Bedenkende*]'. We have to turn towards what is to be thought because, 'since the beginning [*von einsther*]', 'thought turns away [*abwendet*] from man'.[29] Turning towards what has first turned away, thinking starts from what 'withdraws from the beginning [*das einsther entzieht*]'. This withdrawal 'draws us along', draws us 'towards what withdraws': man is what 'points toward what draws away'.[30] As we have seen, after *Glas* Derrida would retranslate Heidegger's evocation of withdrawal as the equivocal origin of proximity. For Heidegger 'what withdraws in such a manner keeps and develops its own incomparable nearness'.[31] Derrida suggests that this withdrawal can be treated as both the possibility *and* the limitation of proximity.

We are still not thinking, Heidegger argues. Drawn towards what withdraws, we must learn to think, to answer and respond to what withdraws. We are drawn to 'nearness of its appeal'. *Was heisst Denken?* Thinking begins with what 'calls us to think'. It puts us 'in question'.[32] Thinking begins with 'an anticipatory reaching out for something that is reached by our call [*heißen*], through our calling'. It is an appeal to what 'remains to be thought' (*bleibt zu bedenken*), a call to what remains – and remains to respond, *to come*. Thought is a 'thinking back which devotes what it thinks to that which is to be thought' (*Gedenken, das sein Gedachtes dem zu-Denkenden zu-denkt*).[33] As Heidegger had first suggested in *Being and Time* (1927), the temporalization of temporality, 'a future which makes present in the process of having been', opens the question of the future possibilities *of* the past: the past always has a future.[34] Thought is the thinking *of* the past *for* the future. Thinking is the gift – without present.[35]

But it is already *too late* to stop, and for Heidegger 'what remains to be thought about' also arises out of 'the gathering of thought' (*die Versammlung des Denkens*), of a 'thinking back' or 'recollection' (*Andenkens*).[36] The *call* to thinking is a call *back* towards a gathering and recollection, *die Versammlung des Denkens*.[37] In asking '*Was heisst Denken?*', Heidegger *gathers* together thinking and memory. Thinking always re-calls, thinks back, re-collects and *centres* the past, the beginning, for the future.[38] Calling *backwards*, thinking is 'the gift given in thinking back' (*einem Andenken Beschenkte*), and somehow we always end up with Socrates, with a thinking without palintropes.[39]

There is something heroic and almost athletic about Heidegger's description of Socrates. He *placed himself* in the 'draft' that draws us towards what withdraws and he *held his position*, not only in life, but even in death: 'All through his life and right into his death, Socrates did nothing else than place himself into this draft [*den Zugwind*], this current, and maintain himself in it. This is why he is the purest thinker [*der reineste Denker*] of the West. This is why he wrote nothing [*deshalb hat er nichts geschrtben*].'[40] Calling backwards takes us back to a memory *without* writing, without the trace or strategic traces of the remainders that resist gathering and recollection. For Heidegger, thinking inexorably takes us back, first to Socrates and then to the *logos* until, finally, we must *start again* with Parmenides.[41]

A decade after *Glas*, in his 1984 memorial lectures for Paul de Man, which explore de Man's attempts to distinguish *Errinerung* (remembrance as interiorization) from *Gedächtnis* (thinking memory), Derrida associates Heidegger's emphasis on 'the gathering of thought' (*die Versammlung des Denkens*) with an originary gathering, a gathering *of* the start, a re-gathering back *to* the start.[42] 'Gathering together (*Versammlung*) is always what Heidegger privileges', Derrida writes the following year in '*Geschlecht* II: Heidegger's Hand' (1985).[43] Two years later in *Of Spirit: Heidegger and the Question* (1987), Derrida will argue that for Heidegger spirit (*Geist*) 'is another name for the One and the *Versammlung*, one of the names of collecting and gathering'.[44] Finally, in 'Heidegger's Ear: Philopolemology (*Geschlecht* IV)' (1989), a paper given at a conference to mark the hundredth anniversary of the birth of Martin Heidegger, Derrida links Heidegger's use of *Versammlung* to a logocentrism: 'At bottom logocentricism is perhaps not so much the gesture that consists in placing the *lógos* at the center as the interpretation of *lógos* as *Versammlung*, that is the gathering [*le rassemblement*] that precisely concenters what it configures.'[45] At the same time, since at least his 1984 lectures for de Man, in this history – of the senses of Martin Heidegger, Derrida also raised the *question* of a 'non-architectonic *Versammlung*' in Heidegger's work, and in 'Heidegger's Ear' he gestures to the *polemos* of an *Auseinandersetzung* (debate) that opens not only 'the joints or couplings' (*les jointures ou les ajointements*) of the *Versammlung*, but also the distances and disjunctions of 'the faults, the intervals, the gaps' (*les failles, les intervalles, les écarts*).[46] Heidegger opens (and attempts to close) the gap.

Derrida's questions about the *weight* of thinking began at least in the mid-1960s, and the gaps in the columns on *What is Called Thinking?* in *Glas* mark an important Hegelian moment in Derrida's later readings of Heidegger.[47] Thinking is *to call*, Heidegger argues in *Was heisst Denken?*, and he draws a *distinction* between to call as 'to be named and to name' and to call as 'to appeal commendingly', to entrust, to shelter. Calling precedes naming. It is the origin of the name and 'by naming, we call on what is present to arrive' (*im nennen heißen wird as Ansesende ankommen*).[48] What is *called* thinking calls *for* thinking. It has still not arrived, it is not yet present. It is still to come. Starting with the name, with the truth of and as the name (the *etymon*), in *Glas* Derrida is *interested* in the 'unavoidable circle' of the question '*qu'appelle-t-on penser?*', '*qu'est-ce qui s'appelle penser?*', which in French turns *back on itself* and states: 'to think is to call, to name oneself' (*penser c'est s'appeler*) (20a; 27a).

'I am interested' (*m'intéresse*) Derrida writes, and recalls that Heidegger's lectures also make a *distinction* between interest and interesting (19a; 26a). Heidegger contrasts the calling back of memory (to the gathering and recollection) to *today*: 'Nobody will deny that there is an interest [*ein Interesse*] in philosophy today [*heute*]. But – is there anything at all left today [*heute*] in which man does not take an interest, in the sense in which he understands "interest" ["*interessieren*"]?' Heidegger defines interest (*inter-esse*) as 'to be among and in the midst of things, or to be at the centre of a thing and to stay with it' (*unter und zwischen den Sachen sein, mitten in einer Sache stehen und bei ihr bleiben*). 'But today's interest' (*das heutige Interesse*), Heidegger goes on to say, 'accepts as valid [*gilt*] only what is interesting [*Interessante*]. And interesting is the sort of thing that can freely be regarded as indifferent [*gleich gültig*] the next moment, and be displaced [*abgelöst*] by something else, which then concerns us just as little as what went before [*das Vorige*]'.[49] While thinking as a calling back to memory gathers and re-collects, 'today's interest', the interest *of* today cannot *hold on to* 'what went before'. Flitting from one interesting indifference to the next (much as the curiosity of everyday *Dasein* in *Being and Time*), 'today's interest' is displaced perpetually by its *lack* of interest (a holding at the centre, a keeping in the middle).

For Derrida, as I have suggested elsewhere, it would be impossible to draw a clear and absolute distinction between interest (a holding at the centre) and interesting (a perpetual displacement).[50] Interest is always interest-ing, always displacing its hold on the centre. When I take an unavoidable and impossible interest – for example in the 'unavoidable circle' of 'to think is to call, to name oneself' – I am *dis*-interested, taken away from myself to the other, for the other. Taking an interest, I can no more freely hold on to the centre than I can freely move from one displacement to the next. A year after *Glas* was published, Derrida remarks in an interview, 'when I write "what interests me" ["*ce qui m'intéresse*"], I am designating not only an *object* of interest, but the place that *I am in the middle of* [*le lieu au* milieu de quoi je suis], and precisely this place that I cannot exceed [*déborder*]'.[51]

As we have seen, Derrida would also later suggest that when I write *today*, and most of all 'today's interest', it can always gesture to *another* today.[52] Interest, today's interest, is always taken *from* the impossible: it constrains, demands and refuses the *good conscience* of an absolute separation or distinction – and between interest and interesting, between the essential gathering of memory *and* the easy indifference of today, between thinking as the calling (back to memory) and naming (oneself), most of all.

In the second gap in the columns of *Glas* devoted to *Was heisst Denken?* Derrida writes: 'one can try to displace this necessity only by thinking – but what is called thinking? [*mais qu'appelle-t-on penser?*] – the remain(s) outside the horizon of essence, outside the thought of being. The remain(s) *n'este pas* [does not come-to-essence]' (22–3a; 30a). The necessity that 'one can try to displace' refers to the reading of Hegel between the two gaps and notches on Heidegger. In the history of spirit (the progress from subjective to objective to absolute spirit) 'the spirit thinks [*l'esprit pense*] and at the same time is conscious of itself. I know the object only insofar as I know myself; I also think it while thinking myself thinking it [*je le pense aussi en me pensant le penser*]' (21a; 28–9a). The 'content of spirit' can only be spiritual. It 'never simply stands outside itself'. Spirit 'in advance interiorizes all content'. And in only repeating *itself*, it 'alone can conceive spirit', can give birth to itself. If 'to think is to call, to name oneself' (*penser c'est s'appeler*), 'to know is to appropriate oneself' (*connaître c'est s'approprier*) (22a; 29a). For Hegel, when thought thinks itself thinking the truth, spirit has always already taken care of the content, of the *matter* or the *weight* of thought.

For Derrida, as we have seen, memory and thinking are marked in French by the strange and strained relation between *penser* (to think) and *peser* (to weigh): *pe(n)ser*. Thinking is at once *neither* simply a weighing up, spirit taking account of matter, *nor* merely a weighing down, matter taking account of spirit. Neither the *weightlessness* of the triumph of spirit *over* matter, nor the profound *weightiness* of spirit *with* matter, thinking remains (and remains to come) always somewhere in *between* the light and the heavy, the mind and the body, flight and ground. *Pe(n)ser* – does not have the weight(lessness) for an idealizing re-collection. And memory is always marked by a finitude of a memory that can never monumemorialize itself.[53]

For Hegel, spirit is absolute and absolutely free, and matter cannot be the *absolute* opposite of spirit. 'Matter is not free. It weighs [*elle pèse*], it goes towards the bottom', Derrida writes, 'but there is a law to its weight, its gravity [*sa pesanteur*]' (22a; 29a). Matter is heavy (*pesant*) and, Derrida suggests, thinking (*pensant*) has its weight: *pe(n)sant*. Obliquely recalling Heidegger's emphasis on thinking as a turning *towards* what turns away or a calling *back* to what has been gathered, Derrida describes Hegel's analysis on the proper relation between spirit and matter: 'If the gravity [*la pesanteur*] and the dispersion of matter to the outside are analyzed, one should recognize there a tendency [*une tendance*], an effort tending toward [*tendu vers*] unity and the gathering of self [*le rassemblement de soi*]' (22a; 29–30a).

Matter is 'a tendency toward [*tendance vers*] the center and unity' and it can neither oppose nor follow this tendency without ceasing to be matter: 'matter then is spirit's opposite only inasmuch as it remains resistant to this tendency, inasmuch as it is opposed to its own tendency. But to be opposed to its own tendency, to itself, to matter, it must be spirit. And if it yields to this tendency it is still spirit' (22a). 'The concept wins against matter that can hold its own against the concept only by relieving itself, only by denying itself in raising itself to spirit' (23a). It is here, in a gap in the column, that Derrida asks 'but what is called thinking?' and suggests that this necessity – matter can only tend towards being *itself* (spirit) by being what it is *not* (spirit) – can only be displaced when 'the remain(s) *n'este pas* [does not come-to-essence]' (22–3a). In the Hegelian configuration, matter is somewhat like not-being for Parmenides: to not be being, it must *be* and there can be no opposite of being. But at the same time, as we have already seen, as Derrida had suggested in 'Violence and Metaphysics', in the *Sophist* the Stranger acknowledges that not-being has a *relative* (and not an absolute) difference in relation to being.[54]

When Hegel argues that in both being *and* not being itself matter can *only* be spirit, he also implies that matter has no essence of its own: 'weight (*la pesanteur*) and dispersion, the essence of matter, could not qualify an essence. Matter has no essence; its essence is its contrary, its essence is not having an essence. Dispersion, like weight (nonunity and nonideality), has no essence' (23a; 31a). For Hegel, this is why matter can only tend *towards* spirit. For Derrida, the *weight* of thinking, weight as thinking, cannot be reduced or elevated to spirit: *le reste n'este pas*. It is only when the 'weight or gravity' (*pesanteur*) of matter is not taken *as* 'the search for unity' that one can perhaps think anything else than spirit thinking itself thinking the truth (22–3a).

Derrida had already hinted at the difficulty of this *pe(n)sant* in *Of Grammatology* (1965–67). He writes:

> Outside of the economic and strategic reference to the name that Heidegger justifies himself in giving to an analogous but not identical transgression of all philosophemes, *thought* is here for me a perfectly neutral name, the blank part of the text [*un blanc textuel*], the necessarily indeterminate index of a future epoch of différance. *In a certain sense*, '*thought*' *means nothing* ['*la pensée*' *ne veut rien dire*] . . . This thought has no weight [*cette pensée ne pèse rien*]. It is, in the play of the system, the very thing which never has weight [*jamais ne pèse rien*]. Thinking is what we already know we have not yet [*pas encore*] begun.[55]

With Derrida, it is always a problem of the weight given to the name, of the gravitational forces of thinking as a *calling back* to gathering. In *Was heisst Denken?* Heidegger asks, 'but how can we have the least knowledge of something that withdraws from the beginning [*das sich einsther entzieht*], how can we even give it a name?'[56] Some 25 years after *Glas*, in *On Touching – Jean-Luc Nancy* (1992–2000), Derrida returns (but has he ever left?) to this question of 'thinking *as* memory' and of '*the unthinkable and unweighable*', *l'impe(n)sable*.[57] Derrida argues that the weight(lessness) of thought can only be defined *through* the resistance *of* the other: thought 'thinks only there where the counterweight [*le contrepoids*] of the other weighs enough so that it begins to think, that is, *in spite of* itself, when it touches or lets itself be touched *against its will* [contre son gré]. That is why it will never think, it will never have begun to think *by itself*'.[58] Thinking is unthinkable, unweighable, startling even, perhaps because it is *already* a thinking *of* and *as* the senses, an *unavoidable* accessibility or hospitality even, an interlacing oscillation, a thinking that turns backwards, once more, always more than once, a thinking of *palintropes*.

I am interested, I am in the middle, Derrida writes: I am still not even halfway through this never-ending text, through the 'ocean of words' that haunted the old Parmenides as he spoke to the young Socrates. One cannot avoid the palintropes of starting with Plato as he turns back, again, at the start, to Parmenides, and that terrible 'ocean of words' that makes all of us feel old. It is too late, and I'll have to start again.

EPILOGUE:

LET'S GO BACK THEN, ONCE MORE

Oedipus: Where did you get it? Your house? Someone else's?
Shepherd: It wasn't mine, no, I got it from . . . someone.
Oedipus: Which one of them?

Looking at the citizens

Whose house?
Shepherd: No
god's sake, master, no more questions!
Oedipus: You're a dead man if I have to ask again.
Shepherd: Then – the child came from the house . . . of Laius.[1]

In this scene from Sophocles' *Oedipus the King*, Oedipus is only a few moments away from knowing the truth. He will ask six more questions, and then he will know everything: origin, lineage, parricide, incest, self-blindness, exile. Oedipus is rushing to the end, forcing out the truth, like Socrates, question by question. 'You're a dead man if I have to ask again [*pálin*]', he tells the shepherd. But it is only by repeating his questions that Oedipus will get to 'the horrible truth'. Having to 'ask again' is both a threat of death to the other *and* the only possibility of getting to the truth.

Years later, in *Oedipus at Colonus*, the exiled Oedipus will say to Theseus, 'my doom is never to return again [*pálin*] – I killed my father'.[2] Now knowing the *truth*, Oedipus can never go back, can never turn back again to the moment when the truth remained only a few questions away. But without going backwards, without turning back, and asking about his origins, there could have been no *thinking* about the truth.

In Book Thirteen of the *Odyssey* – unlike Oedipus – Odysseus *returns* to Ithaca. But at first he does not know – like Oedipus – that he has 'returned home again [*aut' oikónde pálin kion*]'.[3] Homer says, 'Odysseus awoke out of his sleep in his native land, and did not recognize it, having been away so long'.[4] In this pre-Oedipal scene, Pallas Athene has created a mist to slow Odysseus down, to make the familiar unfamiliar, to *make* the (un)familiar, so that 'all things seemed strange [*àlloeidá*]'. In this Homeric birth of the *Unheimlich*, Pallas Athene turns herself into a young man and speaks 'with winged words' to Odysseus, telling him that he is at last home. In this un-homelike homelike moment of returning, Odysseus takes great care in *how he speaks* to Pallas Athene: 'he spoke, and addressed her with winged words; yet he did not speak the truth [*àlethéa*], but checked [*pálin*] the words before it was uttered, always revolving in his breast thoughts [*nóon*] of great cunning'.[5]

Odysseus is cunning (*pholukerdéa*). He holds back (*palín*) the truth while he speaks, and this gives him time to think. *Odysseus is thinking*. This strange movement of the *palintrope*, of the cunning in the mist, of a re-turning, revolving, turning and holding back *while speaking*, makes thinking *possible*. Odysseus is there (speaking) *and* not there (thinking). He re-turns, turns back, and already, once more, he is *more than one*.

'One, two three; but where, my dear Timaeus, is the fourth [*tétartos*] of those who were yesterday my guests and are to be my entertainers to-day [*nun*]?' Socrates asks at the opening of the *Timaeus*.[6] The *Timaeus* begins with a missing fourth, with Socrates pointing out a three-sided square, a square with an opening, an absent side that cannot be accounted for but which *also* begins the narrative, which sets the *Timaeus* on its strange path.[7] It is not today (*sēmeron*), Plato writes, but the present, the now (*nun*) that has been disrupted by this *palintrope*, this *turning back again* to yesterday. One, two, three . . . once again, we are starting, Plato writes, and once again, we are turning back and beginning with an incomplete and open-sided square.

For Plato, this inaugural and unavoidable throw-back to yesterday is a failure of hospitality. The *Timaeus* begins now, with an impossible restitution *from* yesterday: and that's how it always is with Plato, one can never match or pay back the incomparable Socratic hospitality – philosophy itself – *from* yesterday. From the start, it is always yesterday – and we have lost the *logos* of Socrates.

From the start, we are startled by all the chance encounters, by all the beginnings and endings without Socrates. How can one *return* the hospitality (*xenia*) of Socrates?[8] There seems to be no straightforward equivalence to the hospitality of Socrates. One can only begin with the strange arithmetic of a virtual square: one, two and three must *equal* an absent fourth ($1+1+1 = 4$).[9] Socrates says of the absent fourth: 'Then, if he is not coming, you and the two others must supply his place [*anaphleroun méros*]' (17a). Doesn't this improbable maths, this impossible supplement, also suggest how Plato calculates for and on the *absence* of Socrates? One can only return the hospitality of the Socratic dialogue by accounting on the absence of Socrates, by beginning the narrative with $1+1+1 = 4$.[10]

'One, two, three' (*eis, dúo, treis*) – Plato starts to speculate without term on a hospitality that cannot be returned, a hospitality that is always turning backwards, and always starting once more, more than once: the palintrope of hospitality.[11] At the outset, it is already the day after, and before Timaeus can even start to return this impossible hospitality he must ask Socrates if he would be willing to 'recount again [*pálin epánelthe*] . . . briefly from the beginning' yesterday's discourse (17b).[12]

It is perhaps unsurprising that Derrida ends 'Khora', his 1987 reading of the *Timaeus*, with an impossible and inexhaustible desire of Platonism to start again *with itself* that always takes it back, takes it before *and* beyond itself. For Plato, Derrida suggests, this bewildering and imperial urge to go back 'behind and below the origin' is also the elusive imperative of *thinking*. 'In order to think *khora*', Derrida observes, 'it is necessary to go back to a beginning that is older than the beginning.' Derrida brings his reading to a close by quoting Plato: 'Let us go back then, once more, briefly, to the beginning (*pálin ep' arkhēn*)' (69a).[13]

'And what does thinking then mean (to say)?' (*et que veut dire alors penser?*), Derrida asks in the same year, in the preface to his book *Psyche: Inventions of the Other* (1987).[14] He doesn't answer this question, which he had turned back to again and again in the 1960s and 1970s in his readings of Plato, Aristotle, Hegel and Heidegger, but it is a testament to its persistence that some forty years after he first began to study, to read and to write on philosophy, Derrida remains open to its persistent openness. As he later wrote in 'Provocation: Forewords' (2001):

> What remains to be thought: the very thing that resists thought. It resists *in advance*, it gets out ahead. The rest gets there ahead of thought; it remains *in advance* of what is called thought. For we do not know what thought is. We do not know what this word means before or outside of this resistance. It can only be determined from, in the wake of, what resists and remains thus to be thought. Thought remains to be thought.[15]

In reading Derrida reading, one gets a sense, a blow *and* a caress, of a thinking that both turns back *and* startles itself.

NOTES

Full details of the English translations and the French editions of the works of Jacques Derrida are cited in the Bibliography.

PROLOGUE: PALINTROPES

1 Derrida, 'The Villanova Roundtable', 9–10.
2 Derrida, *Of Spirit: Heidegger and the Question*, 132. On the eddying conversation between *Of Spirit* and the *Politics of Friendship*, see David L. Clark, 'Bereft: Derrida's Memory and the Spirit of Friendship', *South Atlantic Quarterly* 106.2 (2007): 291–324. I would like to thank David Clark for his kind and ready support for this book.
3 Derrida, 'Cogito and the History of Madness', 62.
4 I would like to thank Nicholas Royle for bringing the uncanny resonance of physically starting, of being startled, into questioning the orthodoxy of starting and starting again. See, Royle, *The Uncanny* (Manchester: Manchester University Press, 2003), 205–12. See also, Sarah Wood, 'Let's Start Again', *Diacritics* 29.1 (1999): 4–19. It is appropriate that at the beginning of his remarkable meditation on the interruption of the moment of creation, of starting a life and a book, Sterne writes of the *homunculus* which has already been 'ruffled beyond description – and that in this sad and disordered state of nerves, he had laid down a prey to *sudden starts*, or a series of melancholy dreams and fancies for nine long, long months together', *The Life and Opinions of Tristram Shandy*, ed. Graham Petrie, intro. Christopher Ricks (London: Penguin, 1985), 37 (my emphasis).
5 Derrida, *Of Grammatology*, lxxxix.
6 Derrida, 'Before the Law', 190.

1: STARTING WITH PLATO

1 Aristotle, *Poetics*, in *The Complete Works of Aristotle*, ed. Jonathan Barnes, 2 vols (Princeton: Princeton University Press, 1984), I: 1450b.

2 Derrida, *The Problem of Genesis in Husserl's Philosophy*, 191 n. 36.
3 Derrida, *Edmund Husserl's Origin of Geometry: An Introduction*, 45.
4 *An Introduction*, 45 n. 13.
5 *An Introduction*, 59–60, 107.
6 *An Introduction*, 122–4.
7 *An Introduction*, 124–5
8 *An Introduction*, 125, 127.
9 Edmund Husserl, 'Philosophy and the Crisis of European Man', in *Phenomenology and the Crisis of Philosophy*, trans. Quentin Lauer (New York: Harper, 1965), 159, 164. See Gail Soffer, 'Philosophy and the Disdain for History: Reflections on Husserl's *Ergänzungsband* to the *Crisis*', *Journal of the History of Philosophy* 34 (1996): 95–116. I would like to thank Joanna Hodge for bringing this article to my attention and for our many illuminating conversations about Derrida at Blackwell's. This chapter is dedicated to her.
10 'Philosophy and the Crisis of European Man', 165.
11 See Gregory L. Ulmer, 'Op Writing: Derrida's Solicitation of *Theoria*', in *Displacement: Derrida and After*, ed. and intro. Mark Krupnick (Bloomington: Indiana University Press, 1983), 29–58.
12 Aristotle, *Nicomachean Ethics*, ed. and trans. Roger Crisp (Cambridge: Cambridge University Press, 2004), 1177b.
13 'Philosophy and the Crisis of European Man', 171–2.
14 See *Derrida and Disinterest* (London: Continuum, 2005), 32–68.
15 On nineteenth-century idealizations of disinterest, see Matthew Arnold, 'The Function of Criticism at the Present Time', in *Essays in Criticism*, intro. G. K. Chesterton (London: Dent, 1969), 9–34. See also, though I would question his ready acceptance of a canonical concept of disinterestedness, Pierre Bourdieu, *The Field of Cultural Production: Essays on Art and Literature*, ed. Randal Johnson (Cambridge: Polity, 1993).
16 'Philosophy and the Crisis of European Man', 172–3.
17 'Philosophy and the Crisis of European Man', 172, 173.
18 *An Introduction*, 132–3.
19 Miguel de Cervantes, *Don Quixote de la Mancha*, trans. Charles Jarvis, intro. E. C. Riley (Oxford: Oxford University Press, 1998), 74–6 (I: 9).
20 Derrida, 'Violence and Metaphysics: An Essay on the Thought of Emmanuel Levinas', 115.
21 Samuel Johnson and James Boswell, *A Journey to the Western Islands of Scotland and The Journal of a Tour to the Hebrides*, ed. Peter Levi (London: Penguin, 1993), 61.
22 James Boswell, *Life of Johnson*, ed. R. W. Chapman, intro. Pat Rogers (Oxford: Oxford University Press, 1998), 277 n. 1.
23 *Life of Johnson*, 282, 284, 326.
24 *Life of Johnson*, 297.
25 Derrida, *Glas*, 216a.
26 *An Introduction*, 134.
27 Derrida, 'Force and Signification', 27; 'Force et signification', 46.
28 'Cogito and the History of Madness', 307 n. 1; 'Cogito et histoire de la folie', 51 n. 1.

29 See, Derrida, 'Plato's Pharmacy'.
30 'Cogito and the History of Madness', 31; 'Cogito et histoire de la folie', 51.
31 Jean Hyppolite published the first full translation of Hegel's *Phenomenology of Spirit* into French (1939–41). See also his *Genesis and Structure of Hegel's Phenomenology of Spirit*, trans. Samuel Cherniak and John Heckman (Evanston: Northwestern University Press, 1989). Alexandre Kojève gave his influential lectures on Hegel in 1933–39, *Introduction to the Reading of Hegel: Lectures on the Phenomenology of Spirit*, ed. Raymond Queneau and Allan Bloom, trans. James H. Nichols (Ithaca: Cornell University Press, 1991). On the reception of Hegel in France, see John Heckman's introduction to Hyppolite's *Genesis and Structure* (xv–xli), and Michael S. Roth, *Knowing and History: Appropriations of Hegel in Twentieth Century France* (Ithaca: Cornell University Press, 1988). For Derrida's attitude to Kojève's lectures and their influence on reading Hegel, see the *Specters of Marx*, 49–75. For Hegel, the unhappy consciousness is the last stage of self-consciousness before it moves into the first stage of reason, *Phenomenology of Spirit*, trans. A. V. Miller (Oxford: Oxford University Press, 1977), §206–30.
32 'Cogito and the History of Madness', 31; 'Cogito et histoire de la folie', 52.
33 'Cogito and the History of Madness', 32. Translation modified.
34 Nicholas Royle, *Jacques Derrida* (London: Routledge, 2003), 38.
35 'Cogito and the History of Madness', 39.
36 'Cogito and the History of Madness', 40, 42.
37 'Cogito and the History of Madness', 56–7.
38 'Cogito and the History of Madness', 57.
39 Plato, *Republic*, in *The Dialogues of Plato*, trans. Benjamin Jowett, 5 vols (Oxford: Clarendon Press, 1892), III; Plato, *The Republic*, trans. Paul Shory, 2 vols (London; Heinemann, 1963).
40 'Cogito and the History of Madness', 57.
41 'Cogito and the History of Madness', 62. Derrida returns to this passage from *The Republic* in later works, often to distinguish his own sense of excess from the onto-theology of a negative theology that evokes the greater presence of God in his unique absence. See, for example, 'How to Avoid Speaking: Denials'. It is worth noting that in this 1986 paper, where he reiterates the reading of *The Republic* which he had first outlined in his 1961–62 introduction to *The Origin of Geometry*, Derrida also returns to his reading of the *Sophist* from 'Violence and Metaphysics', to which I will come in a moment. See also, 'Sauf le nom (post-scriptum)', 64–5, and 'Faith and Knowledge: Two Sources of "Religion" at the Limits of Reason Alone', §23.
42 'Cogito and the History of Madness', 56.
43 *An Introduction*, 144.
44 *An Introduction*, 144; 'Cogito and the History of Madness', 57.
45 Derrida, 'La parole. Donner, nommer, appeler', 21–2.
46 Plato, *Phaedrus*, in *The Dialogues of Plato*, I: 275d.
47 'Violence and Metaphysics', 101. See also 106.

48 'Violence and Metaphysics', 99–100.
49 'Violence and Metaphysics', 85–6. See also, Derrida, 'The Double Session', 208.
50 Derrida, *Of Grammatology*, 91; 'Plato's Pharmacy', 82. Derrida cites *The Republic*, 515.
51 Jonathan Barnes, *Early Greek Philosophers* (London: Penguin, 1987), 129, 95.
52 Plato, *Sophist*, in *The Dialogues of Plato*, IV; *Plato*, trans. Harold North Fowler (Cambridge, MA: Harvard University Press, 1987). Further references to this work will be cited in the text.
53 *Early Greek Philosophy*, 96–9.
54 *Early Greek Philosophy*, 134.
55 'Cogito and the History of Madness', 62; 'Cogito et histoire de la folie', 96. Translation modified. On the trope of turning, touring and going back in Derrida's later work, see: *Of Grammatology*, 216–29; 'Des tours de Babel'; 'Shibboleth: For Paul Celan'; 'Back from Moscow, in the USSR'; *Specters of Marx*; 'The Reason of the Strongest (Are there Rogue States?)'.
56 Plato, *Parmenides*, in *The Dialogues of Plato*, IV; *Plato*, trans. H. N. Fowler (London: Heinemann, 1953). References to this work will be cited in the text.
57 See the *Cratylus* on the importance of remembering names, *The Dialogues of Plato*, I.
58 Apollodorus in the *Symposium* is more open about the frailty of such a chain of remembering, remarking 'Aristodemus did not recollect all that was said, nor do I recollect all that he related to me', in *The Dialogues of Plato*, trans. Benjamin Jowett, 5 vols (Oxford: Clarendon Press, 1892), I: 178.
59 'Violence and Metaphysics', 89; Emmanuel Lévinas, *Time and the Other*, trans. Richard A. Cohen (Pittsburgh: Duquesne University Press, 1987), 92–3. See also, Emmanuel Lévinas, 'De la description à l'existence', in *En découvrant l'existence avec Husserl et Heidegger*, third edition (Paris: Vrin, 2001), 141–2.
60 Emmanuel Lévinas, *Totality and Infinity: An Essay on Exteriority*, trans. Alphonso Lingis (Pittsburgh: Duquesne University Press, 1996), 293; *Totalité et Infini: Essai sur l'extériorité* (Paris: Le Livre de Poche, 2001), 326.
61 *Totality and Infinity*, 50.
62 *Theaetetus*, in *The Dialogues of Plato*, IV: 152a–e.
63 *Totality and Infinity*, 59–60.
64 *Totality and Infinity*, 277, 64.
65 *Totality and Infinity*, 218, 102.
66 *Totality and Infinity*, 102; *Totalité et Infini*, 105.
67 *Totality and Infinity*, 103.
68 'Violence and Metaphysics', 311 n. 1; Emmanuel Lévinas, 'The Trace of the Other', in *Deconstruction in Context: Literature and Philosophy*, ed. Mark C. Taylor, trans. A. Lingus (Chicago: University of Chicago Press, 1986), 347.

69 *Totality and Infinity*, 103–4.
70 'The Trace of the Other', 347; 'La trace de l'autre', in *En découvrant l'existence avec Husserl et Heidegger*, third edition (Paris: Vrin, 2001), 265.
71 Emmanuel Lévinas, *Otherwise than Being or Beyond Essence*, trans. Alphonso Lingis (Pittsburgh: Duquesne University Press, 2000), 95, 110, 166. See also Emmanuel Lévinas, *Is It Righteous to Be? Interviews with Emmanuel Levinas*, ed. Jill Robbins (Stanford: Stanford University Press, 2001), 278. Derrida refers to the *epekeina tēs ousia* as 'the hyphen, so to speak between Plato and Plotinus' in *On Touching – Jean-Luc Nancy*, 121. See also, 282–3.
72 'The Trace of the Other', 348.
73 Auguste Diès translates these two remarkable triads of negation from the *Sophist* 238c as '*ni prononcer, ni dire, ni penser le non-être en lui-même*' and '*impensable, ineffable, imprononçable, inexprimable*', *Le sophiste*, in *Platon oeuvres complètes* (Paris: Les Belles Lettres, 1955), 7.3. In his reading of this passage Heidegger concludes 'there is no *lógos* about *mē ón*', '*mē ón* is always closed from *lógos*', *Plato's Sophist*, trans. Richard Rojcewicz and André Schuwer (Bloomington: Indiana University Press, 1997), 292.
74 'Cogito and the History of Madness', 62.
75 In *Time and the Other*, Lévinas writes, 'it is toward a pluralism that does not merge into unity that I should like to make my way and, if this can be dared, break with Parmenides' (42).
76 'Violence and Metaphysics', 126; 'Violence et métaphysique', 185. See for example, *Parmenides*, 139.
77 See also, 'Violence and Metaphysics', 147.
78 'Violence and Metaphysics', 89; 'Violence et métaphysique', 133. See also, 'Violence and Metaphysics', 114. Derrida does not offer a source here for his quotation, 'say farewell to an unnameable opposite of Being', which in the French reads, '*dire adieu à je ne sais quel contraire de l'être*' (133). I have not been able to find this quote in Lévinas' *Le temps et l'autre*, which the text suggests could be its source. On the other hand, it could be from a French translation of the *Sophist*. The very indeterminacy of this citation (Lévinas *or* Plato) amply illustrates the lack of clear determination in the relationship between Plato, Parmenides, the *Parmenides* and the *Sophist*.
79 'Violence and Metaphysics', 127.
80 *The Problem of Genesis in Husserl's Philosophy*, 191 n. 36. See the *Sophist*, 253. In an interview from 1981 with Richard Kearney, Derrida reiterates the importance of starting with the *Republic* and the *Sophist* in his reading of Plato: 'From the very beginning of Greek philosophy the self-identity of the *Logos* is already fissured and divided. I think one can discern signs of such fissures of "différance" in every great philosopher: the "Good beyond Being" (*epekeina tēs ousias*) of Plato's *Republic*, for example, or the confrontation with the "Stranger" in *The Sophist* are already traces of an alterity which refuses to be totally domesticated', in Derrida, 'Deconstruction and the Other', 117.
81 'Plato's Pharmacy', 163–7. See also, *Of Grammatology*, 20.

82 Plato, *Charmides*, in *The Dialogues of Plato*, I; *Plato*, trans. W. R. M. Lamb (London: Heinemann, 1955).
83 Plato, *Lysis*, in *The Dialogues of Plato*, I.
84 Plato, *Protagoras*, in *The Dialogues of Plato*, I.
85 Plato, *Euthydemus*, in *The Dialogues of Plato*, I; *Plato*, trans. W. R. M. Lamb (Cambridge, MA: Harvard University Press, 1977).
86 Plato, *Gorgias*, in *The Dialogues of Plato*, II; Plato, trans. W. R. M. Lamb (Cambridge, MA: Harvard University Press, 1991).
87 *Phaedrus*; *Plato*, trans. Harold North Fowler (London: Heinemann, 1953).
88 Plato, *Symposium*, in *The Dialogues of Plato*, I.
89 Plato, *Timaeus*, in *The Dialogues of Plato*, III; *Plato*, trans. R. G. Bury (London: Heinemann, 1961).
89 'Plato's Pharmacy', 65; 'La pharmacie de Platon', 82.

2: HERODOTUS: ALMOST PRE-SOCRATIC

1 Derrida, '*Ousia* and *Grammē*: Note on a Note from *Being and Time*', 63.
2 Jean-Pierre Vernant and Pierre Vidal-Naquet, *Myth and Tragedy in Ancient Greece*, trans. Janet Lloyd (New York: Zone Books, 1990).
3 A. R. Burn, 'Introduction' to Herodotus, *The Histories*, trans. Aubrey de Sélincourt (London: Penguin, 1972), 10–15.
4 Diogenes Laertius, *Lives of Eminent Philosophers*, trans. R. D. Hicks, 2 vols (Cambridge, MA: Harvard University Press, 1980), I. 12, 40. Hegel cites these distinctions in his *Lectures on the History of Philosophy I: Greek Philosophy to Plato*, trans. E. S. Haldane, intro. Frederick C. Beister (Lincoln: University of Nebraska Press, 1995), 156, 199.
5 Jonathan Barnes, *Early Greek Philosophers* (London: Penguin, 1987), 13.
6 A. R. Burn, 'Introduction', 7.
7 *Early Greek Philosophy*, 19–22.
8 Martin Heidegger, 'Anaximander's Saying', in *Off the Beaten Track*, ed. and trans. Julian Young and Kenneth Hynes (Cambridge: Cambridge University Press, 2002), 243. It is interesting that in *Being and Time* Heidegger links Thucydides to 'the ontological sections' of Plato's the *Parmenides* and Aristotle's *Metaphysics*. He makes no mention of Herodotus: *Being and Time*, trans. John Macquarrie and Edward Robinson (Oxford: Blackwell, 1990), 63 (H 39). On the differences of the reception of Herodotus and Thucydides, see Arnaldo Momigliano, 'The Place of Herodotus in the History of Historiography', in *Studies in Historiography* (New York: Harper Torchbooks, 1966), 127–42.
9 'Anaximander's Saying', 244.
10 Martin Heidegger, 'What Calls for Thinking', in *Basic Writings*, ed. David Farrell Krell (San Francisco: Harper, 1993), 375–6. See Carol J. White, 'Heidegger and the Greeks', in *A Companion to Heidegger*, ed. Hubert L. Dreyfus and Mark A. Wrathall (Oxford: Blackwell, 2005), 121–40, and David C. Jacobs (ed.) *The Presocratics After Heidegger* (Albany: State University of New York Press, 1999).

11 Hegel, *Lectures on the History of Philosophy I*, 167. Aristotle, *Metaphysics*, in *The Complete Works of Aristotle*, ed. Jonathan Barnes, 2 vols (Princeton: Princeton University Press, 1984), I. See also, Harold Cherniss, *Aristotle's Criticism of Presocratic Philosophy* (Baltimore: Johns Hopkins University Press, 1935).
12 Hegel, *Lectures on the History of Philosophy I*, 163; *Vorlesungen über die Geschichte der Philosophie I* (Frankfurt am Main: Suhrkamp, 1986), 188.
13 Martin Heidegger and Eugen Fink, *Heraclitus Seminar*, trans. Charles H. Seibert (Evanston: Northwestern University Press, 1993), 7.
14 *Heraclitus Seminar*, 24. See also, Erin O'Connell, *Heraclitus and Derrida: Presocratic Deconstruction* (New York: Peter Lang, 2005).
15 Rosalind Thomas, *Herodotus in Context: Ethnography, Science and the Art of Persuasion* (Cambridge: Cambridge University Press, 2000), 7, 74.
16 Cicero, *De Legibus*, trans. Clinton Walker Keyes (London: Heinemann, 1928), 1. 1. 3–5.
17 Momigliano, 'The Place of Herodotus in the History of Historiography', 141.
18 François Hartog, *The Mirror of Herodotus: The Representation of the Other in the Writing of History*, trans. Janet Lloyd (Berkeley: University of California Press, 1988); Thomas, *Herodotus in Context*; Rosaria Vignolo Munson, *Telling Wonders: Ethnographic and Political Discourse in the Work of Herodotus* (Ann Arbor: University of Michigan Press, 2001).
19 Hans-Georg Gadamer, *The Beginning of Philosophy*, trans. Rod Coltman (New York: Continuum, 2001), 10.
20 Martin Heidegger, *Plato's Sophist*, trans. Richard Rojcewicz and André Schuwer (Bloomington: Indiana University Press, 1997), 9, 157.
21 Derrida, 'Cogito and the History of Madness', 40.
22 Derrida, 'Some Statements and Truisms about Neologisms, Newisms, Postisms, Parasitisms, and other Small Seismisms'.
23 '*Ousia* and *Grammē*', 63. See also, Derrida, *Of Spirit*, 23–7.
24 Derrida, *Of Grammatology*, 3; *De la grammatologie*, 12.
25 Derrida, 'Heidegger's Ear: Philopolemology (*Geschlecht* IV)', 173. See also, 190–3.
26 Derrida, 'Plato's Pharmacy', 61–171. See also Geoffrey Bennington, 'Mosaic Fragment: If Derrida were an Egyptian . . .', in *Derrida: A Critical Reader*, ed. David Wood (Oxford: Blackwell, 1992), 97–119.
27 Herodotus, *The History*, trans. David Grene (Chicago: University of Chicago Press, 1988), 665–6.
28 G. W. F. Hegel, *Science of Logic*, trans. A. V. Miller (London: Allen & Unwin, 1969), 106–7.
29 Barnes, *Early Greek Philosophers*, 84.
30 Diogenes Laertius, *Lives of Eminent Philosophers*, I: 35–6.
31 Hegel, *Lectures on the History of Philosophy I*, 156; *Vorlesungen über die Geschichte der Philosophie I*, 180. Translation modified.
32 Derrida, 'Envois', 20; 'Envois' [French], 25.
33 Derrida, *Specters of Marx*, 17; *Spectres de Marx*, 41.

34 Aristotle, *Physics*, in *The Complete Works of Aristotle*, ed. Jonathan Barnes, 2 vols (Princeton: Princeton University Press, 1984); *The Physics*, trans. Philip H. Wicksteed and Francis M. Cornford (London: Heinemann, 1928).
35 Herodotus, *The Histories*, trans. Aubrey de Sélincourt (London: Penguin, 1972), 43.
36 The Greek for both Grene and de Selincourt's translations is taken from *Herodotus*, trans. A. D. Godley, 4 vols (London: Heinemann, 1961).
37 'Cogito and the History of Madness', 36; 'Cogito et histoire de la folie', 59. Translation modified.
38 'Cogito and the History of Madness', 43.
39 See also, *Of Grammatology*, 219.
40 'Cogito and the History of Madness', 43; 'Cogito et histoire de la folie', 68. Translation modified.
41 Diogenes Laertius, *Lives of Eminent Philosophers*, I: 47–69.
42 Diogenes, III: 277.
43 Hegel, *Lectures on the History of Philosophy I*, 158.
44 Hegel, *Lectures on the History of Philosophy I*, 162; *Vorlesungen über die Geschichte der Philosophie I*, 186.
45 Herodotus, *The History*, trans. A. D. Godley, I: 1. 5.
46 Derrida, 'Typewriter Ribbon: Limited Ink (2)', 73.
47 Sophocles, *The Three Theban Plays*, trans. Robert Fagles, intro. Bernard Knox (London: Penguin, 1984), 215 (lines 1069–71). See also, Vernant and Vidal-Naquet, *Myth and Tragedy in Ancient Greece*, 44–8, 124–6. On Derrida's reading of chance, see 'My Chances/Mes Chances: A Rendezvous with some Epicurean Sterophonies', 1–32.
48 On Derrida's reading of Heidegger's re-gathering the *logos*, see 'Heidegger's Ear', 187. On the future of the past, see Heidegger, *Being and Time*, H 383–5.
49 Derrida, *The Other Heading: Reflections on Today's Europe*, 17–18.
50 See *The Histories*, trans. de Sélincourt, 280.
51 Derrida, 'Violence and Metaphysics', 117; 'Violence et métaphysique', 173.

3: THE HISTORY – OF LITERATURE

1 Immanuel Kant, *Critique of Pure Reason*, trans. Paul Guyer (Cambridge: Cambridge University Press, 1998), 258 [B154]. A shorter version of this chapter appeared as 'Derrida and the History – of Literature', in *Textual Practice* 21.2 (2007): 313–34. I would like to thank Routledge for permission to reprint this work. See http://www.tandf.co. uk/journals.
2 Derrida, 'Violence and Metaphysics', 117.
3 Derrida, 'Outwork, Prefacing', 54, 56; 'Hors livre: préfaces', 71–2, 74. See also Derrida, 'This Strange Institution Called Literature', 33–75. See, Timothy Clark, *Derrida, Heidegger, Blanchot: Sources of Derrida's Notion and Practice of Literature* (Cambridge: Cambridge University Press, 1992), 111–16.

4 See, Peter Fenves, 'Derrida and History: Some Questions Derrida Pursues in His Early Writings', in *Jacques Derrida and the Humanities: A Critical Reader*, ed. Tom Cohen (Cambridge: Cambridge University Press, 2001), 271–95; Joshua Kates, *Essential History: Jacques Derrida and the Development of Deconstruction* (Evanston: Northwestern University Press, 2005), 158–217.
5 Derrida, 'The Double Session', 191; 'La double séance', 235.
6 On the line in literature, see J. Hillis Miller, 'Line', in *Ariadne's Thread: Story Lines* (New Haven: Yale University Press, 1992), 1–27; William Watkin, 'The line that does not lie down: enjambment, the tomb and the body', in *On Mourning: Theories of Loss in Modern Literature* (Edinburgh: Edinburgh University Press, 2004), 84–119.
7 'The Double Session', 191; 'La double séance', 235.
8 Derrida, *Artaud le Moma*, 18, 89. Derrida first refers to the hyphen in this way in 'The Double Session', 221. See also, *Monolingualism of the Other*, 11. See also Peggy Kamuf, 'Singular Sense, Second-Hand', in *Book of Addresses* (Stanford: Stanford University Press), 268–81
9 Derrida, *Glas*, 45a.
10 See, for example, Paul Crumbley, *Inflections of the Pen: Dash and Voice in Emily Dickinson* (Lexington: University of Kentucky Press, 1997).
11 Emily Dickinson, *The Complete Poems*, ed. Thomas H. Johnson (London: Faber & Faber, 1987), 8 (no. 6).
12 Dickinson, 44 (no. 86).
13 Dickinson, 50 (no. 103). In 'Heidegger's Ear: Philopolemology (*Geschlecht* IV)', Derrida writes of two words being separated by a hyphen, 'as if to make the heard better heard in the unheard of what is not heard' (210).
14 Dickinson, 118 (no. 258).
15 Dickinson, 129 (no. 280).
16 Dickinson, 88 (no. 187).
17 Derrida, *Of Grammatology*, lxxxix.
18 See, for example, Derrida, *Genèses, généalogies, genres et le génie*, 67.
19 Derrida writes of 'le tiret suspendant le mot *Distanz*' in Nietzsche's text in *Spurs: Nietzsche's Styles/Éperons: Les Styles de Nietzsche*, 48.
20 'The Double Session', 183; 'La double séance', 225.
21 I have attempted to address Derrida's reading of the history of truth, of the historicity of ideal objectivity (Husserl) and the speculative history of philosophy (Hegel), in *The Impossible Mourning of Jacques Derrida* (London: Continuum, 2006), 20–73. See also, Derrida, 'The Law of Genre'.
22 'The Double Session', 183; 'La double séance', 226.
23 'The Double Session', 191; 'La double séance', 235.
24 'The Double Session', 193; 'La double séance', 238.
25 *Spurs/Éperons*, 86–7. My translation.
26 Derrida, *Edmund Husserl's Origin of Geometry: An Introduction*, 87–8.
27 *An Introduction*, 88–90.
28 *An Introduction*, 93–5. On the catastrophic in Derrida' s work, see

Catherine Malabou, 'The Parting of the Ways: Drift, Arrival, Catastrophe', in *Counterpath: Travelling with Jacques Derrida*, trans. David Wills (Stanford: Stanford University Press, 2004).

29 *An Introduction*, 123, 128.

30 Aristotle, *On the Soul*, in *The Complete Works of Aristotle*, ed. Jonathan Barnes, 2 vols (Princeton: Princeton University Press, 1984), II: 409a.

31 Derrida, 'Force and Signification', 16.

32 'Force and Signification', 19; 'Force et signification', 33.

33 'Force and Signification', 15; 'Force et signification', 27.

34 *Of Grammatology*, lxxxix–xc; *De la grammatologie*, 8.

35 *Of Grammatology*, 85–7, 72, 289–91.

36 Heidegger, *Being and Time*, H 420–1, H 428. See also note xxx, pp. 500–501.

37 Derrida, '*Ousia* and *Grammē*', 57–8.

38 *Critique of Pure Reason*, 163; *Kritik der Reinen Vernunft* (Frankfurt am Main: Im Insel, 1964) [A33–4; B49–50]. All further references to the German text will be from this edition. Derrida cites this passage in '*Ousia* and *Grammē*', 49 n. 28. In *Of Grammatology*, Derrida had already noted that Kant cannot avoid the line: 'And from my present point of view, there is much to say on the concept of the *line* [ligne] which so intervenes in the Kantian critique. (Time, the form of all sensible phenomena, internal *and* external, seems to dominate space, the form of external sensible phenomena; but it is a time that one may always represent by a line and the "refutation of idealism" will reverse this order)' (290; 410). On the reversal of this order, see *Critique of Pure Reason*, 326–8 [B274–9].

39 *Critique of Pure Reason*, 258 [B154].

40 Aristotle, *Physics*, in *The Complete Works of Aristotle*, ed. Jonathan Barnes, 2 vols (Princeton: Princeton University Press, 1984) I: 223a, 222a.

41 '*Ousia* and *Grammē*', 59; '*Ousia* et *Grammè*', 68.

42 In Derrida's French translation of Aristotle, 'a pause is necessary' becomes 'l'arrêt est nécessaire', '*Ousia* et *Grammè*', 68. Derrida's reading of Aristotle here can perhaps be seen as a first glimpse of his later reading of the totality that *stops* itself in *Glas*, 106–7a. See also Derrida's reading of Blanchot's *L'Arrêt de mort*, in 'LIVING ON. Border Lines', 75–176.

43 '*Ousia* and *Grammē*', 59–60.

44 '*Ousia* and *Grammē*', 65–7. See also, 'Différance', 24.

45 *Of Grammatology*, 203; *De la grammatologie*, 289.

46 Derrida, 'Ellipsis', 300; 'Ellipse', 436.

47 *Of Grammatology*, 74–5; *De la grammatologie*, 110.

48 Derrida, 'Avertissement', in *La Vérité en peinture*, 4. This is quoted on the back cover of the English translation of *The Truth in Painting*.

49 Derrida, *Memoirs of the Blind*, 3.

50 Derrida, *The Problem of Genesis*, xvii–xix; *Edmund Husserl's Origin of Geometry: An Introduction*, 26, 51. See Paola Marrati, *Genesis and*

Trace: Derrida Reading Husserl and Heidegger, trans. Simon Sparks (Stanford: Stanford University Press, 2005).

51 Derrida, 'Parergon', 20–1 (trans. modified); 'Parergon' [French], 25. The last sentence of the quote ends without a full stop, marking one of the gaps in the text, of the gap between the seminar and the published fragment. See also, Georges Didi-Huberman, *L'image survivante: Histoire de l'art et le temps des fantômes selon Aby Warburg* (Paris: Minuit, 2002). I would like to thank Gretchen Schiller for bringing this work to my attention.

52 Derrida, 'Passe-Partout', 4; 'Passe-Partout' [French], 8.

53 See *The Impossible Mourning of Jacques Derrida*, 74–124.

54 *Being and Time*; *Sein und Zeit*, H 43, H 62.

55 *Being and Time*, H 104–6.

56 *Spurs*, 48–51; Derrida, 'Pas', in *Parages*, 28, 31. See also, Malabou, 54–5.

57 Martin Heidegger, 'The Origin of the Work of Art', in *Basic Writings*, ed. David Farrell Krell, trans. Albert Hofstadter, revised and expanded edition (San Fransisco: Harper, 1993), 188; 'Der Ursprung des Kunstwerkes', in *Holzwege* (Frankfurt am Main: Vittorio Klostermann, 1950), 51.

58 'Passe-Partout', 6; 'Passe-Partout', 10.

59 'Parergon', 32, 121, 128–9. Martin Heidegger, 'The Way to Language', in *Basic Writings*, ed. and trans. David Farrell Krell (San Fransisco: Harper, 1993), 407–12. See also, Derrida, *Of Spirit: Heidegger and the Question*, 129–36.

60 Derrida, 'Restitutions of the Truth in Pointing', 280.

61 Derrida, 'Cartouches', 193–4.

62 'Restitutions', 303; 'Restitutions' [French], 346. See also (in the English edition), 318–19, 324, 336–7, 340, 354.

63 'Passe-Partout', 6–7; 'Passe-Partout' (French), 11.

64 'Passe-Partout', 11; 'Passe-Partout' (French), 16.

65 Derrida, 'The Retrait of Metaphor', 119; 'Le retrait de la métaphore', 82. See also, Philip Lewis, 'Vers la traduction abusive', in *Les fins de l'homme: à partir du travail de Jacques Derrida* (Paris: Galilée, 1981), 253–61. Derrida comments on his translation in the discussion that follows Lewis' paper (268). See also his earlier remarks on *le retrait* (160).

66 'The Retrait of Metaphor', 117. On the re-mark, see also Rodolphe Gasché, *The Tain of the Mirror: Derrida and the Philosophy of Reflection* (Cambridge [MA]: Harvard University Press, 1986), 217–24.

67 'The Retrait of Metaphor', 127. See also Malabou, *Counterpath*, 125–33.

68 'The Retrait of Metaphor', 123; 'Le retrait de la métaphore', 87. Translation modified.

69 'The Retrait of Metaphor', 124; 'Le retrait de la métaphore', 88.

70 Derrida, 'This Strange Institution Called Literature', 54, 68.

71 John Dryden, *Annus Mirabilis: The Year of Wonders, 1666*, in *The Major Works*, ed. Keith Walker (Oxford: Oxford University Press, 2003), 24.

72 *Annus Mirabilis*, 26.
73 John Dryden, *An Essay of Dramatic Poesy*, in *The Major Works*, ed. Keith Walker (Oxford: Oxford University Press, 2003), 92.
74 *An Essay of Dramatic Poesy*, 95.
75 *An Essay of Dramatic Poesy*, 96.
76 Plato, *Symposium*, in *The Dialogues of Plato*, trans. Benjamin Jowett, 5 vols (Oxford: Clarendon Press, 1892), I: 207d–e.
77 I trace this economy *of* death *in* life in *Derrida and Disinterest*, 117–25.
78 Aristotle, *Poetics*, in *The Complete Works of Aristotle*, ed. Jonathan Barnes, 2 vols (Princeton: Princeton University Press, 1984), I: 1451a–b. See also, G. E. M. de Ste Croix, 'Aristotle on History and Poetry (*Poetics*, 9, 1451a36–b11)', in *Essays on Aristotle's Poetics*, ed. Amélie Oksenberg Rorty (Princeton: Princeton University Press, 1992), 23–32.
79 Sir Philip Sidney, *The Defence of Poesy*, in *The Major Works*, ed. Katherine Duncan-Jones (Oxford: Oxford University Press, 2002), 220, 214. See also, Phyllis Rackin, *Stages of History: Shakespeare's English Chronicles* (London: Routledge, 1991), 104–16.
80 G. W. F. Hegel, *Lectures on the History of Philosophy I: Greek Philosophy to Plato*, trans. E. S. Haldane, intro. Frederick C. Beister (Lincoln: University of Nebraska Press, 1995), 9.
81 'Parergon', 23. On Derrida's own remarkable responses to the question of the poem, see 'Che cos' è la poesia?' See, Timothy Clark, *The Theory of Inspiration: Composition as a Crisis of Subjectivity in Romantic and Post-Romantic Writing* (Manchester: Manchester University Press, 1997), 261–71. See also Catherine Malabou, in Malabou and Derrida, *Counterpath*, 261–79; Nicholas Royle, *Jacques Derrida* (London: Routledge, 2003), 129–42.
82 *An Essay of Dramatic Poesy*, 96. In his critical notes, Keith Walker cites both Hesiod, and Homer as the sources for this passage. Hesiod writes, 'we know how to say many false things / that seem like true sayings, / but we know also how to speak the truth / when we wish to', *The Works and Days*; *Theogony*; *The Shield of Herakles*, trans. Richmond Lattimore (Ann Arbor: University of Michigan Press, 1978), 27–30. Homer writes, 'He spoke, and made the many falsehoods of his tale seem like the truth', in *The Odyssey*, trans. A. T. Murray, 2 vols (London: Heinemann, 1966), II: XIX: 203.
83 'Parergon', 80. See also Derrida, 'Economimesis', 263–93.
84 'Parergon', 20; 'Parergon' (French), 24–5.
85 See, *Of Grammatology*, 287–95.
86 David Daiches, *A Critical History of English Literature*, 2 vols (London: Secker and Warburg, 1960), I: 3–11.
87 *Beowulf*, trans. Kevin Crossley-Holland (Oxford: Oxford University Press, 1999), 5. See also, David Sandner, 'Tracking Grendel: The Uncanny in *Beowulf*', *Extrapolation* 40.2 (1999): 162–76.
88 See M. I. Steblin-Kamenskij, *The Saga Mind* (Odense: Odense Universitetsforlag, 1973).
89 J. J. Jusserand, *A Literary History of the English People – from the Origins to the Civil War*, 3 vols (London: C. Fisher Unwin, 1925), 50.

90 *The Cambridge History of English Literature*, ed. A. W. Ward and A. R. Waller, *Volume 1: From the Beginnings to the Cycles of Romance* (Cambridge: Cambridge University Press, 1907), 1–2, 22.
91 Thomas Warton, *History of English Poetry: From the Twelfth to the Close of the Sixteenth Century*, ed. W. Carew Hazlitt, pref. Richard Price, 4 vols (London: Reeves and Turner, 1871), I. Edward Gibbon, *The History of the Decline and Fall of the Roman Empire*, ed. David Womersley, 3 vols (London: Penguin, 1994), I: 1.
92 *History of English Poetry*, 3.
93 *Critique of Pure Reason*, 228 [A98].
94 *History of English Poetry*, 4.
95 *History of English Poetry*, 4–6.
96 Derrida, 'At This Very Moment in This Work Here I Am', 30.
97 *Edmund Husserl's Origin of Geometry: An Introduction*, 61
98 *History of English Poetry*, 92–3, 103–5, 110. See also Claude Kappler, *Monstres, Démons, et Merveilles à la fin du Moyen Age* (Paris: Payot, 1980).
99 On Derrida's Notion of monstrosity, see Royle, *Jacques Derrida*, 103–18.
100 Derrida, 'Negotiations', 13. See also, Simon Morgan Wortham, *Counter-institutions: Jacques Derrida and the Question of the University* (New York: Fordham, 2006).

4. *ENTER* TIME

1 Derrida, 'The Time is Out of Joint', 18.
2 William Shakespeare, *The Tragedy of Hamlet, Prince of Denmark*, in *The Norton Shakespeare, Based on the Oxford Edition*, ed. Stephen Greenblatt and others (New York: Norton, 1997), I. 1. 188–9.
3 William Shakespeare, *The Winter's Tale*, in *The Norton Shakespeare, Based on the Oxford Edition*, ed. Stephen Greenblatt and others (New York: Norton, 1997), IV. 1. 1–8.
4 Frederick Kiefer, 'The Iconography of Time in *The Winter's Tale*', *Renaissance and Reformation* 23 (1999): 49.
5 Brian Vickers (ed.), *Shakespeare: The Critical Heritage*, 6 vols (London: Routledge, 1974–81), IV: 207–18 (Garrick), 229–42 (Marsh).
6 Vickers, IV: 244.
7 Vickers, IV: 256. See also Dr Johnson's comments on Thursday 19 October 1769 in James Boswell, *Life of Johnson*, ed. R. W. Chapman, intro. Pat Rogers (Oxford: Oxford University Press, 1998), 416.
8 G. V. Coyne, M. A. Hoskin and O. Pedersen, *Gregorian Reform of the Calendar: Proceedings of the Vatican Conference to Commemorate its 400th Anniversary 1582–1982* (Vatican: Pontificia Academia Scientiarum, 1983), 268–73. The reference to 'that calendar trick' (*coup de calendrier*) is taken from Derrida, *Glas*, 107b. On his reading of the date and dating, see 'Shibboleth: For Paul Celan'.
9 *Gregorian Reform of the Calendar*, 22–30.

10 Paul Alkon, 'Changing the Calendar', *Eighteenth-Century Life* 7 (1982): 1–18; Robert Poole, '"Give Us Our Eleven Days!": Calendar Reform in Eighteenth-Century England', *Past and Present* 149 (1995): 95–139.
11 Chesterfield, Philip Dormer Stanhope, Earl of, *Lord Chesterfield's Letters*, ed. David Roberts (Oxford: Oxford University Press, 1992).
12 David Garrick, *The Letters of David Garrick*, ed. David M. Little and George M. Kahrl, 2 vols (London: Oxford University Press, 1963).
13 Samuel Johnson, *The Letters of Samuel Johnson, Volume 1: 1731–1772*, ed. Brue Redford (Princeton: Princeton University Press, 1992), 58.
14 Joseph Ames, *A Collection of Notes of journeys, memoranda, copies of inscriptions, drawings of antiquities, etc., entitled on cover, 'Mr. Ames's Minute book'* (Bodleian MS. Top. gen. e. 58).
15 Horace Walpole, *The Yale Edition of the Correspondence of Horace Walpole: Horace Walpole's Correspondence with Hannah More*, ed. W. S. Lewis, Robert A. Smith and Charles H. Bennet, 48 vols (London: Oxford University Press, 1961), 31: 306; *The Yale Edition of the Correspondence of Horace Walpole: Horace Walpole's Correspondence with Mary and Agnes Berry*, ed. W. S. Lewis and A. Dayle Wallace, 48 vols (London: Oxford University Press, 1944), 12: 152–3.
16 Henry Fielding, *The History of Tom Jones, A Foundling*, ed. R. P. C. Mutter (London: Penguin, 1985), 167.
17 Fielding, *The History of Tom Jones*, 59–60.
18 See Paul Ricoeur, *Time and Narrative*, III, trans. Kathleen Blamey and David Pellauer (Chicago: University of Chicago Press, 1990).
19 Vickers, *The Critical Heritage*, II 222–3.
20 William Shakespeare, *The Second Part of Henry the Fourth*, in *The Norton Shakespeare, Based on the Oxford Edition*, ed. Stephen Greenblatt and others (New York: Norton, 1997), Introduction.
21 William Shakespeare, *The Life of Henry the Fifth*, in *The Norton Shakespeare, Based on the Oxford Edition*, ed. Stephen Greenblatt and others (New York: Norton, 1997), Prologue 8–15.
22 Vickers, *The Critical Heritage*, V: 180.
23 Vickers, IV: 287.
24 Theresa M. Kriek, 'The Triumph of Time: Paradox in *The Winter's Tale*', *Centennial Review* 26 (1982): 347; Kiefer, 'The Iconography of Time in *The Winter's Tale*', 53; Nevill Coghill, 'Six Points of Stage-Craft in *The Winter's Tale*', *Shakespeare Survey* 11 (1958): 36; Inga-Stina Ewbank, 'The Triumph of Time in *The Winter's Tale*', *A Review of English Literature* 5 (1964): 84, 90; William Blissett, 'The Wide Gap of Time: *The Winter's Tale*', *English Literary Renaissance* 1 (1971): 55–6.
25 Michael D. Bristol, 'In Search of the Bear: Spatiotemporal Form and the Heterogeneity of Economies in *The Winter's Tale*', *Shakespeare Quarterly* 42 (1991): 145–67.
26 Aristotle, *Poetics*, in *The Complete Works of Aristotle*, ed. Jonathan Barnes, 2 vols (Princeton: Princeton University Press, 1984), I; Aristotle, *Poetics*, trans. Stephen Halliwell (Cambridge, MA: Harvard University Press, 1995). Further references to this work will be cited in the text.

27 John Dryden, *An Essay of Dramatic Poesy*, in *The Major Works*, ed. Keith Walker (Oxford: Oxford University Press, 2003), 79–83, 87, 107.
28 Ludovico Castelvetro, *Castelvetro on the Art of Poetry*, trans. Andrew Bongiorno (New York: Medieval and Renaissance Texts and Studies, 1984). I would like to thank Paige Newmark for bringing this edition to my attention. Castelvetro's *Poetica d'Aristotele vulgarizzata et sposta* was first published in Vienna in 1570. A second posthumous edition appeared in Basel in 1576. See, Thora Burnley Jones and Barnard de Bear Nicol, *Neo-Classical Dramatic Criticism 1560–1770* (Cambridge: Cambridge University Press, 1976), 27–34.
29 Pierre Corneille, *Trois Discours sur le poème dramatique*, ed. Bénédicte Louvat and Marc Escola (Paris: Flammarion, 1999), 65. My translation. For a brief history of the reception of the *Poetics* see, Stephen Halliwell, *Aristotle's Poetics* (London: Duckworth, 2000), 293–309.
30 *An Essay of Dramatic Poesy*, 86–8, 107–8.
31 Virginia Woolf, *Orlando: A Biography*, ed. Brenda Lyons, intro. Sandra M. Gilbert (London: Penguin, 1993), 16.
32 Erich Auerbach, *Mimesis: The Representation of Reality in Western Literature*, trans. Willard R. Trask (Princeton: Princeton University Press, 1991), 472.
33 *The Tragedy of Hamlet*, V. 1. 70, 170–5.
34 William Shakespeare, *The Life of Timon of Athens*, in *The Norton Shakespeare, Based on the Oxford Edition*, ed. Stephen Greenblatt and others (New York: Norton, 1997), 2252. This is in the list of 'The Persons of the Play'.
35 *The Life of Timon of Athens*, I. 1. 257–9.
36 In the midst of his discussion of *Hamlet*, Derrida notes that Marx himself had written on *Timon of Athens*, in *Specters of Marx*, 41–4.
37 Plato, *Symposium*, in *The Dialogues of Plato*, trans. Benjamin Jowett, 5 vols (Oxford: Clarendon Press, 1892), I: 174–5. Derrida discusses the *Symposium* (*le Banquet*) in 'To Speculate – on "Freud"', 344, 369–75.
38 William Shakespeare, *Troilus and Cressida*, in *The Norton Shakespeare, Based on the Oxford Edition*, ed. Stephen Greenblatt and others (New York: Norton, 1997), II. 2. 162–6.
39 Aristotle, *Nicomachean Ethics*, ed. and trans. Roger Crisp (Cambridge: Cambridge University Press, 2004), 1094b–1095a.
40 Michelle and Charles Martindale, *Shakespeare and the Uses of Antiquity: An Introductory Essay* (London; Routledge, 1990), 95; W. R. Elton, 'Aristotle's *Nicomachean Ethics* and Shakespeare's *Troilus and Cressida*', *Journal of History of Ideas* 58 (1997): 331–7.
41 Nicholas Royle, *After Derrida* (Manchester: Manchester University Press, 1995); *Jacques Derrida* (London: Routledge, 2003); *The Uncanny* (Manchester: Manchester University Press, 2003); 'The Poet: Julius Caesar and the Democracy to Come', *Oxford Literary Review* 25 (2003): 39–61; 'Not Now', *Epoché* 10.2 (2006): 379–93; *How To Read Shakespeare* (London: Granta, 2005). See also, Derrida, 'Aphorism Countertime'; *Specters of Marx*; 'The Time is Out of Joint'; 'What is a "Relevant" Translation?' I have been fortunate to hear a

number of Nicholas Royle's illuminating papers on Derrida and Shakespeare and would like to dedicate this chapter to him and to his work.

42 Thomas M. Greene, *The Vulnerable Text: Essays on Renaissance Literature* (New York: Columbia University Press, 1986), 218–27. See also, Phyllis Rackin, *Stages of History: Shakespeare's English Chronicles* (London: Routledge, 1991), 1–12, 86–145.
43 Peter Burke, *The Renaissance Sense of the Past* (London: Edward Arnold, 1969), 138–41.
44 *The Tragedy of Hamlet*, IV. 4. 9.25–9.29. My emphasis.
45 Aristotle, *Physics*, in *The Complete Works of Aristotle*, ed. Jonathan Barnes, 2 vols (Princeton: Princeton University Press, 1984), I; *The Physics*, trans. Philip H. Wicksteed and Francis M. Cornford (London: Heinemann, 1928). Further references to this work will be cited in the text.
46 Ursula Coope, *Time for Aristotle: Physics IV: 10–14* (Oxford: Clarendon Press, 2005), 1.
47 Derrida, '*Ousia* and *Grammē*', 61. Derrida is referring to *Physics* 220b. See also, Derrida, *Politics of Friendship*, 1–25. In his *Lectures on the History of Philosophy I*, Hegel remarks that for the Pythagoreans, 'number is the substance or the essence of things; number is not sensuous, nor is it pure thought, but it is a non-sensuous object of sense' (170). See also, 194–239.
48 Michel Foucault, *The Order of Things: An Archaeology of the Human Sciences*, trans. Alan Sheridan (London: Routledge, 2002), xviii.
49 *Being and Time*; *Sein und Zeit*, H 420–1, H 428. See also note xxx, 500–501 in the English edition.
50 Derrida, *Of Grammatology*, 72.
51 '*Ousia* and *Grammē*', 39–40. As Derrida notes, Hegel will illustrate this problem by arguing that time is the *Aufhebung* of space (42–3). Derrida returned to his reading of the *Physics* in his 1977–78 seminars, which formed the basis of his 1991 text *Given Time: 1. Counterfeit Money*, 8–9, 27–8. Accounts of '*Ousia* and *Grammē*' include: Timothy Clark, ' "Time after Time": Temporality, Temporalization', *Oxford Literary Review* 9 (1987): 119–34; John Protevi, *Time and Exteriority: Aristotle, Heidegger, Derrida* (Lewisburg: Bucknell University Press, 1994).
52 '*Ousia* and *Grammē*', 46, 61, 64.
53 '*Ousia* and *Grammē*', 55.
54 Derrida, 'Différance', 8.
55 Derrida, 'Force and Signification', 13, 15–16.
56 '*Ousia* and *Grammē*', 39.
57 '*Ousia* and *Grammē*', 47.
58 *The Winter's Tale*, I. 2. 63–6.
59 William Shakespeare, *Riverside Shakespeare*, second edition (Boston: Houghton Mifflin Company, 1997).
60 *The Tragedy of Hamlet*, III. 4. 179.
61 I have attempted to follow this in *The Impossible Mourning of Jacques Derrida*, 101–12.

62 Jean-Pierre Vernant and Pierre Vidal-Naquet, *Myth and Tragedy in Ancient Greece*, trans. Janet Lloyd (New York: Zone Books, 1990), 43.
63 Kiefer, 'The Iconography of Time in *The Winter's Tale*', 50–3.
64 Plotinus, *The Enneads*, trans. Stephen Mackenna, intro. and ed. John Dillon (London: Penguin, 1991), III. 7. 10. Derrida refers to Plotinus in '*Ousia* and *Grammē*', 66 n. 41.
65 *Of Grammatology*, 143.
66 '*Ousia* and *Grammē*', 66 n. 41.
67 Derrida, 'Form and Meaning, 172 n. 16; 'La forme et le vouloir-dire', 206 n. 14. The translation has been modified.
68 Derrida questions Heidegger's association of time with justice as 'joining, adjoining, adjustment, articulation of accord or harmony' in *Specters of Marx*, 23–9.
69 Coghill, 'Six Points of Stage-craft in *The Winter's Tale*', 35.
70 Derrida, '*Ousia* and *Grammē*', 40, 47, 53.
71 Blissett, 'The Wide Gap of Time: *The Winter's Tale*', 55; Kiefer, 'The Iconography of Time in *The Winter's Tale*', 57.
72 *Of Grammatology*, 67; *De la grammatologie*, 98. See also, Derrida, 'Tympan', xvii.
73 *The Tragedy of Hamlet*, I. 1. 188–9. *Specters of Marx*, 17–29.
74 *Specters of Marx*, 3. See Royle, 'Not Now', and Geoffrey Bennington, 'Is it Time?', in *Interrupting Derrida* (London: Routledge, 2000), 128–40.
75 *The Winter's Tale*, I. 1. 25, 30–1.
76 *The Winter's Tale*, I. 2. 12.
77 *The Winter's Tale*, IV. 2. 18–20, 26–7.
78 *The Winter's Tale*, IV. 2. 37.
79 *The Winter's Tale*, I. 2. 64.
80 *The Winter's Tale*, V. 3. 31.

5: A 'NEW' HISTORY – OF THE SENSES

1 John Dryden, *To My Honoured friend Dr Charleton*, in *The Major Works*, ed. Keith Walker (Oxford: Oxford University Press, 2003), 21 (lines 1–8). On the declining reputation of Aristotle in this period see Richard Tuck, *Philosophy and Government 1572–1651* (Cambridge: Cambridge University Press, 1993), and Wilbur Samuel Howell, *Eighteenth Century British Logic and Rhetoric* (Princeton: Princeton University Press, 1971).
2 Derrida, *Edmund Husserl's Origin of Geometry: An Introduction*, 138.
3 *Edmund Husserl's Origin of Geometry: An Introduction*, 150.
4 *An Introduction*, 139, 141.
5 *An Introduction*, 138; *L'origine de la géométrie*, 152.
6 *An Introduction*, 106.
7 Derrida, 'Force and Signification', 27.
8 Derrida, *Glas*, 169a.

9 Aristotle, *On the Soul*, in *The Complete Works of Aristotle*, ed. Jonathan Barnes, 2 vols (Princeton: Princeton University Press, 1984), II; Aristotle, *On the Soul*, trans. W. S. Hett (Cambridge, MA: Harvard University Press, 1986). References to this work will be cited in the text.
10 Derrida, 'Cogito and the History of Madness', 55; 'Cogito et histoire de la folie', 85. Translation modified. See also Derrida, 'Edmond Jabès and the Question of the Book', 70.
11 Derrida, 'The Theatre of Cruelty and the Closure of Representation', 333.
12 Giorgio Agamben, 'On Potentiality', in *Potentialities*, ed. and trans. Daniel Heller-Roazen (Stanford: Stanford University Press, 1999), 180. See also, '*Pardes*: The Writing of Potentiality', in *Potentialities*, ed. and trans. Daniel Heller-Roazen (Stanford: Stanford University Press, 1999), 218. I elaborate on this in a forthcoming article, 'The Potential of the Diaphanous: Agamben, Derrida and Aristotle'.
13 Derrida, 'Violence and Metaphysics', 103.
14 Derrida, *Speech and Phenomena*, 14; *La voix et le phénomène*, 14. My translation.
15 Derrida, *The Problem of Genesis in Husserl's Philosophy*, 85; ' "Genesis and Structure" and Phenomenology', 162–3.
16 *The Problem of Genesis*, 85–6.
17 *The Problem of Genesis*, 86–7.
18 *The Problem of Genesis*, 89–90.
19 ' "Genesis and Structure" and Phenomenology', 163–4.
20 Derrida, 'Form and Meaning', 157–8, 170–2.
21 Aristotle, *Physics*, in *The Complete Works of Aristotle*, ed. Jonathan Barnes, 2 vols (Princeton: Princeton University Press, 1984), I: 218a.
22 Derrida, '*Ousia* and *Grammē*', 48–9.
23 Derrida, *Of Grammatology*, 290. In '*Ousia* and *Gramme*' (48–9), Derrida cites the *Physics* 219a, and *Critique of Pure Reason*, 156 [A20–1; B34–5], 162–3 [A30–6; B46–52].
24 *Critique of Pure Reason*, 156 [A20; B34].
25 *Critique of Pure Reason*, 157 [A22; B36]. My emphasis.
26 *Critique of Pure Reason*, 238 [A118].
27 One can nonetheless discern traces of the problem of memory in the *Critique of Pure Reason*. See, for example, 230, 239–40, 305, 327–8.
28 Immanuel Kant, *Anthropology From a Pragmatic Point of View*, ed. and trans. Robert B. Louden (Cambridge: Cambridge University Press, 2006), 75.
29 Thomas Hobbes, *Leviathan; or, The Matter, Forme, & Power of a Common-Wealth Ecclesiastical and Civill*, ed. Richard Tuck (Cambridge: Cambridge University Press, 1996), 16; John Locke, *Two Treatises of Government*, ed. Peter Laslett (Cambridge: Cambridge University Press, 1996), 96, 335, 338, 346.
30 David Hume, *A TREATISE of Human Nature: BEING An ATTEMPT to introduce the experimental Method of Reasoning into Moral Subjects*, ed. L. A. Selby-Bigge and P. H. Nidditch (Oxford: Oxford University Press, 1978), 8–9.

31 *Critique of Pure Reason*, 220–1; *Kritik der Reinen Vernunft* (Frankfurt am Main: Im Insel, 1964), A86–7; B118–19.
32 Derrida has written on the gap between form and content in Hegel's prefaces in 'Outwork, Prefacing'.
33 *Critique of Pure Reason*, 228 [A98].
34 *Critique of Pure Reason*, 104 [Axx].
35 Derrida, 'The Pit and the Pyramid', 75; 'Le puits et la pyramide', 86.
36 G. W. F. Hegel, *Hegel's Philosophy of Mind, Being Part Three of the Encyclopaedia of The Philosophical Sciences (1830)*, trans. William Wallace, foreword J. N. Findlay (Oxford: Clarendon, 1971), §378.
37 'The Pit and the Pyramid', 75–87.
38 'The Pit and the Pyramid', 73.
39 *An Introduction*, 141.
40 'Violence and Metaphysics', 99–100.
41 *Speech and Phenomena*, 78–9.
42 Derrida, 'Différance', 5
43 In the preface to part one of *Either/Or* (1843), Kierkegaard writes: 'Little by little, hearing became my favourite sense; for just as it is the voice that reveals the inwardness which is incommensurable with the outer, so the ear is the instrument whereby that inwardness is grasped, hearing the sense by which it is appropriated', *Either/Or: A Fragment of Life*, ed. Victor Eremita, trans. Alastair Hannay (London: Penguin, 1992), 27.
44 Derrida, 'Tympan', xv, xiii n. 5.
45 'Tympan', xv–xvi; 'Tympan' [French], viii.
46 'Tympan', xxv–xxvi. Derrida returned to the question of the ear in later readings of Nietzsche and Heidegger: 'Otobiographies: The Teaching of Nietzsche and the Politics of the Proper Name'; 'Heidegger's Ear: Philopolemology (*Geschlecht* IV)'.
47 On the senses as mediation and the diaphanous, see T. K. Johansen, *Aristotle on the Sense-organs* (Cambridge: Cambridge University Press, 1998).
48 *On Touching Jean Luc Nancy*, 155.
49 *On Touching*, 6.
50 See *The Impossible Mourning of Jacques Derrida*, 4–6, 12–15, 97–8.
51 *On Touching*, 24.
52 *On Touching*, 181, 229.
53 *On Touching*, 34; *Le toucher, Jean-Luc Nancy*, 47.
54 *On Touching*, 92.
55 *On Touching*, 104, 108–9.
56 *On Touching*, 119–22. Derrida refers to the *Phaedo* 65c. See the *Phaedo*, in *The Dialogues of Plato*, trans. Benjamin Jowett, 5 vols (Oxford: Clarendon Press, 1892), II. See also, *Derrida and Disinterest*, 119–21.
57 *On Touching*, 120.
58 *Critique of Pure Reason*, 227 [A95], 230 [A102], 238 [A119].
59 *Critique of Pure Reason*, 247 [B132], 260 [260], 163 [A33/B49].
60 *On Touching*, 7–8.

61 *An Introduction*, 132–3. See also, *On Touching*, 24.
62 Derrida, 'Le facteur de la vérité', 428–9; 'Le facteur de la vérité' [French], 456.
63 'Le facteur de la vérité', 420 n. 4. Derrida refers to Nancy's first book, written with Philippe Lacoue-Labarthe, *Le titre de la lettre: une lecture de Lacan* (Paris: Galilée, 1973); *The Title of the Letter: A Reading of Lacan*, trans. François Raffeisl and David Pettigrew (Albany: State University of New York Press, 1992).
64 *On Touching*, 26, 46. See also, 73.
65 *On Touching*, 47, 67–9.
66 *On Touching*, 69.
67 *On Touching*, 18. Derrida begins his reading of Nancy in 1992 with the Aristotelian question of the eye. One can see this question already at work in 1983 in Derrida's, 'The Principle of Reason: The University in the Eyes of its Pupils'.
68 *On Touching*, 19, 56, 127.
69 *On Touching*, 128–9.
70 *On Touching*, 17, 49, 50. See, for example, *Glas*, 151–62a, 202–5a, 223–5a.
71 *On Touching*, 218–19.
72 *On Touching*, 59, 60, 54. See also, Jacques Derrida and Jean-Luc Nancy, 'Responsabilité – du sens à venir', in *Sens en tous sens: Autour des travaux de Jean-Luc Nancy*; 'Avant-propos', in *Chaque fois unique, la fin du monde*, 11.
73 *On Touching*, 47.
74 *On Touching*, 18. At the outset of *On Touching*, Derrida asks, 'May I, even before starting out again [*avant même un nouveau départ*], be permitted the space and the freedom of a long parenthesis here to announce, at some remove, a possible destination?' (20; 33). A hundred and twenty pages later he writes: 'Let us start again' (*Repartons*) (139; 160).
75 *On Touching*, 120.
76 '*Ousia* and *Grammē*', 60; '*Ousia* et *Grammè*', 69–70.
77 William Shakespeare, *A Midsummer Night's Dream*, in *The Norton Shakespeare, Based on the Oxford Edition*, ed. Stephen Greenblatt and others (New York: Norton, 1997), IV. 1. 204–8.

6: LEAPING TO PLATO

1 Michel Foucault, 'The Discourse on Language', in *The Archaeology of Knowledge*, trans. Rupert Swyer (New York: Pantheon, 1972), 235. The original title of Foucault's paper in French was 'L'ordre du discours'.
2 Derrida, 'Violence and Metaphysics', 81; 'Violence et métaphysique', 120.
3 See *The Impossible Mourning of Jacques Derrida*, 19–73. I also take account here of the problem of the various different editions of the German text and of the different translations available in English as

emblematic of a *history* of philosophy. Needless to say, I have tried to negotiate as best I can through the discrepancies between the English translation and the German text. See Frederick C. Beister, 'Introduction', in G. W. F. Hegel, *Lectures on the History of Philosophy I: Greek Philosophy to Plato*, trans. E. S. Haldane, intro. Frederick C. Beister (Lincoln: University of Nebraska Press, 1995), xxxi–xxiv. See also, Alfredo Ferrarin, *Hegel and Aristotle* (Cambridge: Cambridge University Press, 2001), 31–3.

4 G. W. F. Hegel, *Lectures on the History of Philosophy I: Greek Philosophy to Plato*, trans. E. S. Haldane, intro. Frederick C. Beister (Lincoln: University of Nebraska Press, 1995), 38–9; *Vorlesungen über die Geschichte der Philosophie I* (Frankfurt am Main: Suhrkamp, 1986), 58. Further references to this work will be cited in the text, the page number of the English edition being followed, where necessary, by the page numbers of the German edition. See also, Timothy Bahti, *Allegories of History: Literary Historiography after Hegel* (Baltimore: Johns Hopkins University Press, 1992), 68–133.

5 On *restance*, see Derrida, 'Outwork, Prefacing', 7–8.

6 Derrida, *Glas*, 11a; *Glas*, 18a.

7 *Glas*, 14a.

8 Marie Joanus Kurrik, *Literature and Negation* (New York: Columbia University Press, 1979), 59. See also, Sanford Budick and Wolfgang Iser, *Languages of the Unsayable: The Play of Negativity in Literature and Literary Theory* (New York: Columbia University Press, 1989).

9 *Glas*, 36a; *Glas* [French], 45a.

10 See Nicholas Royle, *The Uncanny* (Manchester: Manchester University Press, 2003).

11 *Glas*, 51a.

12 Martin Heidegger, *What is Called Thinking?*, trans. Fred D. Wieck and J. Glenn Gray (New York: Harper and Row, 1968), 11; *Was heisst Denken?* (Frankfurt am Main: Vittoria Klostermann, 2002), 13. See also, David Farrell Krell, *Of Memory, Reminiscence, and Writing: On the Verge* (Bloomington: Indiana University Press, 1990), 262–8; Martin Donougho, 'Hegel's Art of Memory', in *Endings: Questions of Memory on Hegel and Heidegger*, ed. Rebecca Comay and John McCumber (Evanston: Northwestern University Press, 1999), 142–3.

13 *Glas*, 89a; *Glas* [French], 103a.

14 *Glas*, 90a.

15 *Glas*, 95a; *Glas* [French], 110a.

16 *Glas*, 109a; *Glas* [French], 125a.

17 *Glas*, 233b; *Glas* [French], 260b.

18 *Glas*, 216a; *Glas* [French], 242a.

19 See Gaston, *Derrida and Disinterest*, 92–4.

20 *Glas*, 151a–162a. This is also a leap of translation, as the jump differs slightly in the French, leaping not through the tran-scendental, but through 'the abyss playing / an almost transcendental role' (l'abîme jouant [171a] un rôle quasi transcendental [183a]).

21 Jonathan Barnes, *Early Greek Philosophy* (London: Penguin, 1987), 117.

7: SENSE CERTAINTY, OR

1 G. W. F. Hegel, *Lectures on the History of Philosophy I: Greek Philosophy to Plato*, trans. E. S. Haldane, intro. Frederick C. Beister (Lincoln: University of Nebraska Press, 1995), 88.
2 See Derrida, *Who's Afraid of Philosophy: The Right to Philosophy I*, and *Eyes of the University: The Right to Philosophy 2*.
3 Derrida, 'Between Brackets I', 11; 'Entre crochets I', 19. See also, John P. Leavey, Jr, *Glassary* (Lincoln: University of Nebraska Press, 1986), 48–52, 135.
4 Derrida, 'Outwork, Prefacing', 54, 56; 'Hors livre', 74.
5 G. W. F. Hegel, *Phenomenology of Spirit*, trans. A. V. Miller (Oxford: Oxford University Press, 1977), §73; *Phänomenologie des Geistes* (Frankfurt am Main: Suhrkamp, 1986), 68. References to the paragraph sections for the English translation and, where necessary, the page numbers for the German edition will be cited in the text.
6 Derrida, 'Violence and Metaphysics', 302 n. 91.
7 Derrida, *Of Grammatology*, 329 n. 34.
8 Catherine Malabou, *The Future of Hegel: Plasticity, Temporality and Dialectic* (London: Routledge, 2005), 15. See also Derrida's preface, 'A Time of Farewells: Heidegger (read by) Hegel (read by) Malabou', xix.
9 Derrida, '*Ousia* and *Grammē*', 41–3; '*Ousia* et *Grammè*', 46.
10 '*Ousia* and *Gramme*', 44 n. 16.
11 Derrida, 'The Pit and the Pyramid', 75; G. W. F. Hegel, *Hegel's Philosophy of Mind, Being Part Three of the Encyclopaedia of The Philosophical Sciences (1830)*, trans. William Wallace, foreword J. N. Findlay (Oxford: Clarendon, 1971), §378. On Hegel's reading of Aristotle, see also Malabou, *The Future of Hegel*, 39–56.
12 Aristotle, *On the Soul*, in *The Complete Works of Aristotle*, ed. Jonathan Barnes, 2 vols (Princeton: Princeton University Press, 1984), II; Aristotle, *On the Soul*, trans. W. S. Hett (Cambridge, MA: Harvard University Press, 1986). References to this work will be cited in the text. See also Alfredo Ferrarin, *Hegel and Aristotle* (Cambridge: Cambridge University Press, 2001), 234–61.
13 Plato, *Symposium*, in *The Dialogues of Plato*, trans. Benjamin Jowett, 5 vols (Oxford: Clarendon Press, 1892), I (200). My emphasis.
14 Derrida, 'Form and Meaning'; 'La forme et le vouloir-dire'.
15 Derrida, 'The Ends of Man', 120.
16 'The Ends of Man', 120 n. 13.
17 *Lectures on the History of Philosophy I*, 293–4.
18 *Being and Time*, H 5.
19 Ten years after his seminar on sensible certainty, Derrida would give a series of seminars on The Thing (*La Chose*). Traces of these unpublished seminars can be found in most of his works from the late 1970s onwards, including *La Vérité en peinture* (1978), *La carte postale* (1980), *Parages* (1986), *Signéponge* (1988), *Donner le temps* (1991), and *Spectres de Marx* (1993). To only gesture towards the immense labour, care and patience needed to respond to these traces, Derrida refers in a footnote in 'To

Speculate – on "Freud" ' to seminars 'organized for three years running, under the title of *La Chose* (The Thing) (Heidegger / Ponge, Heidegger / Blanchot, Heidegger / Freud), at Yale University and in Paris', in *The Post Card*, 401 n. 8. See also, 'LIVING ON: Border Lines', 156.

20 'The Ends of Man', 136; 'Les fins de l'homme', 166.

21 Derrida, 'From Restricted to General Economy', 275–6; 'De l'économie restreinte à l'économie générale', 406. The translation has been modified.

22 'The Ends of Man', 121–3.

23 *Of Grammatology*, 3, 10–18. For Derrida's account of Hegel's conception of writing, see 'The Pit and the Pyramid', 98–108.

24 Derrida, *Edmund Husserl's Origin of Geometry: An Introduction*, 115. See Derrida, *Glas*, 29–30a; 'Parergon', 15–147. See also Andrzej Warminski, 'Reading for Example: "Sense-certainty" in Hegel's *Phenomenology of Spirit*', *Diacritics* 11.2 (1981): 83–96.

25 Jean Hyppolite, *Genesis and Structure of Hegel's Phenomenology of Spirit*, trans. Samuel Cherniak and John Heckman (Evanston: Northwestern University Press, 1989), 88.

26 *Being and Time*, H 420–1, H 428, n. xxx (500–501).

27 I have attempted to explore the question of today in *Derrida and Disinterest*, 103–7, and in *The Impossible Mourning of Jacques Derrida*, 2, 36–41, 54, 77.

28 Derrida, 'After.rds, or, at least, less than a letter about a letter less', 202.

29 Derrida, *Speech and Phenomena*.

30 G. W. F. Hegel, *Science of Logic*, trans. A. V. Miller (London: Allen & Unwin), 106–7. See also, *Glas*, 12a.

31 This passage can be seen as a first trace of Derrida's later essay on Heidegger and Schapiro, 'Restitutions of the Truth in Pointing'.

32 'Parergon', 27; 'Parergon' [French], 33.

33 From first tracing Husserl's endless oscillations between psychologism and empiricism in the 1950s to starting again with Hegel in the 1960s, Derrida would come to define his work through that which gave itself to *neither* a phenomenology *nor* an empiricism. In 'Parergon', on the example of and as the frame (*parergon*) that supplements the work (*ergon*) and is at once neither simply inside nor merely outside, Derrida writes: 'No "theory" no "practice", no "theoretical practice" can intervene effectively in this field if it does not weigh up and bear on the frame, which is the decisive structure of what is at stake, at the invisible limit to (between) the interiority of meaning (put under shelter by the whole hermeneuticist, semioticist, phenomenologicalist, and formalist tradition) *and* (to) all the empiricisms of the extrinsic which, incapable of either seeing or reading, miss the question completely' (61).

34 'The Pit and the Pyramid', 77; 'Le puits et la pyramide', 88.

35 Derrida, 'Plato's Pharmacy', 105, 107.

36 *Of Grammatology*, 91; 'Plato's Pharmacy', 82; 'White Mythology: Metaphor in the Text of Philosophy', 242–57.

37 'From Restricted to General Economy', 259; 'De l'économie restreinte à l'économie générale', 381. Derrida writes, 'In naming the without-reserve of absolute expenditure "abstract negativity", Hegel, through

precipitation, blinded himself to that which he had laid bare under the rubric of negativity. And did so through precipitation toward the seriousness of meaning and the security of knowledge.'

38 *Glas*, 169a.
39 *Glas*, 1a; *Glas*, 7a.

8: CUT *GLAS*

1 *Glas* [French], 7a; *Glas*, 1a. All further references to *Glas* will be cited in the text, giving the page numbers of the English edition and followed, where necessary, by the page numbers of the French edition.
2 Derrida, 'The Pit and the Pyramid', 90.
3 Derrida, 'Between Brackets I', 11; G. W. F. Hegel, *Phenomenology of Spirit*, trans. A. V. Miller (Oxford: Oxford University Press, 1977), §110; *Phänomenologie des Geistes* (Frankfurt am Main: Suhrkamp, 1986), 91.
4 Plato, *Cratylus*, in *The Dialogues of Plato*, trans. Benjamin Jowett, 5 vols (Oxford: Clarendon Press, 1892), I: 411b–c. On the drift of derivation, see Catherine Malabou, in Catherine Malabou and Jacques Derrida, *Counterpath: Traveling with Jacques Derrida*, trans. David Wills (Stanford: Stanford University Press, 2004).
5 G. W. F. Hegel, *Science of Logic*, trans. A. V. Miller (London: Allen & Unwin, 1969), 106–7. On Derrida's retranslation of the *Aufhebung*, see 'The Pit and the Pyramid', 88; 'What is a "Relevant" Translation?' See also Jean-Luc Nancy, *The Speculative Remark (One of Hegel's bon mots)*, trans. Celine Surprenant (Stanford: Stanford University Press, 2001).
6 The translation here has been slightly modified.
7 See Derrida, 'Countersignature', 11. See also, Geoffrey Hartman, 'Homage to *Glas*', *Critical Inquiry* 33.2 (2007): 244–61.
8 On *écarts* in *Glas*, see also Jacques Derrida, 'Proverb: "He that would Pun . . ."', 18–19.
9 The translation has been modified.
10 On monu-memorialization see, *The Impossible Mourning of Jacques Derrida*, 2, 15, 25, 47, 74, 94, 123. On mourning in *Glas*, see also David Farrell Krell, *The Purest of Bastards: Work of Mourning; Art, and Affirmation in the Thought of Jacques Derrida* (Pennsylvania: Pennsylvania State University Press, 2000), 149–73.
11 See, Derrida, 'LIVING ON. Border lines'; 'To Speculate – on "Freud"'. See also, Gaston, *Derrida and Disinterest*, 109–25.
12 Martin Heidegger, *Identity and Difference*, trans. Joan Stambaugh (Chicago: University of Chicago Press, 2002), 32–5.
13 Martin Heidegger, *What is Called Thinking?*, trans. Fred D. Wieck and J. Glenn Gray (New York: Harper and Row, 1968), 12; *Was heisst Denken?* (Frankfurt am Main: Vittoria Klostermann, 2002), 15.
14 *What is Called Thinking?*, 12; *Was heisst Denken?*, 15.
15 See Derrida, '*Qual Quelle*: Valéry's Sources'.
16 James Joyce, *Finnegans Wake*, intro. Seamus Deane (London: Penguin, 1992), 149.

17 On the crypt, see 'The Pit and the Pyramid'; 'Fors: The Anglish Words of Nicolas Abraham and Maria Torok'; *Archive Fever: A Freudian Impression*.

18 See also 68b (and 84b), where Derrida links *derrière le rideau* to his father's (and his own) name.

19 Derrida, *Mémoires – for Paul de Man*, 35–7, 51–6, 65, 71, 106–7. Derrida will return to de Man and the questions of memory and matter which begin in *Glas* in 'Typewriter Ribbon: Limited Ink (2)', 71–160.

20 'The Pit and the Pyramid', 77.

21 See Werner Hamacher, *Pleroma – Reading Hegel: The Genesis and Structure of a Dialectical Hermeneutics in Hegel*, trans. Nicholas Walker and Simon Jarvis (London: Athlone, 1998).

22 On *il* or *elle*, see Derrida, 'At this Very Moment in this Work Here I am', 11–48.

23 Derrida, 'How to Avoid Speaking: Denials', 96.

24 On the question of women and the sexual difference, see the essays collected in *Feminist Interpretations of Jacques Derrida*, ed. Nancy J. Holland (Pennsylvania: Pennsylvania State University Press, 1997).

25 See also Derrida, 'Tympan', xv–xvi; 'Tympan' [French], viii.

26 See also, Derrida, '*Geschlecht*: Sexual Difference, Ontological Difference'; '*Geschlecht* II: Heidegger's Hand'; *Of Spirit: Heidegger and the Question*; 'Heidegger's Ear: Philopolemology (*Geschlecht* IV)'.

27 See also, Derrida, 'The Reason of the Strongest', 18.

28 *Lectures on the History of Philosophy I*, 221.

29 *What is Called Thinking?*, 4, 6, 7; *Was heisst Denken?*, 5, 6, 8. See also, Joanna Hodge, *Heidegger and Ethics* (London: Routledge, 1995), 47, 84, 115.

30 *What is Called Thinking?*, 8, 9; *Was heisst Denken?*, 10.

31 *What is Called Thinking?*, 17.

32 *What is Called Thinking?*, 17, 121, 116.

33 *What is Called Thinking?*, 117, 120–1, 142; *Was heisst Denken?*, 124, 146. See also, Alexander García Düttmann, *The Memory of Thought: An Essay on Heidegger and Adorno*, trans. Nicholas Walker (London: Continuum, 2002), 151–2, 264–5.

34 Heidegger, *Being and Time*, H 350, 380–6.

35 On the gift, see Derrida, *Given Time: 1. Counterfeit Money*.

36 See also Dominique Janicaud's remarks on Heidegger's use of 'the step back' (*der Schritt zurück*) in his reading of Hegel, 'Heidegger and Hegel: An Impossible "Dialogue"?', in *Endings: Questions of Memory on Hegel and Heidegger*, ed. Rebecca Comay and John McCumber, trans. Nina Belmonte (Evanston: Northwestern University Press, 1999), 29–30.

37 *What is Called Thinking?*, 3, 11; *Was heisst Denken?*, 5, 13. See David Farrell Krell, *Of Memory, Reminiscence, and Writing: On the Verge* (Bloomington: Indiana University Press, 1990), 172, 263, 267, 298; Michel Haar, 'The History of Being and Its Hegelian Model', in *Endings: Questions of Memory on Hegel and Heidegger*, ed. Rebecca Comay and John McCumber, trans. Reginald Lilly (Evanston: Northwestern University Press, 1999), 49–50.

38 *What is Called Thinking?*, 143–7.
39 *What is Called Thinking?*, 4; *Was heisst Denken?*, 5. I have followed Krell's revised translation for this passage, 'What Calls for Thinking', in *Basic Writings*, ed. David Farrell Krell (San Francisco: Harper, 1993), 369.
40 *What is Called Thinking?*, 11; *Was heisst Denken?*, 20.
41 In 'The End of Philosophy and the Task of Thinking', Heidegger asks 'is there a *first* possibility for thinking apart from the *last* possibility that we characterized (the dissolution of philosophy in the technologized sciences), a possibility from which the thinking of philosophy would have to start, but which as philosophy it could nevertheless not expressly experience and adopt?', in *Basic Writings*, ed. David Farrell Krell (San Francisco: Harper, 1993), 435.
42 *Mémoires – for Paul de Man*, 73, 91–3, 141. See Derrida's comments on Heidegger's return to Socrates (111). See also Paul de Man, 'Sign and Symbol in Hegel's *Aesthetics*', in *Aesthetic Ideology*, ed. Andrzej Warminski (Minneapolis: University of Minnesota Press, 1996), 91–104.
43 '*Geschlecht* II: Heidegger's Hand', 182.
44 *Of Spirit: Heidegger and the Question*, 9. See also, 76–80, 106–7.
45 'Heidegger's Ear', 187; 'L'oreille de Heidegger', 378. See also, Derrida, *The Politics of Friendship*, 244; *Specters of Marx*, 27–8.
46 'Heidegger's Ear', 209; 'L'oreille de Heidegger', 410. See also Derrida's comments in *Arguing With Derrida*, ed. Simon Glendinning (Oxford: Blackwell, 2001), 55–6.
47 On a different aspect of Heidegger in *Glas*, see Simon Critchley, 'A Commentary upon Derrida's Reading of Hegel in *Glas*', in *Hegel After Derrida*, ed. Stuart Barnett (London: Routledge, 1998), 219–20.
48 *What is Called Thinking?*, 116–18, 120; *Was heisst Denken?*, 124. I have followed Krell's translation for these passages, 'What Calls for Thinking', 386–7, 390.
49 *What is Called Thinking?*, 5; *Was heisst Denken?*, 6–7. On Heidegger's use of today in *Being and Time*, see Gaston, *The Impossible Mourning of Jacques Derrida*, 37–41.
50 See Gaston, *Derrida and Disinterest*.
51 Derrida, 'Ja, or the *faux-bond* II', 67; 'Ja, ou le faux-bond', 72.
52 See Derrida, 'Shibboleth: For Paul Celan'. See also, Gaston, *Derrida and Disinterest*, 103–7.
53 Krell, *Of Memory*, 283–99.
54 Derrida, 'Violence and Metaphysics', 89.
55 Derrida, *Of Grammatology*, 93; *De la grammatologie*, 142.
56 *What is Called Thinking?*, 8–9; *Was heisst Denken?*, 10.
57 Derrida, *On Touching – Jean-Luc Nancy*, 35, 62. See also, 71–4, 293–9, 306. See also Jean-Luc Nancy, *Le poids d'une pensée* (Sainte-Foy: Le Griffon d'argile, 1991), partially translated in *The Gravity of Thought*, trans. François Raffoul and Gregory Recco (Atlantic Highlands: Humanities Press, 1997). Derrida's concern with *pe(n)ser*

from *Of Grammatology*, predates Jean-Luc Nancy's work on this problem. See also, Derrida, 'Rams', 141–2; *Béliers*, 27–9.

58 *On Touching*, 299; *Le Toucher*, 335.

EPILOGUE: LET'S GO BACK THEN, ONCE MORE

1 Sophocles, *Oedipus the King*, in *The Three Theban Plays*, trans. Robert Fagles, intro. Bernard Knox (London: Penguin, 1984), 230 (lines 1161–7).

2 Sophocles, *Oedipus at Colonus*, in *The Three Theban Plays*, trans. Robert Fagles, intro. Bernard Knox (London: Penguin, 1984), 321 (lines 667–78).

3 Homer, *Odyssey*, trans. A. T. Murray and George E. Dimock, 2 vols (Cambridge, MA: Harvard University Press, 1995), II: 13: 125.

4 *Odyssey*, II: 13: 187–9

5 *Odyssey*, II: 13: 252–5.

6 Plato, *Timaeus*, in *The Dialogues of Plato*, III; *Plato*, R. G. Bury (London: Heinemann, 2005), 17a. See also, Derrida, 'Khora', 117.

7 See also, Derrida, 'Dissemination', 352.

8 On Derrida's extensive work on hospitality, see for example: *Adieu: To Emmanuel Levinas*, trans. Anne Pascale-Brault and Michael Naas (Stanford: Stanford University Press, 1999); *Of Hospitality, Anne Dufourmantelle Invites Jacques Derrida to Respond*, trans. Rachel Bowlby (Stanford: Stanford University Press, 2000); 'Hostpitality', in *Acts of Religion*, trans. Gil Anidjar (London: Routledge, 2002), 356–71.

9 Derrida, *Of Grammatology*, 36.

10 See also Michal Ben Naftali on the 1+1+ 'ça', 'Histoire d'une amitié: L'archive et la question de la Palestine', in *Judéités: Questions pour Jacques Derrida*, sous la direction de Joseph Cohen et Raphael Zagury-Orly (Paris: Galilée, 2003), 95.

11 In 'To Speculate – on "Freud"', Derrida writes 'one two three – speculation without term', 283. He explores the question of hospitality in Plato most explicitly in *Of Hospitality*.

12 I have used R. G. Bury's translation here.

13 'Khora', 126–7. I have used the quoted translation of Plato's text. In *The Space of Literature*, Maurice Blanchot suggests that 'the writer's solitude, that condition which is the risk he runs, seems to come from his belonging, in the work, to what precedes the work. Through him, the work comes into being; it constitutes the resolute solidity of a beginning. But he himself belongs to a time ruled by the indecisiveness inherent in beginning over again.' Compelled by 'a privileged theme, which obliges him to say over again what he has already said', the writer cannot avoid 'starting over what for him never starts', trans. Ann Smock (Lincoln: University of Nebraska Press, 1989), 24.

14 Derrida, 'Avant-propos', in *Psyché: inventions de l'autre*, 10.

15 Derrida, 'Provocation: Forewords', xxxii–iii. See also Rudolphe Gasché, 'Thinking Without Wonder', in *The Horror of Thinking: Critique,*

Theory, Philosophy (Stanford: Stanford University Press, 2007), 348–63. I would like to thank Nicholas Royle, David Clark, Peter Otto, David Punter, Joanna Hodge, Maria Stamatopoulou, William Watkin, Simon Morgan Wortham, Sarah Campbell, Nick Fawcett, Leif Isaksen, Jean and Jasper Rose, David and Bea Hackel, Avi Lifschitz, Adrianne Rubin, Sheera and Erga Sutherland, Etai and Maya Koren, and Carmella Elan-Gaston. This book is dedicated to Viviane de Charrière, translator, writer, reader, heroine and tireless volunteer for over 25 years for the French telephone support service, *S-O-S Amitié*. See www.sos-amitie.com.

BIBLIOGRAPHY

Agamben, Giorgio, 'On Potentiality', in *Potentialities*, ed. and trans. Daniel Heller-Roazen (Stanford: Stanford University Press, 1999), 177–84.

Agamben, Giorgio, '*Pardes*: The Writing of Potentiality', in *Potentialities*, ed. and trans. Daniel Heller-Roazen (Stanford: Stanford University Press, 1999), 205–19.

Alkon, Paul, 'Changing the Calendar', *Eighteenth-Century Life* 7 (1982): 1–18.

Ames, Joseph, *A Collection of Notes of journeys, memoranda, copies of inscriptions, drawings of antiquities, etc., entitled on cover, 'Mr. Ames's Minute book'* (Bodleian MS. Top. gen. e. 58).

Aristotle, *Metaphysics*, in *The Complete Works of Aristotle*, ed. Jonathan Barnes, 2 vols (Princeton: Princeton University Press, 1984), I.

Aristotle, *Nicomachean Ethics*, ed. and trans. Roger Crisp (Cambridge: Cambridge University Press, 2004).

Aristotle, *On the Soul*, in *The Complete Works of Aristotle*, ed. Jonathan Barnes, 2 vols (Princeton: Princeton University Press, 1984), II; Aristotle, *On the Soul*, trans. W. S. Hett (Cambridge, MA: Harvard University Press, 1986).

Aristotle, *Physics*, in *The Complete Works of Aristotle*, ed. Jonathan Barnes, 2 vols (Princeton: Princeton University Press, 1984), I; *The Physics*, trans. Philip H. Wicksteed and Francis M. Cornford (London: Heinemann, 1928).

Aristotle, *Poetics*, in *The Complete Works of Aristotle*, ed. Jonathan Barnes, 2 vols (Princeton: Princeton University Press, 1984), I; Aristotle, *Poetics* trans. Stephen Halliwell (Cambridge, MA: Harvard University Press, 1995).

Arnold, Matthew, 'The Function of Criticism at the Present Time', in *Essays in Criticism*, intro. G. K. Chesterton (London: Dent, 1969), 9–34.

Auerbach, Erich, *Mimesis: The Representation of Reality in Western Literature*, trans. Willard R. Trask (Princeton: Princeton University Press, 1991).

Bahti, Timothy, *Allegories of History: Literary Historiography after Hegel* (Baltimore: Johns Hopkins University Press, 1992).

Barnes, Jonathan, *Early Greek Philosophers* (London: Penguin, 1987).

Beister, Frederick C., 'Introduction', in G. W. F. Hegel, *Lectures on the History of Philosophy I: Greek Philosophy to Plato*, trans. E. S. Haldane (Lincoln: University of Nebraska Press, 1995), xi–xl.

Ben Naftali, Michal, 'Histoire d'une amitié: L'archive et la question de la Palestine', in *Judéités: Questions pour Jacques Derrida*, sous la direction de Joseph Cohen et Raphael Zagury-Orly (Paris: Galilée, 2003), 85–118.

Bennington, Geoffrey, 'Is it Time?', in *Interrupting Derrida* (London: Routledge, 2000), 128–40.

Bennington, Geoffrey, 'Mosaic Fragment: If Derrida were an Egyptian . . .', in *Derrida: A Critical Reader*, ed. David Wood (Oxford: Blackwell, 1992), 97–119.

Beowulf, trans. Kevin Crossley-Holland (Oxford: Oxford University Press, 1999).

Blanchot, Maurice, *The Space of Literature*, trans. Ann Smock (Lincoln: University of Nebraska Press, 1989).

Blissett, William, 'The Wide Gap of Time: *The Winter's Tale*', *English Literary Renaissance* 1 (1971): 52–70.

Boswell, James, *Life of Johnson*, ed. R. W. Chapman, intro. Pat Rogers (Oxford: Oxford University Press, 1998).

Bourdieu, Pierre, *The Field of Cultural Production: Essays on Art and Literature*, ed. Randal Johnson (Cambridge: Polity, 1993).

Bristol, Michael D., 'In Search of the Bear: Spatiotemporal Form and the Heterogenity of Economies in *The Winter's Tale*', *Shakespeare Quarterly* 42 (1991): 145–67.

Budick, Sanford and Wolfgang Iser, *Languages of the Unsayable: The Play of Negativity in Literature and Literary Theory* (New York: Columbia University Press, 1989).

Burke, Peter, *The Renaissance Sense of the Past* (London: Edward Arnold, 1969).

Burn, A. R., 'Introduction' to Herodotus, *The Histories*, trans. Aubrey de Sélincourt (London: Penguin, 1972), 7–37.

Castelvetro, Ludovico, *Castelvetro on the Art of Poetry*, trans. Andrew Bongiorno (New York: Medieval and Renaissance Texts and Studies, 1984).

Cervantes, Miguel de, *Don Quixote de la Mancha*, trans. Charles Jarvis, intro. E. C. Riley (Oxford: Oxford University Press, 1998).

Cherniss, Harold, *Aristotle's Criticism of Presocratic Philosophy* (Baltimore: Johns Hopkins University Press, 1935).

Chesterfield, Philip Dormer Stanhope, Earl of, *Lord Chesterfield's Letters*, ed. David Roberts (Oxford: Oxford University Press, 1992).

Cicero, *De Legibus*, trans. Clinton Walker Keyes (London: Heinemann, 1928).

Clark, David L., 'Bereft: Derrida's Memory and the Spirit of Friendship', *South Atlantic Quarterly* 106.2 (2007): 291–324.

Clark, Timothy, *Derrida, Heidegger, Blanchot: Sources of Derrida's Notion and Practice of Literature* (Cambridge: Cambridge University Press, 1992).

Clark, Timothy, *The Theory of Inspiration: Composition as a Crisis of Subjectivity in Romantic and Post-Romantic Writing* (Manchester: Manchester University Press, 1997).

Clark, Timothy, '"Time after Time": Temporality, Temporalization', *Oxford Literary Review* 9 (1987): 119–34.

Coghill, Nevill, 'Six Points of Stage-craft in *The Winter's Tale*', *Shakespeare Survey* 11 (1958): 31–41.

Coope, Ursula, *Time for Aristotle: Physics IV: 10–14* (Oxford: Clarendon Press, 2005).

Corneille, Pierre, *Trois Discours sur le poème dramatique*, ed. Bénédicte Louvat and Marc Escola (Paris: Flammarion, 1999).

Coyne, G. V., M. A. Hoskin, O. Pedersen, *Gregorian Reform of the Calendar: Proceedings of the Vatican Conference to Commemorate its 400th Anniversary 1582–1982* (Vatican: Pontificia Academia Scientiarum, 1983).

Critchley, Simon, 'A Commentary upon Derrida's Reading of Hegel in *Glas*', in *Hegel After Derrida*, ed. Stuart Barnett (London: Routledge, 1998), 197–226.

Croix, G. E. M. de Ste., 'Aristotle on History and Poetry (*Poetics*, 9, 1451a36–b11)', in *Essays on Aristotle's Poetics*, ed. Amélie Oksenberg Rorty (Princeton: Princeton University Press, 1992), 23–32.

Crumbley, Paul, *Inflections of the Pen: Dash and Voice in Emily Dickinson* (Lexington: University of Kentucky Press, 1997).

Daiches, David, *A Critical History of English Literature*, 2 vols (London: Secker and Warburg, 1960).

De Man, Paul, 'Sign and Symbol in Hegel's Aesthetics', in *Aesthetic Ideology*, ed. Andrzej Warminski (Minneapolis: University of Minnesota Press, 1996), 91–104.

Derrida, Jacques, *Adieu: To Emmanuel Levinas*, trans. Anne Pascale-Brault and Michael Naas (Stanford: Stanford University Press, 1999).

Derrida, Jacques, 'After.rds, or, at least, less than a letter about a letter less', in *Afterwards*, ed. Nicholas Royle (Tampere: Outside Books, 1992), 197–216.

Derrida, Jacques, 'Aphorism Countertime', in *Acts of Literature*, trans. Nicholas Royle, ed. Derek Attridge (London: Routledge, 1992), 14–33; 'L'aphorisme à contretemps', in *Psyché: Inventions de l'autre* (Paris: Galilée, 1987), 519–33.

Derrida, Jacques, *Archive Fever: A Freudian Impression*, trans. Eric Prenowitz (Chicago: University of Chicago Press, 1996); *Mal d'Archive: une impression freudienne* (Paris: Galilée, 1995).

Derrida, Jacques, *Artaud le Moma: Interjections d'appel* (Paris: Galilée, 2002).

Derrida, Jacques, 'At This Very Moment in This Work Here I Am', in *Re-Reading Lévinas*, trans. Ruben Berezdivin, ed. Robert Bernasconi and Simon Critchley (Bloomington: Indiana University Press, 1991), 11–48; 'En ce moment même dans cet ouvrage me voici,' in *Psyché: Inventions de l'autre* (Paris: Galilée, 1987), 159–202.

Derrida, Jacques, 'Avant-propos', in *Chaque fois unique, la fin du monde*, présenté par Pascale-Anne Brault et Michael Naas (Paris: Galilée, 2003), 9–11.

Jacques Derrida, 'Avant-propos', in *Psyché: inventions de l'autre*, nouvelle édition augmentée (Paris: Galilée, 1987–98), 9–10.

Derrida, Jacques, 'Avertissement', in *La Vérité en peinture* (Paris: Flammarion, 1978), 3–4.
Derrida, Jacques, 'Back from Moscow, in the USSR', in *Politics, Theory, and Contemporary Culture*, ed. Mark Poster, trans. Mary Quaintaire (New York: Columbia University Press, 1993), 197–235; *Moscou aller-retour* (Paris, Éditions de l'Aube, 1995).
Derrida, Jacques, 'Before the Law', in *Acts of Literature*, ed. Derek Attridge (London: Routledge, 1992), 181–220; 'Préjugés: devant la loi', in *La faculté de juger* (Paris: Minuit, 1985), 87–139.
Derrida, Jacques, 'Between Brackets I', in *Points: Interviews 1974–1994*, ed. Elisabeth Weber (Stanford: Stanford University Press, 1995), 5–29; 'Entre crochets I', in *Points de suspension: Entretiens*, choisis et présentés par Elisabeth Weber (Paris: Galilée, 1992), 13–36.
Derrida, Jacques, 'Cartouches', in *The Truth in Painting*, trans. Geoff Bennington and Ian McLeod (Chicago: University of Chicago Press, 1989), 183–253; 'Cartouches', in *La Vérité en peinture* (Paris: Flammarion, 1978), 211–90.
Derrida, Jacques, 'Che cos' è la poesia?', in *Points. . . Interviews, 1974–1994*, ed. Elisabeth Weber, trans. Peggy Kamuf (Stanford: Stanford University Press, 1995), 289–99; 'Che cos' è la poesia?', in *Points de suspension: Entretiens*, choisis et présentés par Elisabeth Weber (Paris: Galilée, 1992), 303–8.
Derrida, Jacques, 'Cogito and the History of Madness', in *Writing and Difference*, trans. Alan Bass (Chicago: University of Chicago Press, 1989), 31–63; 'Cogito et histoire de la folie', in *L'écriture et la différence* (Paris: Seuil, 2001), 51–97.
Derrida, Jacques, 'Countersignature', in *Genet*, ed. Mairéad Hanrahan, *Paragraph* 27.2 (Edinburgh: Edinburgh University Press, 2004), 7–42.
Derrida, Jacques, 'Deconstruction and the Other', in Richard Kearney, *Dialogues with Contemporary Continental Thinkers: The Phenomenological Heritage* (Manchester: Manchester University Press, 1984), 105–26.
Derrida, Jacques, 'Des tours de Babel', in *Difference in Translation*, ed. Joseph F. Graham (Ithaca: Cornell University Press, 1985), 165–248; 'Des tours de Babel', in *Psyché: Inventions de l'autre*, nouvelle édition revue et augmentée, 2 vols (Paris: Galilée, 1987–2003), I: 203–36.
Derrida, Jacques, 'Différance', in *Margins of Philosophy*, trans. Alan Bass (Chicago: University of Chicago Press, 1990), 1–27; 'La différance', in *Marges – de la philosophie* (Paris: Minuit, 2003), 1–29.
Derrida, Jacques, *Dissemination*, trans. Barbara Johnson (Chicago: University of Chicago Press, 1988); *La dissémination* (Paris: Seuil, 2001).
Derrida, Jacques, 'Dissemination', in *Dissemination*, trans. Barbara Johnson (Chicago: University of Chicago Press, 1988), 287–366; 'La dissémination', in *La dissémination* (Paris: Seuil, 2001), 349–445.
Derrida, Jacques 'The Double Session', in *Dissemination*, trans. Barbara Johnson (Chicago: University of Chicago Press, 1988), 173–285; 'La double séance', in *La dissémination* (Paris: Seuil, 2001), 215–346.

Derrida, Jacques, 'Economimesis', in *The Derrida Reader*, ed. Julian Wolfreys, trans. Richard Klein (Edinburgh: Edinburgh University Press, 1998), 263–93; 'Economimesis', in *Mimesis des articulations* (Paris: Aubier-Flammarion, 1975), 55–93.

Derrida, Jacques, 'Edmond Jabès and the Question of the Book', in *Writing and Difference*, trans. Alan Bass (Chicago: University of Chicago Press, 1989), 64–78; 'Edmond Jabès et la question du livre', in *L'écriture et la différence* (Paris: Seuil, 2001), 99–118.

Derrida, Jacques, *Edmund Husserl's Origin of Geometry: An Introduction*, trans. John P. Leavey, Jr (Lincoln: University of Nebraska Press, 1989); *Edmund Husserl, L'origine de la géométrie: Introduction et traduction* (Paris: Presses Universitaires de France, 1974).

Derrida, Jacques, 'Ellipsis', in *Writing and Difference*, trans. Alan Bass (Chicago: University of Chicago Press, 1989), 294–300; 'Ellipse', in *L'écriture et la différence* (Paris: Seuil, 2001), 429–36.

Derrida, Jacques, 'The Ends of Man', in *Margins of Philosophy*, trans. Alan Bass (Chicago: University of Chicago Press, 1990), 109–36; 'Les fins de l'homme', in *Marges – de la philosophie* (Paris: Minuit, 2003), 129–66.

Derrida, Jacques, 'Envois', in *The Post Card: From Socrates to Freud and Beyond*, trans. Alan Bass (Chicago: University of Chicago Press, 1987), 1–256; 'Envois', in *La carte postale: de Socrate à Freud et au-delà* (Paris: Aubier Flammarion, 2003), 5–273.

Derrida, Jacques, *Eyes of the University: Right to Philosophy II*, trans. Jan Plug (Stanford: Stanford University Press, 2005); second part of *Du droit à la philosophie* (Paris: Galilée, 1990).

Derrida, Jacques, 'Le facteur de la vérité', in *The Post Card: From Socrates to Freud and Beyond*, trans. Alan Bass (Chicago: University of Chicago Press, 1987), 411–96; 'Le facteur de la vérité', in *La carte postale: de Socrate à Freud et au-delà* (Paris: Aubier Flammarion, 2003), 439–524.

Derrida, Jacques, 'Faith and Knowledge: Two Sources of "Religion" at the Limits of Reason Alone', in *Religion*, ed. Jacques Derrida and Gianni Vattimo, trans. Sam Weber (Oxford: Polity Press, 1998), 1–78; *Foi et Savoir, suivi de Le Siècle et le Pardon* (Paris: Seuil, 2000).

Derrida, Jacques, 'Force and Signification', in *Writing and Difference*, trans. Alan Bass (Chicago: University of Chicago Press, 1989), 3–30; 'Force et signification', in *L'écriture et la différence* (Paris: Seuil, 2001), 9–49.

Derrida, Jacques, 'Form and Meaning: A Note on the Phenomenology of Language', in *Margins of Philosophy*, trans. Alan Bass (Chicago: University of Chicago Press, 1990), 155–73; 'La forme et le vouloir-dire: Note sur la phénoménologie du langage', in *Marges – de la philosophie* (Paris: Minuit, 2003), 185–207.

Derrida, Jacques, 'Fors: The Anglish Words of Nicolas Abraham and Maria Torok', in Abraham and Torok, *The Wolf Man's Magic Word: A Cryptonymy*, trans. Nicholas Rand (Minneapolis: University of Minnesota Press, 1986), xi–xlviii; 'Fors: Les mots anglés de Nicolas Abraham et Maria Torok', in Abraham and Torok, *Cryptonomie: le verbier de l'homme aux loups* (Paris: Aubier-Flammarion, 1976), 7–73.

Derrida, Jacques, 'From Restricted to General Economy: A Hegelianism Without Reserve', in *Writing and Difference*, trans. Alan Bass (Chicago: University of Chicago Press, 1989), 251–77; 'De l'économie restreinte à l'économie générale: un hegelianisme sans réserve', in *L'écriture et la différence* (Paris: Seuil, 2001), 369–407.

Derrida, Jacques, *Geneses, Genealogies, Genres and Genius: The Secrets of the Archive*, trans. Beverly Bie Brahic (Edinburgh: Edinburgh University Press, 2006); *Genèse, généalogies, genres et le génie: Les secrets de l'archive* (Paris: Galilée, 2003).

Derrida, Jacques, ' "Genesis and Structure" and Phenomenology', in *Writing and Difference*, trans. Alan Bass (Chicago: University of Chicago Press, 1989), 154–68; ' "Genèse et structure" et la phénomenologie', in *L'écriture et la différence* (Paris: Seuil, 2001), 409–28.

Derrida, Jacques, '*Geschlecht*: Sexual Difference, Ontological Difference', trans. Ruben Berezdivin, *Research in Phenomenology* 13 (1983): 65–83; '*Geschlecht*: différence sexuelle, différence ontologique', in *Psyché: Inventions de l'autre*, nouvelle édition revue et augmentée, 2 vols (Paris: Galilée, 1987–2003), I: 15–33.

Derrida, Jacques, '*Geschlecht* II: Heidegger's Hand', in *Deconstruction and Philosophy: The Texts of Jacques Derrida*, ed. John Sallis, trans. John P. Leavey (Chicago: University of Chicago Press, 1987), 161–96; 'La main de Heidegger (*Geschlecht* II)', in *Psyché: Inventions de l'autre*, nouvelle édition revue et augmentée, 2 vols (Paris: Galilée, 1987–2003), I: 35–68.

Derrida, Jacques, *Given Time: 1. Counterfeit Money*, trans. Peggy Kamuf (Chicago: University of Chicago Press, 1992); *Donner le temps: I. La fausse monnaie* (Paris: Galilée, 1991).

Derrida, Jacques, *Glas*, trans. John P. Leavey, Jr and Richard Rand (Lincoln: University of Nebraska Press, 1990); *Glas* (Paris: Galilée, 1995).

Derrida, Jacques, 'Heidegger's Ear: Philopolemology (*Geschlecht* IV)', in *Reading Heidegger: Commemorations*, ed. John Sallis, trans. John Leavey, Jr (Bloomington: Indiana University Press, 1992), 163–218; 'L'oreille de Heidegger: Philopolémologie (*Geschlecht* IV)', in *Politiques de l'amitié* (Paris: Galilée, 1994), 341–419.

Derrida, Jacques, 'Hostpitality', in *Acts of Religion*, trans. Gil Anidjar (London: Routledge, 2002), 356–71.

Derrida, Jacques, 'How to Avoid Speaking: Denials', in *Derrida and Negative Theology*, trans. Ken Frieden, ed. Harold Coward and Toby Foshay (Albany: SUNY, 1992), 73–142; 'Comment ne pas parler: Dénégations', in *Psyché: Inventions de l'autre*, nouvelle édition revue et augmentée, 2 vols (Paris: Galilée, 1987–2003), I: 145–200.

Derrida, Jacques, 'Ja, or the *faux-bond* II', in *Points . . . Interviews 1974–1994*, ed. Elisabeth Weber, trans. Peggy Kamuf (Stanford: Stanford University Press, 1995), 30–77; 'Ja, ou le faux-bond', in *Points de suspension: Entretiens*, choisis et présentés par Elisabeth Weber (Paris: Galilée, 1992), 37–81.

Derrida, Jacques, 'Khora', in *On the Name*, trans. Ian Mcleod (Stanford: Stanford University Press, 1995), 87–127; *Khora* (Paris: Galilée, 1993), 19.

Derrida, Jacques, 'The Law of Genre', *Critical Inquiry* 7.1 (1980): 55–81; 'La loi du genre', in *Parages*, nouvelle édition revue et augmentée (Paris: Galilée, 2003), 231–66.

Derrida, Jacques, 'LIVING ON. Border Lines', in *Deconstruction and Criticism*, trans. James Hulbert (New York: Continuum, 1979), 75–176; 'Survivre' in *Parages*, nouvelle édition revue et augmentée (Paris: Galilée, 2003), 109–203.

Derrida, Jacques, *Mémoires – for Paul de Man*, trans. Cecile Lindsay, Jonathan Culler and Eduardo Cadava (New York: Columbia University Press, 1986); *Mémoires – pour Paul de Man* (Paris: Galilée, 1988).

Derrida, Jacques, *Memoirs of the Blind: The Self-Portrait and Other Ruins*, trans. Pascale-Anne Brault and Michael Naas (Chicago: University of Chicago Press, 1993); *Mémoires d'aveugle: L'autoportrait et autres ruines* (Paris: Réunion des musées nationaux, 1990).

Derrida, Jacques, *Monolingualism of the Other; or, The Prothestic Origin*, trans. Patrick Menash (Stanford: Stanford University Press, 1998); *Le monolinguisme de l'autre, ou la prothèse d'origine* (Paris: Galilée, 1996).

Derrida, Jacques, 'My Chances/Mes Chances: A Rendezvous with some Epicurean Sterophonies', in *Taking Chances: Derrida, Psychoanalysis and Literature*, ed. Joseph H. Smith and William Kerrigan (Baltimore: Johns Hopkins University Press, 1984), 1–32; 'Mes Chances: Au rendez-vous de quelques stéréophoniees épicuriennes', in *Psyché: Inventions de l'autre*, nouvelle édition revue et augmentée, 2 vols (Paris: Galilée, 1987–2003), I: 353–84.

Derrida, Jacques, 'Negotiations', in *Negotiations: Interventions and Interviews 1971–2001*, trans. Elizabeth Rottenberg (Stanford: Stanford University Press, 2002), 11–40.

Derrida, Jacques, *Of Grammatology*, trans. Gayatri Chakravorty Spivak (Baltimore: Johns Hopkins University Press, 1990); *De la grammatologie* (Paris: Minuit, 2004).

Derrida, Jacques, *Of Hospitality, Anne Dufourmantelle invites Jacques Derrida to Respond*, trans. Rachel Bowlby (Stanford: Stanford University Press, 2000).

Derrida, Jacques, *Of Spirit: Heidegger and the Question*, trans. Geoffrey Bennington and Rachel Bowlby (Chicago: University of Chicago Press, 1989); 'De l'esprit', in *Heidegger et la question* (Paris: Champs/Flammarion, 1990), 9–143.

Derrida, Jacques, *On Touching – Jean-Luc Nancy*, trans. Christine Irizarry (Stanford: Stanford University Press, 2005); *Le toucher, Jean-Luc Nancy* (Paris: Galilée, 2000).

Derrida, Jacques, *The Other Heading: Reflections on Today's Europe*, trans. Pascale-Anne Brault and Michael Naas (Bloomington: Indiana University Press, 1992); *L'autre cap: Mémoires, réponses et responsabilités* (Paris: Minuit, 1991).

Derrida, Jacques, 'Otobiographies: The Teaching of Nietzsche and the Politics of the Proper Name', in *The Ear of the Other*, ed. Christie McDonald, trans. Avital Ronell (Lincoln: University of Nebraska Press, 1988), 1–38; *Otobiographies: l'enseignement de Nietzsche et la politique du nom propre* (Paris: Galilée, 1984).

Derrida, Jacques, '*Ousia* and *Grammē*: Note on a Note from *Being and Time*', in *Margins of Philosophy*, trans. Alan Bass (Chicago: University of Chicago Press, 1990), 29–67; '*Ousia* et *Grammè*: note sur une note de *Sein und Zeit*', in *Marges – de la philosophie* (Paris: Minuit, 2003), 31–78.

Derrida, Jacques, 'Outwork, Prefacing', in *Dissemination*, trans. Barbara Johnson (Chicago: University of Chicago Press, 1988), 1–59; 'Hors livre: préfaces', in *La dissémination* (Paris: Seuil, 2001), 7–68.

Derrida, Jacques, *Parages*, nouvelle édition revue et augmentée (Paris: Galilée, 2003).

Derrida, Jacques, 'Parergon', in *The Truth in Painting*, trans. Geoff Bennington and Ian McLeod (Chicago: University of Chicago Press, 1989), 15–147; 'Parergon', in *La Vérité en peinture* (Paris: Flammarion, 1978), 23–168.

Derrida, Jacques, 'La Parole. Donner, nommer, appeler', in *Ricoeur, Cahiers de l'Herne 81* (Paris: l'Herne, 2004), 19–25.

Derrida, Jacques, 'Pas', in *Parages*, nouvelle édition revue et augmentée (Paris: Galilée, 2003), 17–108.

Derrida, Jacques, 'Passe-Partout', in *The Truth in Painting*, trans. Geoff Bennington and Ian McLeod (Chicago: University of Chicago Press, 1989), 1–13; 'Passe-Partout', in *La Vérité en peinture* (Paris: Flammarion, 1978), 5–18.

Derrida, Jacques 'The Pit and the Pyramid: Introduction to Hegel's Semiology', in *Margins of Philosophy*, trans. Alan Bass (Chicago: University of Chicago Press, 1990), 69–108; 'Le puits et la pyramide: introduction à la sémiologie de Hegel', in *Marges – de la philosophie* (Paris: Minuit, 2003), 79–127.

Derrida, Jacques, 'Plato's Pharmacy', in *Dissemination*, trans. Barbara Johnson (Chicago: University of Chicago Press, 1988), 61–171; 'La pharmacie de Platon', in *La dissémination* (Paris: Seuil, 2001), 69–167.

Derrida, Jacques, *The Politics of Friendship*, trans. George Collins (London: Verso, 2005); *Politiques de l'amitié* (Paris: Galilée, 1994).

Derrida, Jacques, *The Post Card: From Socrates to Freud and Beyond*, trans. Alan Bass (Chicago: University of Chicago Press, 1987); *La carte postale: de Socrate à Freud et au-delà* (Paris: Flammarion, 2003), 275–437.

Derrida, Jacques, 'The Principle of Reason: The University in the Eyes of its Pupils', in *Eyes of the University: Right to Philosophy 2*, trans. Catherine Porter and Edward P. Morris (Stanford: Stanford University Press, 2005), 129–55; 'Les pupilles de l'Université: Le principe de raison et l'idée de l'Université', in *Du droit à la philosophie* (Paris: Galilée, 1990), 461–98.

Derrida, Jacques, *The Problem of Genesis in Husserl's Philosophy*, trans. Marian Hobson (Chicago: University of Chicago Press, 2003); *Le problème de la genèse dans la philosophie de Husserl* (Paris: Presses Universitaires de France, 1990).

Derrida, Jacques, 'Proverb: "He that would Pun . . ."', in John P. Leavey, Jr, *Glassary* (Lincoln: University of Nebraska Press, 1986), 17–20.

Derrida, Jacques, 'Provocation: Forewords', in *Without Alibi*, trans. Peggy Kamuf (Stanford: Stanford University Press, 2002), xv–xxxv.

Derrida, Jacques, 'Qual Quelle: Valéry's Sources', in *Margins of Philosophy*, trans. Alan Bass (Chicago: University of Chicago Press, 1990), 273–306; 'Qual Quelle: Les sources de Valéry', in *Marges – de la philosophie* (Paris: Minuit, 2003), 325–63.

Derrida, Jacques, 'Rams: Uninterrupted Dialogue – Between Two Infinities, the Poem', in *Sovereignties in Question: The Poetics of Paul Celan*, ed. Thomas Dutoit and Outi Pasanen (New York: Fordham University Press, 2005), 135–63; *Béliers – Les dialogue ininterrompu: entre deux infinis, le poème* (Paris: Galilée, 2003).

Derrida, Jacques, 'The Reason of the Strongest (Are There Rogue States?)', in *Rogues: Two Essays on Reason*, trans. Rachel Bowlby (Stanford: Stanford University Press, 2005), 1–114; 'La raison du plus fort (Y a-t-il des états voyous?)', in *Voyous: Deux essais sur la raison* (Paris: Galilée, 2003), 19–161.

Derrida, Jacques, 'Restitutions of the Truth in Pointing', in *The Truth in Painting*, trans. Geoff Bennington and Ian McLeod (Chicago: University of Chicago Press, 1989), 255–382; 'Restitutions de la vérité en pointure', in *La Vérité en peinture* (Paris: Flammarion, 1978), 291–436.

Derrida, Jacques, 'The Retrait of Metaphor', in *The Derrida Reader*, ed. Julian Wolfreys, trans. F. Gasdner (Edinburgh: Edinburgh University Press, 1998), 102–29; 'Le retrait de la métaphore', in *Psyché: Inventions de l'autre* (Paris: Galilée, 1987), 63–93.

Derrida, Jacques, 'Sauf le nom (post-scriptum)', in *On the Name*, trans. John P. Leavey, ed. Thomas Dutoit (Stanford: Stanford University Press, 1995), 33–85; *Sauf le nom* (Paris: Galilée, 1993).

Derrida, Jacques, 'Shibboleth: For Paul Celan', in *Sovereignties in Question: The Poetics of Paul Celan*, ed. Thomas Dutoit and Outi Pasanen (New York: Fordham University Press, 2005), 1–64; *Schibboleth – pour Paul Celan* (Paris: Galilée, 1986).

Derrida, Jacques, *Signéponge/Signsponge*, trans. Richard Rand (New York: Columbia University Press, 1988).

Derrida, Jacques, 'Some Statements and Truisms about Neologisms, Newisms, Postisms, Parasitisms, and Other Small Seismisms', in *The States of 'Theory': History, Art and Critical Discourse*, ed. and intro. David Carroll, trans. Anne Tomiche (New York: Columbia University Press, 1990), 63–94.

Derrida, Jacques, *Specters of Marx: The State of the Debt, the Work of Mourning, and the New International*, trans. Peggy Kamuf (London: Routledge, 1994); *Spectres de Marx: L'État de la dette, le travail du deuil et la nouvelle Internationale* (Paris: Galilée, 1993).

Derrida, Jacques, *Speech and Phenomena and Other Essays on Husserl's Theory of Signs*, trans. David B. Allison (Evanston: Northwestern University Press, 1973); *La voix et le phénomène: Introduction au problème du signe dans la phénoménologie de Husserl* (Paris: Presses Universitaires de France, 1993).

Derrida, Jacques, *Spurs: Nietzsche's Styles/Éperons: Les Styles de Nietzsche*, trans. Barbara Harlow, intro. Stefano Agosti (Chicago: University of Chicago Press, 1979).

Derrida, Jacques, 'The Theatre of Cruelty and the Closure of Representation', in *Writing and Difference*, trans. Alan Bass (Chicago: University of Chicago Press, 1989), 232–50; 'Le théâtre de la cruauté et la clôture de la représentation', in *L'écriture et la différence* (Paris: Seuil, 2001), 341–68.

Derrida, Jacques, 'The Time is Out of Joint', in *Deconstruction is/in America: A New Sense of the Political*, ed. Anslem Haverkamp, trans. Peggy Kamuf (New York: New York University Press, 1995), 14–38.

Derrida, Jacques, 'A Time of Farewells: Heidegger (read by) Hegel (read by) Malabou', in Catherine Malabou, *The Future of Hegel: Plasticity, Temporality and Dialectic* (London: Routledge, 2005), vii–xlvii; 'Le temps des adieux: Heidegger (lu par) Hegel (lu par) Malabou', *La Revue Philosophique* 1 (1998) (Paris: P. U. F.), 3–47.

Derrida, Jacques, 'To Speculate – on "Freud" ', in *The Post Card: From Socrates to Freud and Beyond*, trans. Alan Bass (Chicago: University of Chicago Press, 1987), 257–409; 'Spéculer – sur "Freud" ', in *La carte postale: de Socrate à Freud et au-delà* (Paris: Flammarion, 2003), 275–437.

Derrida, Jacques, *The Truth in Painting*, trans. Geoff Bennington and Ian McLeod (Chicago: University of Chicago Press, 1989); *La Vérité en peinture* (Paris: Flammarion, 1978).

Derrida, Jacques, 'Tympan', in *Margins of Philosophy*, trans. Alan Bass (Chicago: University of Chicago Press, 1990), ix–xxix; 'Tympan', in *Marges– de la philosophie* (Paris: Minuit, 2003), i–xxv.

Derrida, Jacques, 'Typewriter Ribbon: Limited Ink (2)', in *Without Alibi*, trans. Peggy Kamuf (Stanford: Stanford University Press, 2002), 71–160; 'Le ruban de machine à écrire. Limited Ink II', in *Papier Machine* (Paris: Galilée, 2001), 33–147.

Derrida, Jacques, 'The Villanova Roundtable', in *Deconstruction in a Nutshell: A Conversation with Jacques Derrida*, ed. and comm. John D. Caputo (New York: Fordham University Press, 1997), 3–28.

Derrida, Jacques, 'Violence and Metaphysics: An Essay on the Thought of Emmanuel Levinas', in *Writing and Difference*, trans. Alan Bass (Chicago: University of Chicago Press, 1989), 79–153; 'Violence et métaphysique: Essai sur la pensée d'Emmanuel Levinas', in *L'écriture et la différence* (Paris: Seuil, 2001), 117–228.

Derrida, Jacques, 'What is a "Relevant" Translation?', *Critical Inquiry* 27 (2001): 174–200; 'Qu'est-ce qu'une traduction "relevante"?', in *Derrida, Cahiers de l'Herne 83*, ed. Marie-Louise and Ginette Michaud (Paris: L'Herne, 2004), 561–76.

Derrida, Jacques, 'White Mythology: Metaphor in the Text of Philosophy', in *Margins of Philosophy*, trans. Alan Bass (Chicago: University of Chicago Press, 1990), 207–71; 'La mythologie blanche: la métaphore dans le texte philosophique', in *Marges – de la philosophie* (Paris: Minuit, 2003), 247–324.

Derrida, Jacques, *Who's Afraid of Philosophy? Right to Philosophy I*, trans. Jan Plug (Stanford: University of Stanford Press, 2002); first part of *Du droit à la philosophie* (Paris: Galilée, 1990).

Derrida, Jacques, *Writing and Difference*, trans. Alan Bass (Chicago: University of Chicago Press, 1989); *L'écriture et la différence* (Paris: Seuil, 2001).

Derrida, Jacques, and Derek Attridge, 'This Strange Institution Called Literature: An Interview with Jacques Derrida', in *Acts of Literature*, ed. Derek Attridge (New York: Routledge, 1992), 33–75.

Derrida, Jacques and Jean-Luc Nancy, 'Responsabilité – du sens à venir', in *Sens en tous sens: Autour des travaux de Jean-Luc Nancy*, sous la direction de Francis Guibal et Jean-Clet Martin (Paris: Galilée, 2004), 165–200.

Dickinson, Emily, *The Complete Poems*, ed. Thomas H. Johnson (London: Faber & Faber, 1987).

Didi-Huberman, Georges, *L'image survivante: Histoire de l'art et le temps des fantômes selon Aby Warburg* (Paris: Minuit, 2002).

Donougho, Martin, 'Hegel's Art of Memory', in *Endings: Questions of Memory on Hegel and Heidegger*, ed. Rebecca Comay and John McCumber (Evanston: Northwestern University Press, 1999), 139–59.

Dryden, John, *Annus Mirabilis: The Year of Wonders, 1666*, in *The Major Works*, ed. Keith Walker (Oxford: Oxford University Press, 2003), 23–70.

Dryden, John, *An Essay of Dramatic Poesy*, in *The Major Works*, ed. Keith Walker (Oxford: Oxford University Press, 2003), 70–130.

Dryden, John, *To My Honoured friend Dr Charleton*, in *The Major Works*, ed. Keith Walker (Oxford: Oxford University Press, 2003), 21–2.

Düttmann, Alexander García, *The Memory of Thought: An Essay on Heidegger and Adorno*, trans. Nicholas Walker (London: Continuum, 2002).

Elton, W. R., 'Aristotle's *Nicomachean Ethics* and Shakespeare's *Troilus and Cressida*', *Journal of History of Ideas* 58 (1997): 331–7.

Ewbank, Inga-Stina, 'The Triumph of Time in *The Winter's Tale*', *A Review of English Literature* 5 (1964): 83–100.

Fenves, Peter, 'Derrida and History: Some Questions Derrida Pursues in His Early Writings', in *Jacques Derrida and the Humanities: A Critical Reader*, ed. Tom Cohen (Cambridge: Cambridge University Press, 2001), 271–95.

Ferrarin, Alfredo, *Hegel and Aristotle* (Cambridge: Cambridge University Press, 2001).

Fielding, Henry, *The History of Tom Jones, A Foundling*, ed. R. P. C. Mutter (London: Penguin, 1985).

Foucault, Michel, 'The Discourse on Language', in *The Archaeology of Knowledge*, trans. Rupert Swyer (New York: Pantheon, 1972), 215–37.

Foucault, Michel, *The Order of Things: An Archaeology of the Human Sciences*, trans. Alan Sheridan (London: Routledge, 2002).

Gadamer, Hans-Georg, *The Beginning of Philosophy*, trans. Rod Coltman (New York: Continuum, 2001).

Garrick, David, *The Letters of David Garrick*, ed. David M. Little and George M. Kahrl, 2 vols (London: Oxford University Press, 1963).

Gasché, Rodolphe, 'Thinking Without Wonder', in *The Horror of Thinking: Critique Theory, Philosophy* (Stanford, Stanford University Press, 2007), 348–63.

Gasché, Rodolphe, *The Tain of the Mirror: Derrida and the Philosophy of Reflection* (Cambridge, MA: Harvard University Press, 1986).
Gaston, Sean, *Derrida and Disinterest* (London: Continuum, 2005).
Gaston, Sean, *The Impossible Mourning of Jacques Derrida* (London: Continuum, 2006).
Gibbon, Edward, *The History of the Decline and Fall of the Roman Empire*, ed. David Womersley, 3 vols (London: Penguin, 1994).
Glendinning, Simon (ed.), *Arguing With Derrida* (Oxford: Blackwell, 2001).
Greene, Thomas M., *The Vulnerable Text: Essays on Renaissance Literature* (New York: Columbia University Press, 1986).
Haar, Michel, 'The History of Being and Its Hegelian Model', in *Endings: Questions of Memory on Hegel and Heidegger*, ed. Rebecca Comay and John McCumber, trans. Reginald Lilly (Evanston: Northwestern University Press, 1999), 45–56.
Halliwell, Stephen, *Aristotle's Poetics* (London: Duckworth, 2000).
Hamacher, Werner, *Pleroma – Reading Hegel: The Genesis and Structure of a Dialectical Hermeneutics in Hegel*, trans. Nicholas Walker and Simon Jarvis (London: Athlone, 1998).
Hartman, Geoffrey, 'Homage to *Glas*', *Critical Inquiry* 33.2 (2007): 244–61.
Hartog, François, *The Mirror of Herodotus: The Representation of the Other in the Writing of History*, trans. Janet Lloyd (Berkeley: University of California Press, 1988).
Heckman, John, 'Introduction', in Jean Hyppolite, *Genesis and Structure of Hegel's Phenomenology of Spirit*, trans. Samuel Cherniak and John Heckman (Evanston: Northwestern University Press, 1989), xv–xli.
Hegel, G. W. F., *Lectures on the History of Philosophy I: Greek Philosophy to Plato*, trans. E. S. Haldane, intro. Frederick C. Beister (Lincoln: University of Nebraska Press, 1995); *Vorlesungen über die Geschichte der Philosophie I* (Frankfurt am Main: Suhrkamp, 1986).
Hegel, G. W. F., *Phenomenology of Spirit*, trans. A. V. Miller (Oxford: Oxford University Press, 1977); *Phänomenologie des Geistes* (Frankfurt am Main: Suhrkamp, 1986).
Hegel, G. W. F., *Philosophy of Mind, Being Part Three of the Encyclopaedia of The Philosophical Sciences (1830)*, trans. William Wallace, foreword J. N. Findlay (Oxford: Clarendon, 1971).
Hegel, G. W. F., *Science of Logic*, trans. A. V. Miller (London: Allen & Unwin, 1969).
Heidegger, Martin, 'Anaximander's Saying', in *Off the Beaten Track*, ed. and trans. Julian Young and Kenneth Hynes (Cambridge: Cambridge University Press, 2002), 242–81.
Heidegger, Martin, *Being and Time*, trans. John Macquarrie and Edward Robinson (Oxford: Blackwell, 1990); *Sein und Zeit* (Frankfurt am Main: Vittorio Klostermann, 1977).
Heidegger, Martin, 'The End of Philosophy and the Task of Thinking', in *Basic Writings*, ed. David Farrell Krell, trans. Joan Stambaugh (San Francisco: Harper, 1993), 425–49.
Heidegger, Martin, *Identity and Difference*, trans. Joan Stambaugh (Chicago: University of Chicago Press, 2002),

Heidegger, Martin, 'The Origin of the Work of Art', in *Basic Writings*, ed. David Farrell Krell, trans. Albert Hofstadter (San Francisco: Harper, 1993), 139–212; 'Der Ursprung des Kunstwerkes', in *Holzwege* (Frankfurt am Main: Vittorio Klostermann, 1950), 7–68.

Heidegger, Martin, *Plato's Sophist*, trans. Richard Rojcewicz and André Schuwer (Bloomington: Indiana University Press, 1997).

Heidegger, Martin, *Unterwegs zur Sprache* (Pfullingen: Neske, 1959); translations collected in *On the Way to Language*, trans. Peter D. Hertz and Joan Stambaugh (New York: Harper and Row, 1971), and *Poetry, Language and Thought*, trans. Albert Hofstadter (New York: Harper and Row, 1975).

Heidegger, Martin, 'The Way to Language', in *Basic Writings*, ed. and trans. David Farrell Krell (San Francisco: Harper, 1993), 397–426.

Heidegger, Martin, *What is Called Thinking?*, trans. Fred D. Wieck and J. Glenn Gray (New York: Harper and Row, 1968); 'What Calls for Thinking', in *Basic Writings*, ed. David Farrell Krell (San Francisco: Harper, 1993), 365–91; *Was heisst Denken?* (Frankfurt am Main: Vittoria Klostermann, 2002).

Heidegger, Martin and Eugen Fink, *Heraclitus Seminar*, trans. Charles H. Seibert (Evanston: Northwestern University Press, 1993).

Herodotus, *The Histories*, trans. Aubrey de Sélincourt (London: Penguin, 1972); *The History*, trans. David Grene (Chicago: University of Chicago Press, 1988); *Herodotus*, trans. A. D. Godley, 4 vols (London: Heinemann, 1961).

Hesiod, *The Works and Days; Theogony; The Shield of Herakles*, trans. Richmond Lattimore (Ann Arbor: University of Michigan Press, 1978).

Hobbes, Thomas, *Leviathan; or, The Matter, Forme, & Power of a Common-Wealth Ecclesiastical and Civill*, ed. Richard Tuck (Cambridge: Cambridge University Press, 1996).

Hodge, Joanna, *Heidegger and Ethics* (London: Routledge, 1995).

Holland, Nancy J. (ed.), *Feminist Interpretations of Jacques Derrida* (Pennsylvania: Pennsylvania State University Press, 1997).

Homer, *Odyssey*, trans. A. T. Murray and George E. Dimock, 2 vols (Cambridge, MA: Harvard University Press, 1995).

Howell, Wilbur Samuel, *Eighteenth Century British Logic and Rhetoric* (Princeton: Princeton University Press, 1971).

Hume, David, *A TREATISE of Human Nature: BEING An ATTEMPT to introduce the experimental Method of Reasoning into Moral Subjects*, ed. L. A. Selby-Bigge and P. H. Nidditch (Oxford: Oxford University Press, 1978).

Husserl, Edmund, 'Philosophy and the Crisis of European Man', in *Phenomenology and the Crisis of Philosophy*, trans. Quentin Lauer (New York: Harper, 1965), 149–92; see also, 'Philosophy and the Crisis of European Humanity', in *The Crisis of European Sciences and Transcendental Phenomenology: An Introduction to Phenomenological Philosophy*, trans. David Carr (Evanston: Northwestern University Press, 1970), 269–99.

Hyppolite, Jean, *Genesis and Structure of Hegel's Phenomenology of Spirit*, trans. Samuel Cherniak and John Heckman (Evanston: Northwestern University Press, 1989).

Jacobs, David C. (ed.), *The Presocratics After Heidegger* (Albany: State University of New York Press, 1999).

Janicaud, Dominique, 'Heidegger and Hegel: An Impossible "Dialogue"?', in *Endings: Questions of Memory on Hegel and Heidegger*, ed. Rebecca Comay and John McCumber, trans. Nina Belmonte (Evanston: Northwestern University Press, 1999), 26–44.

Johansen, T. K., *Aristotle on the Sense Organs* (Cambridge: Cambridge University Press, 1998).

Johnson, Samuel, *The Letters of Samuel Johnson, Volume 1: 1731–1772*, ed. Brue Redford (Princeton: Princeton University Press, 1992).

Johnson, Samuel and James Boswell, *A Journey to the Western Islands of Scotland and The Journal of a Tour to the Hebrides*, ed. Peter Levi (London: Penguin, 1993).

Jones, Thora Burnley and Bernard de Bear Nicol, *Neo-Classical Dramatic Criticism 1560–1770* (Cambridge: Cambridge University Press, 1976).

Joyce, James, *Finnegans Wake*, intro. Seamus Deane (London: Penguin, 1992).

Jusserand, J. J., *A Literary History of the English People – from the Origins to the Civil War*, 3 vols (London: C. Fisher Unwin, 1925).

Kant, Immanuel, *Anthropology From a Pragmatic Point of View*, ed. and trans. Robert B. Louden (Cambridge: Cambridge University Press, 2006).

Kant, Immanuel, *Critique of Pure Reason*, trans. Paul Guyer (Cambridge: Cambridge University Press, 1998); *Kritik der Reinen Vernunft* (Frankfurt am Main: Im Insel, 1964).

Kamuf, Peggy, 'Singular Sense, Second-Hand', *Book of Addresses* (Stanford: Stanford University Press, 2005), 268–81.

Kappler, Claude, *Monstres, Démons, et Merveilles à la fin du Moyen Age* (Paris: Payot, 1980).

Kates, Joshua, *Essential History: Jacques Derrida and the Development of Deconstruction* (Evanston: Northwestern University Press, 2005).

Kiefer, Frederick, 'The Iconography of Time in *The Winter's Tale*', *Renaissance and Reformation* 23 (1999): 47–64.

Kierkegaard, Søren, *Either/Or: A Fragment of Life*, ed. Victor Eremita, trans. Alastair Hannay (London: Penguin, 1992).

Kojève, Alexandre, *Introduction to the Reading of Hegel: Lectures on the Phenomenology of Spirit*, ed. Raymond Queneau and Allan Bloom, trans. James H. Nichols (Ithaca: Cornell University Press, 1991).

Krell, David Farrell, *Of Memory, Reminiscence, and Writing: On the Verge* (Bloomington: Indiana University Press, 1990).

Krell, David Farrell, *The Purest of Bastards: Work of Mourning; Art, and Affirmation in the Thought of Jacques Derrida* (Pennsylvania: Pennsylvania State University Press, 2000).

Kriek, Theresa M., 'The Triumph of Time: Paradox in *The Winter's Tale*', *Centennial Review* 26 (1982): 341–53.

Laertius, Diogenes, *Lives of Eminent Philosophers*, trans. R. D. Hicks, 2 vols (Cambridge, MA: Harvard University Press, 1980).

Leavey, Jr, John P., *Glassary* (Lincoln: University of Nebraska Press, 1986).

Lévinas, Emmanuel, 'De la description à l'existence', in *En découvrant l'existence avec Husserl et Heidegger*, 3rd edn (Paris: Vrin, 2001), 129–51.

Lévinas, Emmanuel, *Is it Righteous to Be? Interviews with Emmanuel Levinas*, ed. Jill Robbins (Stanford: Stanford University Press, 2001).

Lévinas, Emmanuel, *Otherwise than Being or Beyond Essence*, trans. Alphonso Lingis (Pittsburgh: Duquesne University Press, 2000).

Lévinas, Emmanuel, *Time and the Other*, trans. Richard A. Cohen (Pittsburgh: Duquesne University Press, 1987).

Lévinas, Emmanuel, *Totality and Infinity: An Essay on Exteriority*, trans. Alphonso Lingis (Pittsburgh: Duquesne University Press, 1996); *Totalité et Infini: Essai sur l'extériorite* (Paris: Le Livre de Poche, 2001).

Lévinas, Emmanuel, 'The Trace of the Other', in *Deconstruction in Context: Literature and Philosophy*, ed. Mark C. Taylor, trans. A. Lingus (Chicago: University of Chicago Press, 1986), 345–59; 'La trace de l'autre', in *En découvrant l'existence avec Husserl et Heidegger*, 3rd edn (Paris: Vrin, 2001), 261–82.

Lewis, Philip, 'Vers la traduction abusive', in *Les fins de l'homme: à partir du travail de Jacques Derrida* (Paris: Galilée, 1981), 253–61.

Locke, John, *An Essay Concerning Human Understanding*, ed. Peter H. Nidditch (Oxford: Oxford University Press, 1979).

Malabou, Catherine, *The Future of Hegel: Plasticity, Temporality and Dialectic* (London: Routledge, 2005).

Malabou, Catherine and Jacques Derrida *Counterpath: Traveling with Jacques Derrida*, trans. David Wills (Stanford: Stanford University Press, 2004); *Le Contre-allée* (Paris: La Quinzaine littéraire-Louis Vuitton, 1997).

Marrati, Paola, *Genesis and Trace: Derrida Reading Husserl and Heidegger*, trans. Simon Sparks (Stanford: Stanford University Press, 2005).

Martindale, Michelle and Charles, *Shakespeare and the Uses of Antiquity: An Introductory Essay* (London: Routledge, 1990).

Miller, J. Hillis, 'Line', in *Ariadne's Thread: Story Lines* (New Haven: Yale University Press, 1992), 1–27.

Momigliano, Arnaldo, 'The Place of Herodotus in the History of Historiography', in *Studies in Historiography* (New York: Harper Torchbooks, 1966), 127–42.

Munson, Rosaria Vignolo, *Telling Wonders: Ethnographic and Political Discourse in the Work of Herodotus* (Ann Arbor: University of Michigan Press, 2001).

Nancy, Jean-Luc, *Le poids d'une pensée* (Sainte-Foy: Le Griffon d'argile, 1991); partially translated in *The Gravity of Thought*, trans. François Raffoul and Gregory Recco (Atlantic Highlands: Humanities Press, 1997).

Nancy, Jean-Luc, *The Speculative Remark (One of Hegel's bon mots)*, trans. Celine Surprenant (Stanford: Stanford University Press, 2001).

Nancy, Jean-Luc and Philippe Lacoue-Labarthe, *The Title of the Letter: A Reading of Lacan*, trans. François Raffeisl and David Pettigrew (Albany: State University of New York Press, 1992); *Le titre de la lettre: une lecture de Lacan* (Paris: Galilée, 1973).

O'Connell, Erin, *Heraclitus and Derrida: Presocratic Deconstruction* (New York: Peter Lang, 2005).

Plato, *Charmides*, in *The Dialogues of Plato*, trans. Benjamin Jowett, 5 vols (Oxford: Clarendon Press, 1892), I; *Plato*, W. R. M. Lamb (London: Heinemann, 1955).

Plato, *Cratylus*, in *The Dialogues of Plato*, trans. Benjamin Jowett, 5 vols (Oxford: Clarendon Press, 1892), I.

Plato, *Euthydemus*, in *The Dialogues of Plato*, trans. Benjamin Jowett, 5 vols (Oxford: Clarendon Press, 1892), I; *Plato*, trans. W. R. M. Lamb (Cambridge, MA: Harvard University Press, 1977).

Plato, *Gorgias*, in *The Dialogues of Plato*, trans. Benjamin Jowett, 5 vols (Oxford: Clarendon Press, 1892), II.

Plato, *Lysis*, in *The Dialogues of Plato*, trans. Benjamin Jowett, 5 vols (Oxford: Clarendon Press, 1892), I.

Plato, *Parmenides*, in *The Dialogues of Plato*, trans. Benjamin Jowett, 5 vols (Oxford: Clarendon Press, 1892), IV; *Plato*, trans. H. N. Fowler (London: Heinemann, 1953).

Plato, *Phaedo*, in *The Dialogues of Plato*, trans. Benjamin Jowett, 5 vols (Oxford: Clarendon Press, 1892), II.

Plato, *Phaedrus*, in *The Dialogues of Plato*, trans. Benjamin Jowett, 5 vols (Oxford: Clarendon Press, 1892), I; *Plato*, trans. Harold North Fowler (London: Heinemann, 1953).

Plato, *Protagoras*, in *The Dialogues of Plato*, trans. Benjamin Jowett, 5 vols (Oxford: Clarendon Press, 1892), I.

Plato, *Republic*, in *The Dialogues of Plato*, trans. Benjamin Jowett, 5 vols (Oxford: Clarendon Press, 1892), III; Plato, *The Republic*, trans. Paul Shory, 2 vols (London: Heinemann, 1963).

Plato, *Sophist*, in *The Dialogues of Plato*, trans. Benjamin Jowett, 5 vols (Oxford: Clarendon Press, 1892), IV; *Plato*, trans. Harold North Fowler (Cambridge, MA: Harvard University Press, 1987); *Le sophiste*, in *Platon oeuvres complètes*, trans. Auguste Diès (Paris: Les Belles Lettres, 1955), 7.3.

Plato, *Symposium*, in *The Dialogues of Plato*, trans. Benjamin Jowett, 5 vols (Oxford: Clarendon Press, 1892), I.

Plato, *Theaetetus*, in *The Dialogues of Plato*, trans. Benjamin Jowett, 5 vols (Oxford: Clarendon Press, 1892), IV.

Plato, *Timaeus*, in *The Dialogues of Plato*, trans. Benjamin Jowett, 5 vols (Oxford: Clarendon Press, 1892), III; *Plato*, R. G. Bury (London: Heinemann, 2005).

Plotinus, *The Enneads*, trans. Stephen Mackenna, intro. and ed. John Dillon (London: Penguin, 1991).

Poole, Robert, ' "Give Us Our Eleven Days!": Calendar Reform in Eighteenth-century England', *Past and Present* 149 (1995): 95–139.

Protevi, John, *Time and Exteriority: Aristotle, Heidegger, Derrida* (Lewisburg: Bucknell University Press, 1994).

Rackin, Phyllis, *Stages of History: Shakespeare's English Chronicles* (London: Routledge, 1991).

Ricoeur, Paul, *Time and Narrative* III, trans. Kathleen Blamey and David Pellauer (Chicago: University of Chicago Press, 1990).

Roth, Michael S., *Knowing and History: Appropriations of Hegel in Twentieth Century France* (Ithaca: Cornell University Press, 1988).

Royle, Nicholas, *After Derrida* (Manchester: Manchester University Press, 1995).

Royle, Nicholas, *How to Read Shakespeare* (London: Granta, 2005).

Royle, Nicholas, *Jacques Derrida* (London: Routledge, 2003).

Royle, Nicholas, 'Not Now', *Epoché* 10.2 (2006): 379–93.

Royle, Nicholas, 'The Poet: Julius Caesar and the Democracy to Come', *Oxford Literary Review* 25 (2003): 39–61.

Royle, Nicholas, *The Uncanny* (Manchester: Manchester University Press, 2003).

Sandner, David, 'Tracking Grendel: The Uncanny in *Beowulf*', *Extrapolation* 40.2 (1999): 162–76.

Shakespeare, William, *The Life of Henry the Fifth, in The Norton Shakespeare, Based on the Oxford Edition*, ed. Stephen Greenblatt and others (New York: Norton, 1997).

Shakespeare, William, *The Life of Timon of Athens, in The Norton Shakespeare, Based on the Oxford Edition*, ed. Stephen Greenblatt and others (New York: Norton, 1997).

Shakespeare, William, *A Midsummer Night's Dream, in The Norton Shakespeare, Based on the Oxford Edition*, ed. Stephen Greenblatt and others (New York: Norton, 1997).

Shakespeare, William, *Riverside Shakespeare*, second edition (Boston: Houghton Mifflin Company, 1997).

Shakespeare, William, *The Second Part of Henry the Fourth, in The Norton Shakespeare, Based on the Oxford Edition*, ed. Stephen Greenblatt and others (New York: Norton, 1997).

Shakespeare, William, *The Tragedy of Hamlet, Prince of Denmark, in The Norton Shakespeare, Based on the Oxford Edition*, ed. Stephen Greenblatt and others (New York: Norton, 1997).

Shakespeare, William, *Troilus and Cressida, in The Norton Shakespeare, Based on the Oxford Edition*, ed. Stephen Greenblatt and others (New York: Norton, 1997).

Shakespeare, William, *The Winter's Tale*, in *The Norton Shakespeare, Based on the Oxford Edition*, ed. Stephen Greenblatt and others (New York: Norton, 1997).

Sidney, Sir Philip, *The Defence of Poesy*, in *The Major Works*, ed. Katherine Duncan-Jones (Oxford: Oxford University Press, 2002), 212–50.

Soffer, Gail, 'Philosophy and the Disdain for History: Reflections on Husserl's *Ergänzungsband* to the *Crisis*', *Journal of the History of Philosophy* 34 (1996): 95–116.

Sophocles, *Oedipus at Colonus*, in *The Three Theban Plays*, trans. Robert Fagles, intro. Bernard Knox (London: Penguin, 1984).

Sophocles, *Oedipus the King*, in *The Three Theban Plays*, trans. Robert Fagles, intro. Bernard Knox (London: Penguin, 1984).

Steblin-Kamenskij, M. I., *The Saga Mind* (Odense: Odense Universitetsforlag, 1973).

Sterne, Laurence, *The Life and Opinions of Tristram Shandy*, ed. Graham Petrie, intro. Christopher Ricks (London: Penguin, 1985).

Thomas, Rosalind, *Herodotus in Context: Ethnography, Science and the Art of Persuasion* (Cambridge: Cambridge University Press, 2000).

Tuck, Richard, *Philosophy and Government 1572–1651* (Cambridge: Cambridge University Press, 1993).

Ulmer, Gregory L., 'Op Writing: Derrida's Solicitation of *Theoria*', in *Displacement: Derrida and After*, ed. and intro. Mark Krupnick (Bloomington: Indiana University Press, 1983), 29–58.

Vernant, Jean-Pierre and Pierre Vidal-Naquet, *Myth and Tragedy in Ancient Greece*, trans. Janet Lloyd (New York: Zone Books, 1990).

Vickers, Brian (ed.), *Shakespeare: The Critical Heritage*, 6 vols (London: Routledge, 1974–81).

Walpole, Horace, *The Yale Edition of the Correspondence of Horace Walpole*: *Horace Walpole's Correspondence with Hannah More*, ed. W. S. Lewis, Robert A. Smith and Charles H. Bennet, 48 vols (London: Oxford University Press, 1961), 31.

Walpole, Horace, *The Yale Edition of the Correspondence of Horace Walpole*: *Horace Walpole's Correspondence with Mary and Agnes Berry*, ed. W. S. Lewis and A. Dayle Wallace, 48 vols (London: Oxford University Press, 1944), 12.

Ward, A. W. and A. R. Waller (eds), *The Cambridge History of English Literature, Volume 1: From the Beginnings to the Cycles of Romance* (Cambridge: Cambridge University Press, 1907).

Warminski, Andrzej, 'Reading for Example: "Sense-certainty" in Hegel's *Phenomenology of Spirit*', *Diacritics* 11.2 (1981): 83–96.

Warton, Thomas, *History of English Poetry: From the Twelfth to the Close of the Sixteenth Century*, ed. W. Carew Hazlitt, pref. Richard Price, 4 vols (London: Reeves and Turner, 1871).

Watkin, William, 'The line that does not lie down: enjambment, the tomb and the body', in *On Mourning: Theories of Loss in Modern Literature* (Edinburgh: Edinburgh University Press, 2004), 84–119.

White, Carol J., 'Heidegger and the Greeks', in *A Companion to Heidegger*, ed. Hubert L. Dreyfus and Mark A. Wrathall (Oxford: Blackwell, 2005), 121–40.

Wood, Sarah, 'Let's Start Again', *Diacritics* 29.1 (1999): 4–19.

Woolf, Virginia, *Orlando: A Biography*, ed. Brenda Lyons, intro. Sandra M. Gilbert (London: Penguin, 1993).

Wortham, Simon Morgan, *Counter-institutions: Jacques Derrida and the Question of the University* (New York: Fordham, 2006).

INDEX

INDEX